RJ STARR

The Burden of Freedom

Existential Psychology and the Human Struggle with Uncertainty

≋ Depthmark

For those who have wrestled with the weight of choice, who have carried responsibility even when it felt unbearable, and who have faced uncertainty without guarantees: this book is for you. May it honor your struggle, deepen your courage, and remind you that freedom—though heavy—is the very ground of dignity and meaning.

"Man is condemned to be free; because once thrown into the world, he is responsible for everything he does."

—Jean-Paul Charles Aymard Sartre

Contents

Preface

There are certain questions that haunt a teacher's office hours. They are not typically about the course material, at least not directly; they are the questions that hover beneath the surface of the syllabus, the ones that students finally ask after a long pause, when the textbook has been closed and the conversation has turned more personal. For many years, I have noticed a recurring theme in these quiet moments, a question that has taken different forms but always seems to orbit the same anxious core. It is the question of what to do with one's life, but it is asked with a particular kind of modern anguish.

I remember one student in particular, a young woman who was by all accounts brilliant and full of promise. She was a top performer in her classes, engaged in the material, and possessed a sharp, inquisitive mind. Yet when she sat across from me one autumn afternoon, her sense of potential felt to her not like a gift, but like an indictment. "I feel like I'm standing in a room with a thousand doors," she told me, her voice quiet, "and I'm so terrified of choosing the wrong one that I've just been standing in the middle, not moving at all." She spoke of the overwhelming pressure to optimize her life: to find a career that was not just a job but a passion, to build relationships that were not just stable but transformative, to construct an identity that was not just authentic but also admired. The sheer boundlessness of her freedom had become a cage. She was paralyzed by possibility.

Her predicament stayed with me because it was not an anomaly; it was a perfect articulation of a sentiment I was seeing everywhere, not just in my students, but in my clinical work, in my friends, and if I am being honest, in myself. The language of modern psychology, with its focus on behavioral goals, cognitive reframing, and symptom reduction, seemed to fall short in the face of this particular kind of suffering. We could offer strategies for managing anxiety, but we were not addressing the existential dread from which that anxiety seemed to spring. We were teaching people how to choose, but we were not helping them contend with the terrifying, magnificent reality of having to choose at all.

This book began as an attempt to find a better language for that conversation. It grew out of a conviction that to truly understand the paralysis my student described, we needed to look beyond our contemporary psychological models and turn to a tradition of thought that has never shied away from the difficult questions of the human condition: existentialism. I found myself returning to the thinkers who had shaped my own intellectual development, but I was reading them now with new eyes, seeing their century-old insights illuminate the most pressing anxieties of the 21st century.

I revisited Søren Kierkegaard, the Danish philosopher who wrote of the "dizziness of freedom," the profound anxiety that grips us when we gaze into the abyss of our own potential. In his words, I saw the face of my student, frozen in that room of a thousand doors. I turned again to Jean-Paul Sartre, whose stark insistence that we are "condemned to be free" felt less like a dramatic philosophical flourish and more like a simple, sober diagnosis of modern life. His point was not that freedom is bad, but that it is inescapable. Every moment of our lives, even our refusal to choose, is a choice for which we are responsible. This responsibility, he argued, is the price of our existence.

From there, my inquiry expanded into the realm of psychology, where clinicians like Viktor Frankl, Rollo May, and Irvin Yalom had courageously built a bridge between these profound philosophical ideas and the lived reality of human suffering. Frankl, writing from the horrific crucible of the Holocaust, demonstrated that even in the most extreme circumstances of unfreedom, the one freedom that can never be taken away is the freedom to choose one's attitude, to find meaning in suffering. Yalom, in his work with patients confronting death, isolation, and meaninglessness, identified our struggle with freedom as one of the fundamental "givens" of life, an inescapable reality that we must all face. These thinkers provided the crucial link; they showed that our relationship with freedom is not an abstract intellectual problem, but the very stuff of our emotional and psychological lives.

This book is the culmination of that journey. It is my attempt to weave together these two rich traditions—existential philosophy and clinical psychology—to create a framework for understanding why freedom, our most celebrated ideal, so often feels like a burden. This framework did not emerge from a detached, academic space. It was forged in the quiet anxiety of my own life. I remember standing in a bookstore several years ago, in the sprawling "Self-Help" and "Career" section, and feeling not possibility but a crushing weight. The sheer volume of books, each promising a secret path to a better me, a more optimized life, did not illuminate a path forward. It multiplied them into infinity. The pressure to choose the right book, to find the one answer that would finally resolve the underlying unease, was a perfect microcosm of the paralysis I study. In that moment, surrounded by a thousand promises of certainty, I felt the burden of my own freedom with acute clarity. It was not a lack of options that trapped me, but their abundance. This book is the one I needed in that bookstore aisle—not a map to the one right door, but a guide to understanding the dizziness itself, and a call to find the courage to choose a door nonetheless.

The need for such a framework has never felt more urgent. We are living in an age of radical individualization. The collective structures that once provided clear, if often restrictive, maps for living have largely dissolved. Religion, community, tradition, and stable careers once offered guardrails for choice, providing a sense of shared purpose and identity. Today, we are each tasked with the monumental project of creating that purpose and identity for ourselves, often from scratch.

The digital world has compounded this predicament exponentially. We navigate social landscapes of unprecedented scale, curating our lives for an unseen audience and comparing our messy realities to the polished highlight reels of others. We face a marketplace that offers an illusion of infinite choice, a constant stream of products, lifestyles, and experiences designed to satisfy needs we did not know we had. This deluge of options does not, as promised, make us freer; it depletes our cognitive resources, fuels our fear of missing out, and makes the weight of every decision, no matter how trivial, feel heavier. We are freer than any generation in human history to choose our own path, and we are more lost than ever.

It is for this reason that this book is not a guide to finding the "right" door in that room of a thousand possibilities. It is not a self-help manual that offers five easy steps to a life without anxiety. To offer such false promises would be to participate in the very culture of avoidance this book seeks to critique. The anxiety my student felt is not a pathology to be eliminated; it is a vital, albeit painful, signal of her humanity. It is the natural consequence of being a conscious, free being in a world that offers no guarantees.

Instead, this book is an invitation to an honest exploration. It is for anyone who has ever felt the quiet panic of a blank page, a new beginning, or an open-ended future. It is for the person who feels trapped in a life they did not consciously choose, and for the person who is paralyzed by the prospect of choosing a life at all. It is for the parent, the leader, the partner, or the citizen who feels the immense weight of responsibility for others in a world of profound uncertainty. My approach is to blend philosophical inquiry with psychological research and to ground both in stories of ordinary life, in vignettes drawn from the classroom, the therapy office, and the world at large. My hope is that in seeing our own struggles reflected in this long tradition of thought, we might feel less alone in them.

Ultimately, this book is an argument for a different kind of maturity. Not the maturity of having all the answers, but the maturity of being able to live with the questions. It is a call to cultivate an existential courage: the courage to accept our freedom, to take responsibility for our choices, and to create meaning in a world that does not provide it for us. This is not an easy path. It requires us to turn toward the very anxieties we are most inclined to avoid. It requires a willingness to bear the weight of our own lives without illusion or complaint. But it is, I believe, the only path to a life that is not just lived, but chosen. The goal, as the introduction that follows will make clear, is not to lighten the load of freedom, but to develop the strength to carry it with purpose, clarity, and even a measure of grace. I invite you to begin that journey with me now.

* * *

Introduction

Of all the capacities that define our species, none is more celebrated, more foundational, or more profoundly complicated than our freedom to choose. It is the animating principle of our legal systems, the engine of our economies, and the moral bedrock of our most cherished civic ideals. To be free is, in some essential way, to be fully human. We are, as far as we know, the only creatures on this planet who possess the strange and stunning ability to pause the flow of instinct, to stand at a crossroads in time, and to consciously weigh the future. We can imagine different versions of ourselves, project them forward into the world, and then commit to a path in an attempt to bring one of those imagined selves into being. This capacity for self-creation is our unique inheritance: a cognitive and emotional inheritance that allows us, for better or for worse, to become the primary authors of our own lives.

Yet if you listen closely to the quiet hum of our inner lives, you will find that this celebrated freedom often feels less like a gift and more like a weight. It is the low-grade anxiety that surfaces in the most mundane of arenas: the grocery store aisle, where a simple decision about which milk to buy is complicated by a dozen alternatives, each carrying its own subtle claims about health, ethics, and identity. Do you choose the oat milk for its environmental credentials, the almond milk for its low calorie count, or the organic dairy milk for its traditional simplicity? It is a trivial choice, yet it is a choice nonetheless, and it consumes a small portion of a finite reserve of mental energy. It is a microcosm of a much larger predicament.

This predicament unfolds with far greater stakes in the more significant domains of our lives. Consider the modern search for a partner, a process once largely governed by proximity and social convention, now transformed by the digital world into a seemingly infinite marketplace of possibilities. The dating app presents a catalogue of potential futures, an endless scroll of faces and profiles. With each swipe, a choice is made: a decision to foreclose one path in the tentative hope of opening another. The sheer volume of options promises an unprecedented liberty to find the "perfect" match, yet it often produces a paralyzing fear of making the wrong choice, or a lingering sense of dissatisfaction rooted in the fantasy that an even better option might have been just one more swipe away.

Or consider the contemporary career landscape. The stable, linear, lifelong professions that once offered a clear, if sometimes restrictive, sense of identity and purpose have become increasingly rare. Today, we are encouraged to be agile, to pivot, to reinvent ourselves, to become entrepreneurs of our own lives. We are told that our work should not be merely a job, but a passion; a calling; a form of self-actualization. The promise is one of ultimate freedom to design a life of meaning. The reality for many is a state of perpetual instability and a profound sense of personal responsibility for navigating a complex and unpredictable economic world. We are told that we can be anything we want to be; we are seldom coached on how to live with the quiet terror that comes from knowing we are also solely responsible for what we fail to become.

This is the central paradox this book seeks to explore: that the human being is a creature uniquely aware of its own freedom, yet is often crushed by the responsibility that freedom invariably entails. Choice is the mechanism of our freedom, but responsibility is its constant and unavoidable shadow. With every decision, from the trivial to the life-altering, we author a tiny piece of our existence. Each "yes" to one path is an implicit "no" to countless others, and the ghosts of those unlived lives linger in our minds as regret, as curiosity, as the nagging question of "what if?" To be free is to be the artist of one's life, but it is also to be the one who must stand before the canvas and make the first, irrevocable brushstroke, knowing that it can never be undone. This can be a source of profound meaning, but it can also be a source of profound dread.

Our contemporary culture, a culture of radical individualization and technological saturation, has amplified this paradox to an almost unbearable degree. The social, cultural, and religious structures that once guided human choice have become increasingly fluid. For millennia, the maps for a good life were largely drawn by forces outside the individual: by scripture, by tradition, by the rigid expectations of one's community and social class. These structures were often oppressive and stifling, to be sure, but they also provided a kind of psychological scaffolding. They narrowed the field of choice, offering ready-made answers to the great questions of how to live, whom to marry, what work to do, and what to believe. They provided a sense of belonging and a shared moral language.

Over the last few centuries, and with astonishing speed in the last few decades, much of that scaffolding has been dismantled. The moral land-scapes our ancestors navigated were mapped by firm, shared beliefs; today, we each act as our own moral cartographer, drawing our own lines between right and wrong in ambiguous terrain, often without a shared compass. The great project of modernity has been to liberate the individual from the constraints of these external authorities. The unintended consequence of this liberation is that the full weight of constructing a meaningful, ethical, and coherent life has been transferred directly onto the shoulders of the individual. We are now the sole architects of the systems of meaning in which we live, a monumental task for which most of us feel woefully unprepared.

Into this new landscape, the digital age has introduced a set of powerful and disorienting forces. We live a significant portion of our lives in a mediated world, a world of curated profiles and performance. The pressure is not simply to be free, but to perform one's freedom in a way that is visible, admirable, and consistent. We construct an identity online, and then feel the immense pressure to make life choices that align with that curated brand. The digital world also creates a culture of relentless comparison. We are constantly exposed not just to the choices of our immediate peers, but to the seemingly perfect choices of millions of strangers, whose lives are presented as a seamless highlight reel. This exposure does not inspire us as much as it intensifies our own anxieties, making our own hesitant, imperfect, and often confusing life path feel deeply inadequate.

This book, therefore, is an investigation into the psychological and philosophical dimensions of this very modern form of suffering. It is an exploration of the burden of freedom through the specific lens of existential psychology, a field of inquiry that is uniquely suited to this task because it has always taken the difficult truths of the human condition as its starting point. Existentialism is not a psychology of happiness, but a psychology of reality. It begins not with techniques for feeling better, but with an honest confrontation with the fundamental conditions of our existence: our freedom, our mortality, our isolation, and our search for meaning in a world that does not come with a pre-packaged instruction manual.

To guide our inquiry, we will turn to the insights of the great thinkers who have walked this path before us. We will begin with the 19th-century Danish philosopher Søren Kierkegaard, who brilliantly described the "dizziness" and "dread" that accompany our awareness of our own possibilities. We will then journey into the 20th century with the French philosopher Jean-Paul Sartre, whose radical and uncompromising vision of freedom led him to the stark conclusion that we are "condemned to be free," and that to deny this reality is to live in a state of self-deception he called "bad faith."

From these philosophical foundations, we will move into the world of psychology, to see how these ideas have been applied to the real, lived struggles of human beings. We will explore the work of Viktor Frankl, the psychiatrist and Holocaust survivor who taught the world that meaning can be found even in the most unimaginable suffering, and that our ultimate freedom is the freedom to choose our response to our circumstances. We will also draw heavily on the wisdom of the American psychiatrist Irvin Yalom, who has spent a lifetime helping people confront the "ultimate concerns" of life, identifying our inescapable freedom, and the responsibility it brings, as a primary source of our deepest anxieties. These thinkers are not presented here as gurus with all the answers, but as experienced and compassionate guides who can help us navigate this difficult terrain.

Our journey together will be structured to move from the philosophical to the practical, from the abstract to the deeply personal. We will explore how we so often flee from our own autonomy, seeking refuge in conformity, ideology, consumerism, or digital distraction. We will investigate how the weight of responsibility manifests in our most intimate relationships, in our career choices, in our role as parents, and in our relationship with our own health and mortality. We will look at how this struggle changes over the lifespan, from the overwhelming possibilities of youth to the reflective choices of later life.

It is therefore crucial to state clearly what this book is not. It is not a self-help manual that will offer seven easy steps to a life without anxiety. To offer such false promises would be to participate in the very culture of avoidance that this book seeks to critique. The anxiety we feel in the face of our freedom is not a pathology to be cured or a design flaw to be eliminated. It is a vital, albeit painful, signal of our humanity. It is the natural and inevitable consequence of being a conscious, self-aware, and free being in a universe that is indifferent to our choices and offers no ultimate guarantees.

This book is, instead, an invitation to a more honest and courageous conversation with ourselves. It is an attempt to provide a language and a framework for understanding one of the most profound struggles of contemporary life. The promise is not that you will finish these pages with all the answers. The promise is that you will finish with better questions. The goal is not to lighten the load of freedom, a load that is inextricably linked to our dignity as human beings. The goal is to understand the nature of that load, to learn to bear it with strength and with grace, and in doing so, to build the psychological and spiritual muscle required to carry it. It is a journey into the heart of what it means to be human, and I invite you to begin it with me now.

* * *

I

Part One: The Foundations of Freedom

Why does our most celebrated ideal—freedom—so often feel like an unbearable weight? Part 1 journeys to the heart of this paradox. We explore the foundational insights of existential thinkers who first wrestled with the anxiety of choice and the inescapable burden of responsibility that comes with it. This is the groundwork for understanding the human condition in an age of overwhelming possibility.

1

The Discovery of Freedom

To exist as a human being is to live with a constant, often unexamined, awareness of our own freedom. It is a fundamental component of our consciousness, a background hum so persistent that we often fail to notice its presence until it is either threatened or its consequences become too heavy to ignore. We presume our capacity to choose as a given, as elemental as the air we breathe. Yet this was not always the case. For the vast majority of human history, and for the early part of every individual human life, freedom as we understand it does not truly exist. It is not an innate property but a discovery: a slow, unsettling awakening to the reality of our own agency. This chapter is an exploration of that awakening. It charts the journey, both in the history of ideas and in the development of the individual, from a state of unthinking being to one of conscious, responsible choosing.

Let us consider for a moment the state of an animal in the wild. Its life is governed by a complex and elegant dance of instinct, genetics, and environmental cues. A bird does not choose to build a nest; it is compelled to do so by an ancient biological script. A wolf does not deliberate on the ethics of the hunt; it is driven by the urgent demands of hunger. Its world is one of immediacy, of stimulus and response. The animal is completely immersed in its existence, a perfect and seamless part of its environment. It is not burdened with the question of what it ought to be; it simply is. This state, a state of un-freedom, is a kind of grace. There is no anxiety about the future, no regret for the past, and no sense of responsibility for the creature it has become. It is a life without the weight of possibility.

For human beings, this state of grace is temporary. In the early stages of our lives, we experience a similar kind of immersion. A young child's world is structured by external forces: the rules of parents, the routines of the household, the physical laws of the world. Life is a series of directives and consequences that are perceived not as choices, but as the fundamental nature of reality. The child, like the animal, largely lives in a state of unthinking being. But then, slowly and imperceptibly at first, something begins to shift. A new kind of awareness dawns. This is the discovery of freedom. It is the moment a teenager first realizes that the values of their parents are not immutable laws of the universe, but are themselves choices that can be accepted or rejected. It is the moment a young adult, standing at the precipice of their future, grasps that the path forward is not preordained, but must be created, one decision at a time.

This awakening is rarely the purely joyful and liberating experience our culture so often portrays. It is more often a moment of profound dislocation, a dizzying and even terrifying realization. To discover one's freedom is to be cast out from the garden of unthinking certainty. It is to realize that the scripts we have been following are optional, and that we are now responsible for writing our own. It is to understand that with every choice we make, we simultaneously bring one future into being and annihilate countless others. This sudden awareness of the vast expanse of possibility, and the corresponding weight of being the sole agent responsible for navigating it, can be overwhelming. The psychological ground beneath our feet gives way, and we are left floating in an uncharted space.

It was into this disorienting new territory of the inner life that the first existential thinkers ventured. They were the cartographers of this modern consciousness, attempting to map the landscape of a world in which the individual could no longer rely on external authorities like God, king, or tradition to provide a clear sense of purpose and direction. This chapter traces the lineage of their discoveries, beginning with the thinkers who first gave voice to the unsettling feeling of being free.

We will begin our exploration with the 19th-century Danish philosopher Søren Kierkegaard, who can be considered the first great psychologist of the existential condition. More than any thinker before him, Kierkegaard was interested not in abstract systems of logic, but in the subjective, lived reality of the individual. He understood that freedom was not an intellectual concept to be debated, but a psychological state to be experienced, and that its primary emotional texture was anxiety. He gave us the language to describe the "dizziness" of looking down into the abyss of our own possibilities, the profound and unsettling "dread" that is the constant companion of a free being.

From Kierkegaard's deeply personal and psychological insights, we will move to the work of the 20th-century French philosopher Jean-Paul Sartre. Sartre took Kierkegaard's insights and radicalized them, stripping them of their religious context and placing them firmly in the secular, post-war world. For Sartre, freedom is not a feeling or a psychological state; it is the absolute and inescapable condition of human existence. He famously declared that we are "condemned to be free." There is no external script, no human nature, and no divine plan to guide us. We are nothing more and nothing less than the sum of our choices. Even our attempts to avoid choosing, he argued, are themselves choices for which we are fully responsible. Sartre's vision is a stark and demanding one, but it is also one that places the dignity of the human being squarely in our capacity to create our own essence through our actions.

After charting these philosophical origins, we will turn to the world of clinical psychology to see how these profound ideas have been applied to the real, lived struggles of people in search of a more authentic way of being. We will draw on the work of the American psychiatrist Irvin Yalom, who masterfully translated the insights of existential philosophy into a powerful therapeutic framework. Yalom identified a set of fundamental "givens" of the human condition: inescapable truths that we must all confront. Alongside mortality, isolation, and the search for meaning, he placed freedom as a central source of our deepest anxieties. He shows us how the fear of freedom manifests in the therapy room, driving the subtle and unconscious ways we sabotage our own lives to avoid the weight of our own agency.

Finally, we will bring our inquiry into the present day by examining how the intuitions of these existential thinkers are now being confirmed by the empirical findings of modern psychology. While using a different language, researchers in fields like self-determination theory and the study of locus of control have arrived at a remarkably similar conclusion: that a sense of autonomy and personal agency is a fundamental human need, essential for psychological well-being. This research provides a powerful scientific validation for what the existentialists understood through philosophical and psychological inquiry; it demonstrates through data that our relationship with our own freedom is not a peripheral concern, but lies at the very heart of a flourishing human life. This chapter, therefore, serves as the foundation for our entire exploration. It is an intellectual and psychological orientation, an introduction to the core concepts and the key thinkers who have dared to look directly at the dizzying reality of human freedom. Before we can fully understand the burden of freedom, we must first appreciate the profound and unsettling nature of its discovery.

Kierkegaard and the Anxiety of Possibility

To understand the modern experience of freedom, we must begin not in the brightly lit laboratories of contemporary psychology, but in the dim, rain-swept streets of 19th-century Copenhagen, with a philosopher who was in many ways the first true psychologist of the inner life. Søren Kierkegaard stands as a pivotal figure in the history of thought, largely because he so thoroughly rejected the dominant philosophical trends of his time. While his contemporaries, most notably the German idealists, were busy constructing grand, abstract, all-encompassing systems to explain the rational unfolding of history and the universe, Kierkegaard was consumed by a far more intimate and, for our purposes, more important question: what does it mean to be an existing individual? He was not interested in a truth that could be observed from a detached, objective viewpoint; he was interested in the truth that is lived, the truth that is felt, the truth that one must grapple with in the solitude of one's own consciousness. It is this relentless focus on the subjective, passionate, and often paradoxical nature of human existence that makes him the indispensable starting point for any serious inquiry into the burden of freedom.

For Kierkegaard, freedom was not a political right to be granted or a metaphysical concept to be debated. It was a lived, psychological reality, and its primary emotional signature was not joy or liberation, but a profound and unsettling state he termed Angst, a Danish word often translated as "dread" or "anxiety." To grasp the radical nature of this idea, we must first understand the crucial distinction Kierkegaard made between dread and a more common emotion: fear. Fear, as he saw it, is always directed toward something concrete. We are afraid of a venomous snake, of a financial crisis, of a threatening diagnosis. The object of our fear is specific and identifiable. We can, at least in theory, devise a strategy to confront, avoid, or overcome it. Dread, however, is different. Dread is the fear of nothing. Its object is not a thing in the world, but a void, a nothingness. This nothingness is the vast, undefined expanse of our own possibility. Dread is the anxiety that arises not from what is, but from what could be. It is the internal shudder we feel when we become aware of our own capacity to choose, to act, to create and to destroy.

To illustrate this concept, Kierkegaard famously turned to the biblical story of Adam in the Garden of Eden. In his state of innocence, before God's prohibition, Adam is like an animal. He lives in a state of unthinking, un-free grace. He is not burdened by choice because the concept of choice does not yet exist for him. The pivotal moment is not the act of eating the apple, but the moment God issues the command: "You shall not eat of the fruit of the tree of the knowledge of good and evil." It is this prohibition, Kierkegaard argues, that awakens dread. The command introduces into Adam's world something that was not there before: the possibility of disobedience. In that moment, Adam is not yet a sinner; he has done nothing wrong. But he has become aware of a terrifying new power within himself. He has become aware that he *can*. He can obey, or he can disobey. Dread, Kierkegaard writes, is "the reality of freedom as possibility before this possibility has materialized." It is the dawning, terrifying awareness of our own agency.

This experience is not confined to mythical first men; it is a fundamental part of every human awakening into self-consciousness. Kierkegaard offers a more visceral and immediate metaphor to capture this feeling: that of a man standing on the edge of a tall building or a cliff. If this man were to look down, he might experience fear, the fear of accidentally falling. This is an external threat. But then, a more subtle and disturbing feeling might arise. He might become aware of a different possibility, an internal one. He might realize that nothing is stopping him from throwing himself off. The dread he feels in that moment is not the fear of falling, but the terrifying awareness of his freedom to jump. The abyss outside him is frightening, but the abyss of possibility inside him is far more so. It is this internal abyss that is the source of dread. Kierkegaard called it "the dizziness of freedom." It is the vertigo we experience when we gaze into the chasm of our own potential and realize that we are the ones who must choose what to do with it.

This dizziness is a direct consequence of the nature of possibility itself. Every choice we make is both a creative and a destructive act. To choose one path is to bring a particular future into existence, but it is also, at the same instant, to annihilate all the other potential futures that were available to us in that moment. When a young person chooses to pursue a career in medicine, they are not simply choosing a profession; they are choosing a way of life, an identity, a set of values and experiences. At the same time, they are choosing *not* to be the artist, the teacher, the entrepreneur, or the traveler they might have become. The ghosts of these unlived lives are the price of any single, committed choice. Dread, in this context, is the feeling of being overwhelmed by the sheer magnitude of this creative and destructive power. The more possibilities we perceive, the greater the potential for this feeling of being overwhelmed. Our modern world, with its endless array of options for what to be, what to do, and who to love, has turned this existential condition into a chronic, everyday experience.

Let us bring this down from the philosophical heights and into the lived reality of a single individual, the young adult standing in what our student from the preface called "a room with a thousand doors." Imagine a young woman who has just graduated from a good university. She is talented, intelligent, and has been told her entire life that she can be anything she wants to be. On the surface, this is a position of immense privilege and opportunity. The world is laid out before her as a landscape of pure potential. She could go to law school, she could join a tech startup, she could move to another country to teach English, she could try to write a novel. The sheer number of available paths is exhilarating. This exhilaration is the positive, alluring face of freedom. It is the feeling of power, of being the author of a story that has yet to be written. It is the thrill of pure possibility.

But as the days and weeks after graduation turn into months, this feeling of exhilaration begins to curdle. The open field of possibility starts to feel more like a vast, empty, and intimidating desert. The freedom to choose becomes the oppressive necessity of choosing. Each door in her metaphorical room seems to lead to a completely different life, and to walk through one is to lock all the others forever. The weight of this becomes immense. She researches law schools, but the moment she begins an application, she is haunted by the image of the life she would be giving up, the artist she would not become. She starts to write a business plan for a startup, but is paralyzed by the thought of the stability and prestige she would be sacrificing by not pursuing a more traditional path.

Her paralysis is not rooted in a simple fear of failure. She is not primarily afraid that she will be a bad lawyer or that her business will fail. Her anxiety is more profound. It is the dread of the choice itself. It is the dread of committing to one version of herself at the expense of all others. It is the dread of having to take the raw, undefined material of her potential and give it a final, concrete form. And beneath it all is the terrifying realization that there is no one to make this decision for her. There is no objective, external authority that can tell her which door is the "right" one. The responsibility rests entirely on her. This state of anxious indecision, this hovering in the doorway of life, is the quintessential experience of Kierkegaardian dread.

She is dizzy with her own freedom.

So what is to be done? Kierkegaard was not a therapist, and he did not offer simple solutions for alleviating this anxiety. In fact, he viewed dread not as a pathology to be cured, but as an essential and even valuable part of the human spiritual journey. Dread is the teacher that awakens us to our own freedom. The person who has never felt dread, he argued, is like an animal or a child, living in a state of spiritual immaturity. The attempt to escape dread is the source of our most inauthentic modes of being. We flee from the dizziness of freedom by losing ourselves in the crowd, by conforming to the expectations of others, by filling our lives with trivial distractions, or by dogmatically clinging to an ideology that makes our choices for us. These escape routes offer a kind of comfort, a release from the burden of self-creation, but they do so at the cost of our own authentic existence. To flee from dread is to flee from the very thing that makes us human.

The only way forward, in Kierkegaard's view, is not to escape dread, but to pass through it. The answer to the paralysis of possibility is not more analysis or a search for more certainty where none can be found. The answer is a commitment, an act of will, what he famously called a "leap of faith." For Kierkegaard, this was ultimately a religious leap: a passionate, subjective commitment to a Christian life, made not because of rational proof, but in spite of the lack of it. But we can understand this concept in a broader, psychological sense as well. The leap of faith is the courage to make a choice, to walk through one of the thousand doors, and to commit to the path one has chosen, all the while knowing that there was no guarantee it was the right one. It is the act of embracing a finite life in the face of infinite possibility. It is the decision to live, rather than to perpetually prepare to live. The young woman in our example is freed not when she finally figures out the "perfect" career path, but when she courageously chooses one, accepts the loss of the others, and begins the real work of living the life she has chosen.

Kierkegaard's enduring contribution, then, is that he was the first to diagnose the profound psychological ambivalence at the heart of freedom.

He gave us a language to describe why the discovery of our own agency is so often accompanied by a feeling of profound unease. He taught us that the anxiety we feel when faced with an open future is not a sign of weakness or malfunction, but is, in fact, a signal of our most fundamental human capacity. It is the price of our liberation from the unthinking world of instinct. Before we can explore the specific ways this burden manifests in modern life, we must first sit with this foundational insight: that freedom and dread are two sides of the same coin. To be a free, choosing being is to live with the constant, dizzying, and ultimately ennobling awareness of the abyss of our own possibility.

Sartre's Radical Freedom and Condemnation to Choose

If Søren Kierkegaard opened the door to the inner landscape of freedom and its attendant anxieties, it was Jean-Paul Sartre who threw that door wide open and insisted that we step through it, leaving behind every comfort and every illusion of a predetermined path. Moving from the pietistic, introspective world of 19th-century Copenhagen to the secular, war-torn cafes of mid-20th-century Paris is to move from a psychology of faith to an ontology of action. Sartre takes Kierkegaard's deeply personal and psychological dread and strips it of its religious context, transmuting it into a stark, universal, and inescapable condition of human existence itself. For Sartre, freedom is not a feeling we have or a capacity we possess; it is the very stuff of our being. It is the raw, unstructured, and terrifying material from which we must construct our own lives, and from this task, there is no escape.

Sartre's entire philosophy is built upon a single, revolutionary pronouncement that overturns millennia of Western thought: "existence precedes essence." To grasp the magnitude of this statement, we must first understand the tradition it seeks to dismantle. From Plato onward, philosophy has generally held that the essence of a thing—its fundamental nature, its purpose, its definition—comes before its actual, physical existence. Consider an artisan who wishes to create a paper knife. Before the knife exists, the artisan has a clear concept of it in their mind. They know its purpose (to cut paper), its necessary properties (a blade, a handle), and the process by which it will be made. The idea of the knife, its essence, precedes its creation, its existence. This same logic was applied to humanity through a theological lens. God, the ultimate artisan, was said to have a concept of human nature, an essence, in His mind before creating humankind. We were created for a purpose, with a specific nature to fulfill. Our lives were a process of living up to, or failing to live up to, this preordained essence.

Sartre, writing in a world where, for many, the notion of God had ceased to be a viable foundation for meaning, looked at this old formula and inverted it. If there is no divine artisan, he reasoned, then there is no one to conceive of a human nature beforehand. There is no blueprint, no pre-written script, no essential purpose for our lives. We simply find ourselves here, thrown into the world without a definition. We exist first. We appear on the scene, and only afterward, through our actions and our choices, do we define what we are. "Man is nothing else but what he makes of himself," Sartre famously wrote. "Such is the first principle of existentialism." The paper knife has a fixed purpose, but a human being does not. We are born as a blank slate, and every choice we make is a brushstroke that contributes to the portrait of who we are. Our essence is the sum total of our existence, the accumulation of our free acts.

It is from this foundational principle that Sartre derives his most famous and most challenging declaration: we are "condemned to be free." The language is deliberately paradoxical and unsettling. Freedom is typically associated with liberation and joy, yet Sartre pairs it with the language of a prison sentence. The condemnation lies in the fact that we did not choose this condition. We did not ask to be the authors of our own essence. We are simply thrown into this reality at birth, and from that moment forward, we are burdened with a freedom that we can never shed. A prisoner, after all, can dream of a life outside the prison walls. But for us, there is no outside. Freedom is the prison. We are condemned because we are responsible for everything we are, yet we are not responsible for the fact of our own responsibility.

This freedom is absolute and total. For Sartre, there is no such thing as a partial choice or a moment of unfreedom. Every second of our conscious lives, we are choosing. A man who is conscripted into an army and sent to war did not, perhaps, choose to be in that situation, but he is, in every moment, choosing how to respond to it. He can choose to fight, to desert, to comply with sullen resentment, or to find a way to maintain his integrity within the system. Even the decision to passively go along with orders is a choice to be passive and compliant. A person sitting quietly in a room is choosing not to leave, not to speak, not to act. The most dramatic illustration of this is suicide. Even the choice to end one's life is, for Sartre, the ultimate affirmation of one's freedom to choose. There is no escape route. The refusal to choose is itself a choice: the choice to refuse. We are trapped in a state of perpetual self-creation.

This radical freedom brings with it an equally radical sense of responsibility, which Sartre calls "anguish." This is a concept that builds upon Kierkegaard's dread but expands its scope from the individual to the whole of humanity. For Kierkegaard, the dizziness of freedom was a personal, subjective experience related to one's own possibilities. For Sartre, the anguish of freedom comes from the realization that when we choose for ourselves, we are simultaneously choosing for everyone. When we make a decision, we are not just saying, "This is what I will do." We are implicitly saying, "This is what a human being ought to do." We are creating an image of humanity as we believe it should be. When a person chooses to marry and be monogamous, they are not just making a personal life choice; they are affirming the value of monogamous marriage for all of humankind. When another person chooses a life of free love, they are likewise legislating for all. Every act we commit sets a precedent and posits a value.

This realization, if we take it seriously, is crushing. It means that the weight of the world is on our shoulders with every decision we make. There are no pre-written moral guidelines, no divine commandments, no universal ethical systems to which we can appeal for justification. We are alone, without excuses. This is the source of our anguish. It is the profound and total responsibility that comes from knowing that our choices define not only our own essence but also our vision of humanity's essence. Most of us, most of the time, do not live with this acute awareness. We prefer to believe our choices are small, personal matters that affect only ourselves. But for Sartre, this is a form of self-deception, a flight from the true magnitude of our freedom.

This flight from freedom Sartre terms "bad faith" (mauvaise foi). Bad faith is the attempt to escape the anguish of our condemnation by pretending that we are not free. It is a form of lying to ourselves. We engage in bad faith whenever we try to convince ourselves that our actions are determined by forces outside of our control. We treat ourselves not as free, conscious beings—what Sartre calls a "for-itself"—but as inert objects, or things—an "in-itself." An inkwell is an in-itself; it simply is what it is, defined and complete. A human being, a for-itself, is never complete, always in the process of becoming. Bad faith is the act of pretending to be an inkwell. It is the denial of our own transcendence, our capacity to be more than what we currently are.

Sartre provides a brilliant and memorable example of bad faith in his description of a Parisian cafe waiter. The waiter's movements are a little too precise, a little too theatrical. His voice is a little too solicitous. He is playing the role of a waiter with such exaggerated perfection that he seems to have become an automaton. He is, Sartre suggests, acting as if he *is* a waiter in the same way that an inkwell *is* an inkwell. He has submerged his personal freedom, his consciousness, into the social role he is playing. He is trying to convince himself that he has no choice but to be this waiter, that his essence is fixed. The reality, of course, is that he is a free being who is, at every moment, *choosing* to get up, go to work, and perform these actions. He could, in theory, throw the tray on the ground and walk out. His elaborate performance is a sophisticated, unconscious strategy to hide this terrifying freedom from himself.

We see this mechanism everywhere in our daily lives. It is the person who says, "I can't help it, that's just my personality." This statement treats personality as a fixed, unchangeable object, like a piece of furniture, rather than as a dynamic pattern of chosen behaviors. It is the employee who justifies an unethical act by saying, "I had no choice; my boss told me to do it." This is an attempt to transfer responsibility, to deny one's own freedom to refuse. It is the person who feels trapped in an unhappy relationship and says, "I have to stay for the children," treating their situation as an inescapable prison rather than as a difficult choice with painful consequences. In every case, bad faith is a comforting illusion. It allows us to escape the anguish of responsibility by telling ourselves a story in which we are not the protagonist of our lives, but a mere supporting character whose lines have been written by someone else.

However, Sartre's philosophy is not as bleakly absolute as it might first appear. He introduces a crucial dialectic to complicate this picture of total freedom: the interplay between what he calls "facticity" and "transcendence." Facticity comprises the given, unchosen facts of our situation. We do not choose our place of birth, our historical era, our genetic makeup, our childhood experiences, or the language we first learn. These are the brute facts of our existence, the raw material with which we have to work. They are the "in-itself" aspect of our reality. Transcendence, on the other hand, is our freedom to go beyond these facts, to interpret them, to give them meaning, and to choose our attitude and actions in response to them. I cannot choose the fact that I was born into a poor family, but I am free to choose what that poverty will mean to me and what I will do about it. Will it be a source of shame, a motivation for success, an excuse for failure, or a catalyst for social change? The facticity is the situation, but the transcendence is the choice. Our lives are a constant synthesis of these two poles.

Let us return to the modern workplace to see how this plays out. Consider a man named David who works in a mid-level management position at a large corporation. He finds his job unfulfilling, ethically compromising, and emotionally draining. He complains about it constantly to his wife and friends. He feels trapped, powerless, and profoundly unhappy. From a Sartrean perspective, David is living in a state of bad faith. He perceives his job as a prison, an external reality that has been imposed upon him. His facticity includes his mortgage, his children's need for health insurance, his lack of other immediately obvious job prospects, and the current state of the economy. These are real constraints. However, David is focusing solely on this facticity and denying his transcendence. He is denying the fact that every morning, he *chooses* to wake up, get in his car, and drive to that office. He is *choosing* to accept the paycheck. He is *choosing* to remain in this situation.

The anguish he feels is the simmering, unconscious awareness of this denied freedom. His constant complaining is not just an expression of his unhappiness; it is a performance. It is a way of constantly reaffirming to himself and to others that he is a victim, that he is not responsible for his own predicament. The path to an authentic existence for David does not necessarily require him to quit his job tomorrow. It requires a fundamental shift in consciousness. It requires him to abandon the story of his victimhood and to confront his own freedom. He must say to himself, "I am not trapped. I am choosing this. I am choosing the security of this paycheck over the uncertainty of a job search. I am choosing to compromise these values in exchange for providing for my family. This is my choice, and I am responsible for it."

This acknowledgment is terrifying, but it is also profoundly liberating. The moment David owns his choice, he reclaims his agency. The situation may not have changed externally, but his relationship to it has been transformed. He is no longer a passive object being acted upon by the corporation; he is a free subject who is actively choosing his path. And once he accepts that he is choosing to stay, he also awakens to the reality that he is free to choose differently. He can start looking for a new job in the evenings. He can begin to downsize his lifestyle to reduce his financial dependency. He can choose to find small ways to assert his values within his current role. The point is not what he does, but the awareness from which he does it. He moves from being a prisoner of his circumstances to being the author of his response to them.

Sartre's philosophy, then, is a radical call to psychological and existential maturity. He takes the gentle, internal dizziness that Kierkegaard identified and forces it out into the open, into the realm of concrete action and total responsibility. He leaves us with no excuses, no place to hide from the fact that our lives are the product of our choices. He insists that we are what we do. While this vision can feel harsh and unforgiving, its underlying message is one of profound empowerment. It locates human dignity not in any pre-given essence or divine plan, but in our relentless, terrifying, and magnificent capacity to create ourselves, to define our own meaning, and to be the sole authors of the one life we have.

The Ground of Our Freedom: Facticity and Situation

Sartre's proclamation that we are "condemned to be free" can, in its stark brilliance, feel unmoored from the gritty reality of our daily lives. It can sound like a philosophy for a disembodied spirit, a consciousness floating in a vacuum of pure possibility. To accept this radical freedom, we must confront the most common and powerful objection to it: *But I didn't choose this.* I didn't choose to be born into poverty or wealth, into this particular body, in this historical era, with these genetic predispositions. I didn't choose the war that shattered my country or the systemic prejudices that limit my opportunities. To speak of total freedom in the face of such overwhelming facts can seem not just naive, but cruel.

This is where Sartre introduces a crucial, grounding concept that complicates and enriches his vision: facticity. Facticity (from the Latin *factum*, "thing done") comprises all the unchosen, "thing-like" facts of our situation. It is the raw material we are given, the in-itself of our existence. Our facticity includes:

- Our body: Its sex, its race, its innate abilities and disabilities, its susceptibility to certain illnesses, its eventual decay.
- Our past: Our childhood experiences, the traumas we endured, the education we received (or didn't), the relationships that shaped us.
- Our place and time: Our nationality, our social class at birth, the

historical events that form the backdrop of our lives (a pandemic, a war, an economic boom).

- Our relations to others: The fact that we have a mother and a father, that we are someone's child, that we exist in a web of social expectations and obligations.

These are not illusions. They are real, massive, and often impose very real constraints. A person born into a slum does not have the same set of opportunities as a person born into a mansion. A person with a chronic illness does not have the same relationship to their physical potential as an Olympic athlete. To ignore this is to engage in a privileged fantasy.

However—and this is Sartre's critical point—facticity is not a *determinism*. We are not defined by our facticity alone. Our freedom, our transcendence, lies in what we *do* with this given material. Facticity is the situation, but freedom is our *project* within that situation. We are not merely the sum of our facts; we are the meaning-making, action-taking response to those facts.

Consider two individuals born with the same significant physical disability. This disability is a brute fact of their facticity, an unchosen and difficult reality.

- Person A might interpret this facticity as a prison sentence. They see their life as fundamentally broken, their possibilities foreclosed. They become defined by their disability, using it as the ultimate explanation for all their unhappiness and lack of achievement. They live in a state of resentment and passivity, seeing themselves as a victim of an unfair biological lottery. In Sartrean terms, they are focusing exclusively on their facticity and denying their transcendence. They are treating themselves as an in-itself, a determined object.
- Person B acknowledges the very same facticity with clear-eyed honesty. They feel the pain, the frustration, the very real limitations. But they refuse to be defined by them. They ask, "Given this reality, what is my project? What can I make of this?" Their disability becomes the ground

upon which they build a life of remarkable courage, advocacy, or artistic expression. It might become the motivation to develop immense mental strength, to connect with others in a profound community of support, or to innovate new ways of moving through the world. They have not chosen their disability, but they are absolutely choosing their response to it. They are synthesizing their facticity with their transcendence.

This is the synthesis that defines an authentic life. Our freedom does not operate in a vacuum; it operates in the resistant, dense medium of our facticity. The burden of freedom is not the burden of being able to choose anything, but the burden of having to choose what this specific, given life will mean.

This reframes the entire concept of "limitations." From an existential perspective, a limitation is not merely an obstacle to freedom; it is often the very condition for it. A sculptor is not free because they have an infinite block of marble; they are free because they have a *finite* one. The resistance of the stone, its specific grain and flaws, is what makes the act of sculpting a creative, free engagement rather than a fantasy. Our facticity is our block of marble. It is heavy, it is unwieldy, it has cracks and imperfections we did not choose. But it is ours. And we are the sculptors.

To flee from freedom into bad faith, then, is often to pretend that our facticity is absolute—to say, "I am my poverty," "I am my past trauma," "I am my diagnosis." It is to collapse our dynamic, living "for-itself" into a static, determined "in-itself." Conversely, to pretend our facticity doesn't exist—to live in a delusion of limitless power unaffected by history, body, or social structures—is another, equally inauthentic form of bad faith.

The mature embrace of freedom, therefore, requires a double movement: a courageous acceptance of the facts of our situation, coupled with an even more courageous assertion of our responsibility to act within and upon that situation. We are not free *from* our facticity, but we are free *within* it. Our dignity lies not in the hand we were dealt, but in the unique, unscripted, and deeply personal way we choose to play it. This is the heavy, specific, and ultimately empowering ground of our condemned freedom.

The Existential "Givens" of Life

While the philosophical inquiries of Kierkegaard and Sartre provide an essential and powerful language for understanding the human condition, their work can often feel abstract, uncompromising, and remote from the everyday texture of our lives. They offer a diagnosis of our fundamental situation but provide little in the way of a practical path forward, aside from a call for a courageous, and often lonely, authenticity. It took a new generation of thinkers, those who were both steeped in this philosophical tradition and deeply engaged in the practical, compassionate work of psychotherapy, to build a bridge between these profound ideas and the lived reality of human suffering. Foremost among these bridge-builders is the American psychiatrist and author Irvin Yalom, whose work has masterfully translated the grand themes of European existentialism into a clear, humane, and powerfully effective therapeutic approach.

Yalom's great contribution was to distill the often-dense landscape of existential thought into a workable clinical framework. Through his decades of work with patients, he observed that beneath the vast and varied tapestry of human problems—the relationship conflicts, the career anxieties, the depressive funks, the specific phobias—there lay a deeper, more fundamental layer of concern. He proposed that much of our psychological distress stems not from immediate life stressors or past traumas alone, but from our struggle to confront the basic, unalterable conditions of our existence. He called these conditions the "givens" of life, or our "ultimate concerns." They are not problems to be solved, but realities to be faced. They are the foundational truths of our predicament as self-aware beings, and our attempts to deny, evade, or distort them are, in his view, the primary source of our deepest neuroses. Yalom identified four such ultimate concerns: death, isolation, meaninglessness, and the one that binds them all together, freedom.

To understand the power of this framework, it is useful to think of these givens as a kind of existential gravity. Like physical gravity, they are an invisible but constant and powerful force, exerting their influence on everything we do, think, and feel. We are rarely conscious of gravity's pull, yet it shapes the architecture of our buildings, the biology of our bodies, and the trajectory of every object in motion. In the same way, these ultimate concerns are constantly shaping the architecture of our personalities, the biology of our emotions, and the trajectory of our lives. We can spend our lives pretending this force doesn't exist, but we cannot escape its influence. A truly authentic life, from this perspective, requires us to turn and face these conditions squarely, to learn to live with them, and to find a way to create a life of richness and purpose not in spite of them, but in dialogue with them. Our exploration of freedom, therefore, is incomplete without understanding how it interacts with these other fundamental realities of our existence.

The first and most primal of these givens is death. The awareness of our own mortality is the ultimate shadow that haunts the human experience. We are, as the existentialists are fond of reminding us, the only creatures who live our entire lives with the conscious knowledge of our own inevitable demise. This knowledge is so terrifying that we have developed an elaborate array of psychological defenses to keep it at bay. We repress it, deny it, or seek symbolic forms of immortality through our children, our creative works, our wealth, or our belief in a literal afterlife. The core conflict, as Yalom frames it, is the tension between our awareness of the inevitability of death and our inherent wish to continue to be, to live. This conflict generates a primal anxiety that hums continuously beneath the surface of our lives.

But how does this relate to freedom? The terror of death is inextricably linked to the burden of our freedom to live. If our lives were predetermined, a simple unfolding of a pre-written script, then death would be merely the final page of the book. But because we are free, because our lives are unwritten, death takes on a far more terrifying dimension. Death is the ultimate and absolute cessation of all possibility. It is the door that closes on our freedom forever. The dread of death is therefore not just the fear of non-being, but the fear of having failed to use our freedom well. It is the anxiety of arriving at the end of our lives with the crushing realization that we did not truly live the life that was ours to live. This is the source of so much of what we call midlife crises, the panicked awakening to the fact that time is finite and that many of the choices we have made are irreversible. The awareness of death, then, serves as a powerful, if terrifying, catalyst. It can either paralyze us with fear, causing us to shrink from life and its risks, or it can shock us into a more authentic mode of being. The confrontation with our finitude can liberate us from trivial concerns and focus our freedom on what truly matters. It forces us to ask the ultimate question: given that my time is limited, how will I choose to live?

The second ultimate concern is isolation. Yalom makes a crucial distinction between everyday forms of loneliness and what he calls "existential isolation." We may experience interpersonal loneliness when we lack social connections, or intrapersonal isolation when we are cut off from our own feelings. But existential isolation is a far deeper and more permanent condition. It refers to the unbridgeable gulf that exists between oneself and any other being. We are born alone, we die alone, and we live our lives enclosed within the solitary confinement of our own consciousness. No matter how close we become to another person, we can never fully share their experience, their thoughts, or their feelings. We can empathize, we can communicate, we can love, but we can never completely dissolve the boundary that separates our subjective world from theirs. We are, in Yalom's evocative metaphor, "islands of consciousness."

This fundamental separateness creates a profound tension with our freedom. We are free to reach out, to form connections, to build bridges to other islands. Indeed, our deep-seated need to overcome our isolation is one of the primary drivers of human behavior. But this freedom to connect operates against the constant, unyielding backdrop of our ultimate aloneness. The anguish of this condition is felt most acutely in our most intimate relationships. We yearn for a perfect union, a complete merger with another, a state in which we are fully seen, understood, and accepted. Yet this is an impossible ideal. The friction created when our freedom to love grinds against the unchangeable reality of our separateness is the source of immense relational pain. It leads to attempts to fuse with another person, thereby sacrificing one's own freedom and identity, or to treating the other person as an object to satisfy one's own needs, denying their separate, free existence. A mature relationship, from an existential perspective, is not one that eliminates this isolation, but one in which two free individuals acknowledge their separateness and choose, day after day, to create a shared world together, all the while respecting the mysterious and unbridgeable gap that will always remain between them. The burden of freedom here is the responsibility to connect with others authentically, without demanding that they save us from our fundamental solitude.

This leads us to the third ultimate concern: meaninglessness. If we accept the Sartrean premise that there is no preordained plan for our lives, if we live in a universe that has no inherent meaning, and if we are ultimately alone and heading toward our own annihilation, then we are faced with a profound and deeply unsettling problem: how are we to live? On what basis should we make our choices? What is the point of it all? This is the problem of meaning. The conflict here is between our need to find a sense of purpose and significance in our lives and our existence in a universe that offers no such meaning readymade. We are, in the words of the philosopher Albert Camus, meaning-seeking creatures thrown into a meaningless universe.

Freedom is both the cause of this problem and its only possible solution. We are condemned to meaninglessness precisely because we are free. An animal is not troubled by the question of meaning; its purpose is dictated by its biological instincts. But because we are free from the dictates of instinct, we are cast into a void, a vacuum of meaning that we ourselves must fill. The burden of freedom, in this context, is the monumental task of constructing a life of purpose in a world that provides no blueprint for how to do so. This is perhaps the most daunting of all our responsibilities. It is the reason why people so readily flee their freedom and latch onto externally provided systems of meaning: dogmatic religions, rigid political ideologies, the pursuit of wealth and status, or even codependent relationships. These systems offer ready-made answers to the question of purpose, and in doing so, they relieve us of the terrifying responsibility of having to create our own.

Yalom's clinical work is filled with examples of individuals suffering from a crisis of meaning, often disguised as depression or anxiety. The successful executive who has achieved every external goal—wealth, power, prestige—only to wake up in the middle of the night with a hollow sense of emptiness. He has played the game and won, but now suspects he has been playing the wrong game altogether. The young mother who loves her children but feels she has lost her own identity, that her life's meaning has been entirely subsumed by her role. The individual who drifts from one job to another, one relationship to another, searching for a spark of passion, a sense of purpose that always remains elusive. The existential therapeutic approach to this problem is not to provide the patient with a meaning, but to help them clear away the obstacles that prevent them from creating their own. It is to help them confront their freedom and to understand that the creation of meaning is not a one-time discovery but a lifelong process of engagement with the world. It is found not by looking for it, but by committing oneself to projects, to relationships, to values, and to causes beyond oneself. Meaning, Yalom suggests, is a byproduct of a life actively and freely lived.

Finally, we arrive at freedom itself, which Yalom treats as the fourth ultimate concern. Here, he is in direct dialogue with Kierkegaard and Sartre. The core conflict, as he formulates it for a clinical context, is the clash between our awareness of our freedom and responsibility, and our deep-seated wish for ground, for structure, for certainty. We yearn to be free, but we are terrified of the radical responsibility that freedom entails. We want to be the authors of our lives, but we also want someone else to tell us how the story is supposed to go. This deep ambivalence about our own agency is the engine of so much of our psychological distress. As Yalom writes, "Responsibility may be a glorious concept, a term that inspires us and enhances our feelings of pride and power, but it is a heavy load to bear."

In the therapy room, this conflict rarely presents itself directly. People do not typically come to therapy saying, "I am suffering from the burden of my existential freedom." Instead, they come with complaints about their powerlessness. They feel trapped by their circumstances: their marriage, their job, their personality, their past. They present themselves as the victims of external forces. A central task of existential psychotherapy is to gently and compassionately help the individual move from a position of seeing themselves as a victim of their world to seeing themselves as the creator of it. This involves a meticulous examination of the choices, often subtle and unconscious, that the person is making every day to perpetuate their own unhappiness.

Consider a woman who feels trapped in a verbally abusive relationship. She complains of her partner's cruelty and her own helplessness. The therapeutic work would involve exploring not just the partner's behavior, but her own role in the dynamic. What choices is she making that keep her in this situation? What fears are preventing her from leaving? Perhaps she is afraid of being alone (existential isolation), or of the financial instability that leaving would entail. The therapist helps her to see that her feeling of being "trapped" is, in part, a defense against the terrifying reality of her own freedom to choose differently. To acknowledge this freedom is to become fully responsible for her own life, a responsibility that can feel more frightening than the known misery of her current situation. The goal is not to blame her for her predicament, but to empower her by helping her reclaim her sense of agency. The moment she can say, "I am not trapped; I am choosing to stay out of fear," she has taken the first step from a position of bad faith to one of authenticity. She has moved from being an object to which things happen, to a subject who chooses.

Yalom's framework of the four givens provides us with a profound and practical map of the human psyche. It takes the grand, sweeping insights of existential philosophy and grounds them in the concrete struggles of our everyday lives. It shows us that our anxieties are not just random malfunctions of the brain, but are deeply meaningful responses to the fundamental conditions of our existence. Our fear of death, our struggle with isolation, our quest for meaning, and our profound ambivalence about our own freedom are not separate issues; they are deeply intertwined. Our freedom forces us to confront the reality of our finitude, our ultimate aloneness, and the lack of any inherent purpose in the universe. It is the central dynamic that makes the other givens so psychologically potent. To discover freedom is to be awakened not just to our own power to choose, but to the full, terrifying, and magnificent scope of the human condition.

The Body: The Ambiguous Ground of Freedom

Our exploration of freedom has thus far taken place largely in the theater of the mind. We have spoken of consciousness, choice, and anxiety as if they were phenomena of a pure, disembodied will. But this is an abstraction. The discovery of freedom, the weight of responsibility, the dizziness of possibility—none of these occur in a vacuum. They are experienced through the medium that both grants us access to the world and sets our most fundamental limits: the human body. To be free is to be an *embodied* freedom, a consciousness inextricably tangled with flesh, blood, and bone. This embodiment is not a secondary characteristic of our being; it is the primary, ambiguous ground upon which the drama of our freedom unfolds.

The body is our first and most intimate facticity. We do not *have* a body in the way we have a possession; we *are* our bodies, even as we transcend them through consciousness. It is through the body that we encounter the world—we see the thousand doors, we feel the knot of anxiety in our stomach, we carry the physical weight of exhaustion after a difficult decision. The body is the instrument of our freedom, the means by which our choices are enacted in the world. To write a book, to build a relationship, to walk through a chosen door—all require a body capable of the task.

Yet, simultaneously, the body is the most potent reminder of our *unfreedom*. It is subject to laws we did not write: the law of gravity, the law of decay, the law of mortality. It gets sick, it feels pain, it ages, and it will, inevitably, die. It houses appetites and urges that often feel alien to our conscious will. A pang of hunger can derail a meditation; a surge of fear can paralyze a conscious intention to be brave; a passionate desire can overwhelm our carefully constructed moral codes. In these moments, the body does not feel like an instrument of freedom, but a prison of determinism, a puppet master pulling strings of biology and chemistry that we can neither see nor control.

This ambiguity is the source of a profound and often unspoken anxiety. The body is the living, breathing contradiction of our condition: it is the vehicle of our transcendence and the absolute guarantee of our finitude. We are a "for-itself" that is also, inescapably, an "in-itself." We can project ourselves into future possibilities, but we do so from a body that is rooted in the present and decaying toward a definite end. This is why our relationship with our own physicality is so often fraught with conflict. We seek to master it, optimize it, and control it, desperate to align its stubborn reality with the boundless aspirations of our freedom. The multi-trillion-dollar industries of diet, fitness, and wellness are, in large part, testaments to this existential struggle—attempts to negotiate the terms of our embodiment, to make the body a more perfect and compliant servant of the will.

This struggle manifests in two primary forms of bad faith regarding the body.

First, we can flee from our freedom *by identifying completely with the body*, by reducing ourselves to a mere biological object. This is the person who says, "I can't help it, it's my hormones," or "I'm just not a disciplined person, it's how I'm built." It is the surrender to the body as a deterministic machine, an abdication of the responsibility to bring conscious choice to bear on our physical impulses and habits. It is to live as a creature of pure facticity.

Second, and more commonly in certain modern cultures, we can flee from our facticity *by denying the body's reality and limitations*. This is the fantasy of pure mind, of limitless optimization. It is the belief that with the right biohacking, the perfect supplement regimen, or the ultimate workout, we can transcend aging, vulnerability, and fatigue. It is the attempt to turn the body into a perfect, polished, and permanent object, thereby denying its messy, mortal, and ambiguous nature. This, too, is bad faith. It is a refusal to accept the fundamental condition of being an embodied spirit—that we are fragile, that we will suffer, and that we will die.

An authentic existence requires us to hold this ambiguity without fleeing to either extreme. It means accepting the body in its full reality: as both a powerful, skilled agent of our projects and a vulnerable, finite thing that will ultimately fail us. It means listening to its wisdom—its signals of fatigue, its cries of pain, its expressions of joy—without being enslaved by its every whim. It means recognizing that our freedom is always *situated* in *this* body, with *these* capacities and *these* limits.

The burden of freedom, then, includes the burden of this embodiment. We must choose how to care for this body, how to use it, how to present it to the world, and how to make meaning of its inevitable sufferings and decline. The courage to be free is, therefore, also the courage to be a body—to accept the pleasure and the pain, the strength and the weakness, the vibrant health and the slow decay. It is to understand that every choice we make is not just a choice of the mind, but an act committed by a living, breathing, and dying creature. Our freedom is not abstract. It is lived in the quickened heartbeat of anxiety, the slumped shoulders of defeat, the firm handshake of a commitment, and the final, quiet breath. To embrace our freedom is to embrace this whole, ambiguous, and magnificent corporeal reality.

Modern Psychology's Take on Autonomy

The journey we have taken thus far, from the anxious introspection of Kierkegaard to the radical ontology of Sartre and the compassionate clinical wisdom of Yalom, has charted a rich, deep, and often unsettling map of human freedom. It is a map drawn from the subjective experience of what it means to be an existing individual, a tradition of inquiry that relies on phenomenological insight, philosophical rigor, and therapeutic observation. To a mind trained in the empirical methods of modern science, however, this tradition can at times seem untethered, its claims profound but ultimately unfalsifiable. It is one thing to assert that humans are "condemned to be free"; it is another to prove it. It is therefore both remarkable and deeply significant that in the latter half of the 20th century, working in a completely different tradition and using an entirely different set of tools, the field of psychology began to arrive at a set of conclusions that, in many ways, provide a stunning scientific validation for what the existentialists had intuited all along. While the language is different, the core insight is the same: a sense of authentic, self-directed choice is not a philosophical luxury, but a fundamental and non-negotiable component of human well-being.

One of the most robust and influential frameworks in this area is Self-Determination Theory, or SDT, developed by the psychologists Edward Deci and Richard Ryan. Beginning in the 1970s, Deci and Ryan conducted a series of now-classic experiments that sought to understand the nature of human motivation. They were interested in what drives people to act, to learn, and to grow. Their research led them to propose that all human beings, regardless of culture or background, have three innate and universal psychological needs. Just as our physical bodies require water, food, and shelter to survive, our psyches require the satisfaction of these three needs to thrive. The first is the need for competence, the feeling that we are effective and capable in our actions. The second is the need for relatedness, the feeling that we are connected to and cared for by others. And the third, which is of most interest to us here, is the need for autonomy.

In the context of SDT, autonomy does not mean independence, self-sufficiency, or a detachment from others. It means something far more subtle and psychologically profound. Autonomy is the need to feel that our actions are volitional, that they are an expression of our own authentic self. It is the need to feel that we are the originators of our own behavior, rather than mere pawns being moved about by external forces. An autonomous act is one that we stand behind, one that is congruent with our values and interests. We can be autonomously dependent on another person, for example, if we wholeheartedly and freely choose to be so. Conversely, we can be non-autonomously independent, such as a person who rebels against authority not out of a genuine value, but out of a rigid, compulsive need to defy expectations. The key is not whether we are acting alone or with others, but whether the locus of initiation for the behavior is perceived as internal or external.

This distinction is the psychological bedrock that echoes the existentialists' preoccupation with authenticity. To act autonomously is, in a very real sense, to live in good faith. It is to own one's choices and to act from a place of inner coherence. A non-autonomous act, one driven by external pressures, rewards, or punishments, is the psychological equivalent of Sartrean bad faith. It is behavior that is disowned, behavior for which we feel little personal responsibility. Deci and Ryan's great insight was to demonstrate this empirically. In their early experiments, they found that when people were given an external reward, such as money, for performing an activity they initially found intrinsically interesting, their motivation to perform the activity once the reward was removed actually decreased. The external reward had shifted their locus of causality from internal to external. It had undermined their sense of autonomy. The activity was no longer something they *chose* to do, but something they *had* to do to get the reward. This finding has been replicated hundreds of times and has profound implications. It suggests that many of the motivational strategies used in our schools, workplaces, and even our own attempts at self-improvement—the elaborate systems of rewards and punishments—may in fact be systematically eroding the very sense of autonomy that is essential for genuine, lasting engagement and well-being.

A second, parallel stream of research that reinforces these conclusions comes from the work of the psychologist Julian Rotter and his concept of Locus of Control. Developed in the 1950s and 60s, this theory proposes that individuals differ in their generalized beliefs about the forces that determine the outcomes in their lives. People with a strong internal locus of control believe that they have a significant degree of control over their own lives, that their actions, efforts, and decisions are the primary drivers of what happens to them. They see themselves as the agents of their own fate. In stark contrast, people with a strong external locus of control believe that their lives are primarily determined by forces outside of themselves: by luck, by fate, by powerful other people, or by complex, unpredictable social and economic systems. They perceive themselves not as agents, but as objects to which things happen.

The parallels to existential thought are impossible to miss. A person with a strong internal locus of control is living out the existential ideal of accepting responsibility. They are confronting their freedom and owning the consequences of their choices. A person with a strong external locus of control, on the other hand, is engaged in a psychological strategy that is functionally identical to bad faith. By attributing their successes and, more often, their failures to external factors, they are able to abdicate the heavy burden of personal responsibility. It is a way of fleeing from the anguish of freedom. The story of victimhood, the narrative that one's life is controlled by outside forces, is a powerful psychological defense against the anxiety of having to choose.

The vast body of research that has grown out of this concept over the past half-century has demonstrated in no uncertain terms the profound benefits of cultivating an internal locus of control. People with a more internal locus of control tend to be more academically and professionally successful, as they are more likely to believe that their efforts will pay off. They tend to have better physical health, as they are more likely to engage in healthy behaviors like exercise and proper diet, believing that their actions can influence their well-being. They report higher levels of happiness and lower levels of depression and anxiety, as they feel a sense of agency and empowerment rather than helplessness. This is not to say that external forces are not real and powerful; social and economic structures can and do place very real constraints on people's lives. But even within those constraints, the belief that one has a measure of control, that one's choices matter, is a powerful predictor of psychological flourishing. Science is here confirming what the existentialists knew: while the acceptance of responsibility is a heavy burden, the alternative—a life of perceived powerlessness and abdication—is far heavier.

What this body of modern psychological research provides is a new and powerful language for describing the discovery of freedom. The journey from childhood to adulthood can be seen as a gradual shift from an external to an internal locus of control, a process of learning that we are not simply subject to the world, but are active participants in its creation. A healthy psychological development is one in which our innate need for autonomy is supported and nurtured by our environment, allowing us to develop a robust sense of self and a feeling of volitional engagement with our lives. When this need is thwarted, when we are consistently controlled, coerced, or made to feel that our choices do not matter, the result is not just a lack of motivation, but a deep psychological wounding that can manifest as apathy, anxiety, depression, and a pervasive sense of helplessness.

This chapter began with the unsettling, dizzying discovery of possibility as described by Kierkegaard. It moved through Sartre's stark insistence on our condemnation to a freedom without excuses, and Yalom's compassionate framing of this freedom as one of the ultimate concerns we must all face. And now, we have seen how the dispassionate, data-driven inquiries of modern psychology have converged on a remarkably similar point. The human psyche is not built for a life of passive compliance. We are wired with a deep, intrinsic need to be the authors of our own lives. The discovery of freedom is not just a moment of philosophical awakening; it is the dawning of a fundamental psychological necessity. The existentialists, through their profound and courageous introspection, managed to grasp a fundamental truth of human nature that science has only recently begun to systematically measure and confirm. And it is this very confluence of insight—the philosophical, the clinical, and the scientific—that makes the central paradox of our inquiry so potent. If a sense of autonomy and freedom is so essential to our well-being, then why does it so often feel like such an unbearable burden? Having now established the nature of this freedom and its discovery, we must turn to the other side of the coin: the immense and often overwhelming weight of the responsibility it entails.

* * *

2

The Weight of Responsibility

I n the landscape of the human condition we have just surveyed, the discovery of freedom appears as a monumental and transformative event. It is the moment the ground of certainty falls away, revealing the vast, dizzying expanse of our own possibility. To become aware of one's freedom is to awaken to the reality that we are the artists of our own lives, standing before a blank canvas with the power to create whatever self we choose. It is a moment of profound, and often terrifying, empowerment. But this image is incomplete. Freedom is only one half of a fundamental and indivisible equation. The other half, the inescapable consequence that gives freedom its substance and its gravity, is responsibility. If freedom is the power to author our lives, then responsibility is the unavoidable fact of our authorship. The two are as inseparable as a shadow from its object; where one is present, the other is cast with absolute certainty. This chapter is an inquiry into the nature of that shadow: its composition, its emotional texture, and the immense weight it places upon a life.

When we speak of responsibility in our everyday lives, we typically do so in a conventional, circumscribed sense. We speak of our responsibilities *to* others: the responsibility of a parent to a child, of an employee to an employer, of a citizen to the state. This is a social and ethical framework of duties and obligations, of promises made and rules to be followed. It is a responsibility that involves answering to an external authority. But the existential tradition calls us to consider a far deeper and more radical form of responsibility, one that precedes and underpins all of these social contracts. This is the responsibility not for our specific duties, but for our very existence. It is the responsibility for the person we are actively creating with every choice we make. It is, in the starkest terms, the responsibility for our own life. This is not a responsibility one can be assigned or can accept; it is a condition into which we are thrown by the very fact of our freedom.

This is the central insight that follows directly from the Sartrean premise that existence precedes essence. If there is no preordained human nature, no divine blueprint, no cosmic script for us to follow, then the task of creating our own essence falls entirely to us. We are responsible, as Sartre insisted, for what we are. This is the source of the weight. It is the burden of the artist who must not only paint the picture but must first invent the very concept of art. We must choose not only our path, but the values and principles that will serve as our compass. There is no external authority to which we can appeal for justification. We cannot say we made a particular choice because it was "right" in some absolute, cosmic sense. We can only say that we chose it, and in doing so, we affirmed it as a value. We are the sole legislators of our own moral universe, a task of such magnitude that the impulse to flee from it is not a sign of pathology, but a deeply understandable human response.

This weight is compounded by the irreversible nature of time. Each choice is a brushstroke on the canvas that cannot be fully erased. To choose one career is to foreclose on others; to commit to one partner is to relinquish the possibility of all others; to live in one city is to not live in another. Our lives are a series of such choices, a continuous process of turning possibility into actuality. The responsibility we bear is not just for the life we are living, but for all the unlived lives we have necessarily sacrificed along the way. We are the curators of a single, linear story carved out of an infinity of potential narratives. This awareness, that our choices are final and that we alone are their author, generates a profound and uniquely human form of anxiety. It is the anxiety of being the ultimate cause of our own being, without a safety net and without a guide.

It is no wonder, then, that we have developed such sophisticated and often unconscious strategies for avoiding this burden. The flight from responsibility is one of the most powerful and persistent dynamics in our psychological lives. We attempt to offload our burden onto other people, onto our circumstances, onto our past, onto our genetic predispositions, or onto abstract systems like "the economy" or "society." We adopt the posture of the victim, the martyr, or the passive observer of our own lives. We tell ourselves stories in which we are not the protagonist, but a minor character being acted upon by forces beyond our control. These strategies, which we will explore in detail, are a form of what Sartre called "bad faith." They are a denial of our freedom, an attempt to convince ourselves that we are not the authors of our own lives. This self-deception provides a measure of comfort, a temporary release from the anguish of choosing, but it comes at an immense cost: the forfeiture of an authentic existence and the loss of the very agency that defines our humanity. This chapter is an exploration of that fundamental tension: the clash between the inescapable reality of our responsibility and our deep-seated psychological need to escape from it.

We will begin by delving more deeply into the nature of responsibility as an existential condition, distinguishing it from our more common understandings and exploring what it means to truly "own" one's existence. From there, we will examine the primary emotional consequences of our relationship with responsibility, focusing on the powerful and often misunderstood experiences of guilt and shame. We will see how existential guilt, in particular, can serve as a vital signal, an inner alarm that alerts us to a life unlived and a responsibility avoided. We will then turn our attention to the specific mechanisms of this avoidance, analyzing the common psychological strategies of denial, blame, and projection that we all use to lighten our existential load. Finally, we will ground these concepts in the practical, everyday arenas where the weight of responsibility is most acutely felt: in our intimate relationships, our professional lives, and our moral choices. Here, we will see how the failure to claim ownership of one's role corrodes intimacy, erodes purpose, and hinders the development of a mature and ethical life. The journey through this chapter is a confrontation with the heavy, often uncomfortable, but ultimately ennobling other half of freedom. It is an argument that while the weight of responsibility is immense, the act of choosing to bear it is the very thing that gives a human life its dignity and its meaning.

Responsibility as an Existential Condition

In the common language of our social and moral lives, the concept of responsibility is both ubiquitous and clearly defined. It is a language of contracts, of duties, of obligations owed and debts to be paid. A parent is responsible for the welfare of their child; an engineer is responsible for the structural integrity of a bridge; a citizen is responsible for obeying the laws of the land. This form of responsibility is fundamentally transactional. It operates within a pre-existing framework of rules, roles, and expectations. It involves answering to an external authority, be it a legal system, a professional code of conduct, a set of social norms, or the direct needs of another person. It is a responsibility that is assigned, accepted, and can, in some cases, be discharged. While this conventional understanding is essential for the functioning of any society, it does not touch the deeper, more unsettling layer of responsibility that the existential tradition compels us to confront. It is this deeper layer that concerns us here: responsibility not as a social contract, but as an inescapable ontological condition.

Existential responsibility is not about answering *to* someone for what you have done. It is about answering *for* the simple, stark, and terrifying fact of your own being. It is the direct and unavoidable consequence of the freedom we explored in the previous chapter. If we accept the premise that our existence precedes our essence, that we are born without a preordained purpose or a fixed human nature, then the task of creating that essence falls entirely to us. We are, at every moment, the primary and sole author of the person we are becoming. This is not a role we can accept or decline; it is a condition that is thrust upon us at the moment of our awakening into self-awareness. We are the artist, the canvas, and the brush, and there is no one else to credit or to blame for the final portrait. This is the radical responsibility that Sartre had in mind: a responsibility not for our actions alone, but for our character, our values, our beliefs, our emotions, and even our interpretation of the world. It is the responsibility for the totality of one's own existence.

To grasp the immense weight of this condition, we must first appreciate the profound sense of groundlessness from which it arises. For most of human history, the burden of this ultimate responsibility was softened by a belief in a transcendent order. A divine creator provided a blueprint for humanity, a set of commandments, and a clear purpose for a human life. One's responsibility was primarily to understand and to follow this divine script. But in the modern, secularized world, this external ground has for many become unstable or has disappeared entirely. We find ourselves in the vertiginous position of having to create our own values, to legislate our own moral law. There is no cosmic rulebook to consult, no ultimate authority to which we can appeal for justification. When we make a significant life choice, we cannot defend it by claiming it was the objectively "right" thing to do. We can only claim that it was the thing we chose. In that choice, we simultaneously create a value and reveal the self who holds that value. The anguish of this position is the anguish of the ultimate legislator, who must create the law out of nothing but their own freedom.

This weight is compounded by the irreversible, linear nature of our existence. Time, as it is lived, moves in only one direction. Each choice we make is not a temporary experiment but a permanent mark on the timeline of our lives. It is an act that transforms the open field of possibility into the fixed and unchangeable reality of the past. To choose to become a doctor is to actively choose not to become the musician one might have been. To commit to a life with one person is to actively close the door on a life with any other. We are constantly, through our choices, pruning the branching tree of our potential, leaving a single, unique path in our wake. The responsibility we bear is therefore not just for the life we are living, but for all the unlived lives that our choices have rendered impossible. We are the authors of a single story, and the weight of that authorship comes from the knowledge that we are simultaneously the editors who have cut every other possible plotline. This is a far cry from the conventional responsibility of meeting a deadline or paying a bill. It is the solemn, lifelong task of building a single, finite self out of an infinity of potential selves, and owning the result in its entirety.

So what does it truly mean to "own" one's existence in this way? It means, first and foremost, a radical shift in our internal posture toward life, a movement from a passive stance to an active one. It is the conscious decision to cease seeing oneself as an object to which things happen and to begin seeing oneself as the subject who chooses their response to what happens. This is the crucial distinction that separates a life of authentic engagement from a life of bad faith. The person living in bad faith experiences their life as a series of events imposed upon them by external forces. Their narrative is one of victimhood, of being acted upon by their boss, their spouse, their past, their society. The person who embraces their existential responsibility, however, recognizes that while they cannot always control the events that occur in their life, they are absolutely and unequivocally responsible for the meaning they assign to those events and the actions they take in response to them.

Let us consider the case of a woman named Sarah who, at the age of forty-five, is suddenly laid off from a job she has held for two decades. The company is restructuring, and her position has been eliminated. This event, the layoff itself, is part of her facticity. It is a brute, unchosen fact of her situation. In the initial shock, Sarah's immediate response is one of victimhood. She feels that this has been done *to* her. She blames the callousness of the corporation, the ruthlessness of the economy, the unfairness of her manager. Her internal monologue is a litany of powerlessness: "I've given them the best years of my life, and this is how they repay me. There's nothing I can do. At my age, no one will hire me. My life is ruined." In this state, Sarah has abdicated her responsibility. She has defined herself as an object, a victim of circumstance. She is focusing exclusively on her facticity and denying her transcendence, her freedom to choose her response. Her feeling of being trapped is, in part, a psychological defense. It is a way to avoid the terrifying burden of having to decide what to do next. As long as she is a victim, she is absolved of the responsibility to act.

The act of owning her existence would require a profound internal shift. It would not involve denying the pain or the injustice of the situation. It would involve acknowledging the facts of her situation without defining herself by them. The shift would sound something like this: "I have been laid off. That is a fact. It is painful and it is frightening. But I am not my job. The company has made its choice, and now I am responsible for mine. I am responsible for how I handle this fear. I am responsible for the story I tell myself about this event. Is this the end of my career, or is it an unexpected and unwelcome opportunity to build something new? I am responsible for the effort I put into finding new work. I am responsible for the attitude I bring to my family during this difficult time. This situation is not of my choosing, but my response to it is entirely my own."

Notice the profound change in the locus of control. The narrative has shifted from one of passive victimhood to one of active authorship. Sarah has taken ownership of her feelings, her interpretations, and her future actions. The weight of this responsibility is immense. It is far easier, in the short term, to remain in a state of righteous anger and blame. But the path of ownership, while more difficult, is the only one that reclaims her agency and her dignity. It is the only path that allows her to move forward not as a casualty of her history, but as the creator of her future. This is the essence of owning one's existence. It is the constant, moment-to-moment practice of recognizing our freedom to choose our response, even in situations we did not choose for ourselves.

This concept of responsibility extends even further, beyond the self and into the social world. Sartre argued that in choosing for ourselves, we are simultaneously choosing for all of humanity. This does not mean that we are a role model in the conventional sense. It means that every action we take is an affirmation of a particular value, a presentation of an image of humanity as we believe it ought to be. When we choose to act with integrity in a difficult situation, we are not just making a personal choice; we are positing a world in which integrity is a fundamental human value. When we choose to respond to cruelty with compassion, we are legislating for a world in which compassion is the proper human response. Our individual life, in this view, is a microcosm of our vision for the whole of existence.

This adds another layer of profound weight to our choices. Our responsibility is not just for the self we are creating, but for the image of humanity we are offering to the world. A person who lives a life of cynical self-interest is, in effect, making the statement: "This is what a human being is: a creature of pure self-interest." A person who dedicates their life to a cause beyond themselves is making a different statement: "This is what a human being can be: a creature capable of transcendence and commitment." There is no neutral ground. Every act, every decision, no matter how small or private it may seem, is a vote cast for a particular version of humanity. To become fully conscious of this is to experience what Sartre called "anguish." It is the feeling of being crushed by the weight of this total responsibility, a responsibility for all of humanity that rests on the shoulders of each individual.

In the end, responsibility as an existential condition is the recognition that we are the single point of origin for our own lives. It is the understanding that while we are thrown into a world with a set of unchosen facts, we are forever responsible for the meaning we make of them. It is the acceptance that there are no ultimate excuses, no final appeals to a higher authority that can absolve us of our role as the author of our own essence. This is a heavy, and at times unbearable, burden. But it is also the source of our greatest potential for dignity and meaning. To be responsible for one's own existence is to be a participant in, rather than a spectator of, the unfolding of one's own life. It is the most demanding of all human tasks, and the one from which all others derive their significance.

Guilt, Shame, and the Emotional Consequences of Choice

To accept responsibility for one's own existence is not merely an intellectual exercise or a philosophical posture; it is a profoundly emotional experience. The weight of our authorship, the constant awareness of our role as the creator of our own self, generates a complex and often turbulent inner landscape. Among the most powerful and pervasive emotions in this landscape are guilt and shame. These are words we use frequently, often interchangeably, to describe the painful feeling that follows a transgression. Yet, from an existential perspective, these emotions are far more than simple responses to a broken rule. They are fundamental signals about the state of our relationship with our own freedom, and learning to interpret them correctly is a crucial step toward a more authentic life.

In our conventional understanding, guilt is a straightforward affair. It is the psychological and emotional consequence of violating a known moral, ethical, or social code. We feel guilty when we lie to a loved one, when we betray a trust, when we fail to meet a clear obligation. This type of guilt, which we might call "conventional" or "neurotic" guilt, is specific and directed. It is attached to a particular action or inaction. It serves an important pro-social function, acting as a kind of internal alarm system that alerts us when our behavior has damaged a relationship or violated a shared value. This guilt can, at least in theory, be resolved. We can confess, apologize, make amends, or accept a punishment. The act of reparation can, over time, alleviate the feeling of guilt and restore a sense of moral equilibrium.

The existential tradition, however, invites us to consider a much deeper, more amorphous, and more unsettling form of guilt. This is not the guilt of a specific wrongdoing, but the guilt of a fundamental falling short. It is not a sin against another person or a social code, but a sin against oneself. This is existential guilt. It arises not from what we have done, but from what we have failed to do. It is the guilt of the unlived life, of the possibilities we have neglected, of the potential we have failed to actualize. It is the dull, persistent ache that comes from the awareness, however dim, that we are not the person we could be. The German philosopher Martin Heidegger, a key figure in this tradition, argued that this guilt is a fundamental part of our being. We are, by our very nature, "guilty" in the sense that we are indebted to our own potential, a debt we can never fully repay.

This form of guilt is not tied to a single event. It is a pervasive mood, a background hum of unease. It is the feeling of the man who has spent his life in a safe, respectable, and lucrative career that he chose to please his parents, all the while knowing that his true passion, his true self, lies dormant and undeveloped. He has broken no rules. He is, by all external measures, a "good" and "responsible" person. He has no conventional guilt to pinpoint. Yet he suffers from a chronic sense of emptiness, a low-grade depression he cannot name. This feeling is his existential guilt. It is the quiet mourning for the self he has betrayed. It is the signal from the deepest part of his being that he has abdicated his primary responsibility: the responsibility to live his own life. This guilt cannot be resolved through an apology or an act of penance. It can only be addressed by a courageous turning toward the life he has avoided.

This chronic, nameless emptiness is more than guilt; it is a state of mourning. It is the grief for the unlived life—the quiet, persistent sorrow for the artist, the traveler, the teacher, or the entrepreneur that still lives within us as a phantom of potential. We do not just feel guilty for neglecting this potential; we grieve for it. We feel a sense of loss for the person we might have been, for the loves we might have known, for the contributions we might have made. This grief is unique because its object never truly existed; it is the mourning for a future that was possible but never actualized. And like all grief, it cannot be resolved by rationalization. It can only be honored by acknowledging its truth—that every choice is a beautiful and terrible farewell to a thousand other selves—and then, courageously, by bringing more of that forsaken potential into the one life we are actually living.

A certain amount of this guilt is an unavoidable feature of a conscious human life. Because our existence is finite and our potential is vast, every choice we make is an act of exclusion. To choose to be a dedicated scientist is to choose not to be the concert pianist one might have been. To devote oneself to raising a family is to choose not to live the life of a solitary artist. We cannot be all the things we are capable of being. Therefore, we are always, in some sense, guilty of neglecting some portion of our potential. The person who feels no such guilt, the person who is perfectly content with the self they have created, may not be a picture of mental health, but rather a person who has so narrowed their awareness that they are no longer in touch with the full scope of their own possibilities. A healthy, vibrant life will always contain these faint echoes of our unlived lives, the gentle, bittersweet guilt for the selves we had to sacrifice to become the self we are.

This necessary guilt, however, is different from the corrosive guilt that arises from a life of systemic inauthenticity and avoidance. The latter is a signal not of a difficult choice made, but of a fundamental refusal to choose at all. It is the guilt of the person who drifts through life on a path of least resistance, passively accepting the roles and expectations assigned to them by others without ever consciously and freely committing to them. Their life is not their own creation, but a collage of borrowed pieces. The gnawing feeling of inauthenticity they experience is their existential guilt calling them to account, urging them to take up the difficult but necessary task of authorship.

Closely related to guilt, but in many ways more painful and paralyzing, is the emotion of shame. The classic distinction between the two is a crucial one: guilt is the feeling that "I did something bad," whereas shame is the feeling that "I *am* bad." Guilt is focused on a specific behavior; shame is a global indictment of the self. Guilt motivates us to repair our actions, but shame often motivates us to hide our very being. It is the intensely painful feeling of being seen as flawed, unworthy, and contemptible. Where guilt is a private reckoning with one's own conscience, shame is an inherently social emotion. It is a fear of disconnection, of being cast out from the human community because of some fundamental defect in who we are.

In the context of responsibility, shame functions as a powerful inhibitor of authentic action. The fear of shame is often the primary force that prevents us from embracing our freedom. The aspiring entrepreneur who never launches their business for fear of failure, the writer who keeps their manuscript locked in a drawer for fear of rejection, the person who stays silent in a meeting for fear of saying something foolish—all are paralyzed by the anticipated shame of being seen and found wanting. This paralysis is a form of existential avoidance. It is a retreat from the arena of choice and action into the seemingly safe bunker of invisibility. By refusing to put our true self into the world, by refusing to take the risk of being seen, we shield ourselves from the potential pain of shame. But this safety comes at a terrible price. It is the price of the unlived life. The avoidance of shame becomes a cage that keeps us from the very experiences that are necessary for growth and self-actualization.

Embracing our responsibility for our lives, then, requires a willingness to risk shame. To choose a path is to risk that it will be the wrong one. To speak our truth is to risk that it will be ridiculed. To create something new is to risk that it will be judged as inadequate. The courage to be authentic is inextricably linked to the courage to be vulnerable, to be seen in all our imperfection. A life lived in constant fear of shame is a life lived in a state of perpetual self-censorship, a life in which our choices are dictated not by our own values and aspirations, but by our desperate attempt to manage the perceptions of others.

The great challenge of a mature life is to learn to listen to these powerful emotional signals without being controlled by them. It is to learn to distinguish the healthy, pro-social sting of conventional guilt from the deep, soul-level ache of existential guilt. It is to recognize the paralyzing grip of shame and to find the courage to act in spite of it. The path forward is not to seek a life free from these uncomfortable emotions, for such a life would be a shrunken and impoverished one. The path is to reframe our relationship with them. Existential guilt, in this new frame, ceases to be a sign of our failure and becomes a vital and trustworthy guide. It is the conscience of our potential, the inner compass that points us back toward the life we are meant to be living.

The proper response to this guilt is not to numb it with distraction or to rationalize it away, but to turn toward it with curiosity and respect. We must learn to ask ourselves: what is this feeling trying to tell me? Which part of myself have I abandoned? In what area of my life have I abdicated my freedom and my responsibility? To listen to our existential guilt is to engage in the most important form of dialogue we can have: a dialogue with the self we have not yet become. It is a call to take up our authorship with renewed seriousness, to pick up the pen we have let fall to the side, and to begin, once again, the difficult but magnificent work of writing our own story. This is the process by which the painful weight of guilt is transformed into the empowering posture of responsibility. It is by answering this call that we move from a life of quiet regret to one of integrity, purpose, and wholeness.

Avoidance and Denial

The recognition of our total responsibility for our own existence is a psychologically demanding, and often terrifying, awakening. It is the moment we are made aware of the full weight of our freedom, the moment we understand that we are the sole architects of our lives, standing on a ground of our own making. Given the immense pressure of this condition, it is not only understandable but deeply, fundamentally human that we should develop elaborate strategies to lighten this load. The impulse to hide from responsibility, to deny our authorship, is not a sign of some unique character flaw or moral failing; it is a universal psychic reflex, a deeply ingrained defense mechanism against the anxiety that our freedom provokes. This flight from responsibility is the core dynamic of what Sartre termed "bad faith." It is the myriad ways we lie to ourselves, the sophisticated and often unconscious narratives we construct to convince ourselves that we are not free subjects but determined objects, buffeted by forces beyond our control. This section is an exploration of these common strategies of avoidance and denial, the psychological hiding places where we seek refuge from the burden of our own agency.

Perhaps the most common and straightforward of these strategies is the simple act of blame. Blame is the psychic equivalent of hot potato; it is the rapid offloading of responsibility onto another person, an institution, or the amorphous entity of "circumstance." It is a powerful psychological maneuver because it instantly transforms the blamer from an active participant in their own predicament into a passive, and often righteous, victim. The employee who is passed over for a promotion does not have to confront their own potential shortcomings—their lack of initiative, their underdeveloped skills, their poor interpersonal relationships—if they can construct a compelling narrative in which the primary cause is a biased manager, a toxic work environment, or a system of office politics rigged against them. The person who is chronically unhappy in their relationships does not have to face their own patterns of poor communication, unrealistic expectations, or fear of intimacy if they can consistently locate the fault in their partners, concluding that they simply have bad luck in "picking" people. Blame provides a release from the discomfort of self-examination. It creates an external enemy, and in doing so, it preserves a sense of our own innocence and absolves us of the difficult work of change.

A more complex and insidious form of this externalization is the psychoanalytic mechanism of projection. Where simple blame assigns fault to an external agent, projection takes an unwanted or unacceptable aspect of our own self—a feeling, a trait, a desire—and unconsciously attributes it to someone else. It is a way of disowning a part of our own being and seeing it as coming toward us from the outside world. For example, a person who is struggling with their own unacknowledged anger might perceive the world as a hostile and aggressive place, constantly seeing anger and ill-intent in the neutral actions of others. A manager who is deeply indecisive and anxious about making a difficult decision might accuse their team of being uncooperative and resistant, projecting their own internal paralysis outward. This is a particularly potent form of avoidance because it feels so real. We are not consciously pretending; we genuinely experience the other person as the source of the problem. This allows us to engage in a righteous battle with the external world, all the while avoiding the more terrifying and necessary battle with the disowned parts of ourselves. We flee the responsibility for our own inner conflicts by staging them as dramas in the external world.

Beyond blaming others, we often seek refuge in various forms of determinism, constructing narratives in which our freedom is an illusion and our lives are dictated by forces beyond our control. One of the most popular forms of this in our scientifically-minded age is a kind of crude biological or psychological determinism. We use the language of science to absolve ourselves of responsibility. The person with a volatile temper declares, "I can't help it; I have a short fuse. It's just how my brain is wired." The chronically unmotivated individual explains their inaction by saying, "I probably have an undiagnosed attention disorder; my brain chemistry is working against me." While our biological and genetic predispositions are undeniably part of our facticity, a real and influential part of our given situation, this narrative transforms them from an influence into a verdict. It takes a partial truth—that our biology affects our temperament—and inflates it into a totalizing excuse that negates our freedom to choose how we manage that temperament. It is the difference between saying, "I have a predisposition to anger that I must work hard to manage," which is an act of responsibility, and saying, "I am an angry person, and there's nothing I can do about it," which is an act of bad faith.

A similar strategy is the appeal to historical determinism, the belief that we are the unchangeable products of our past. We use our personal history, particularly our childhood traumas and formative experiences, as the ultimate justification for our present behavior. A man who is emotionally distant and unable to commit in his relationships explains, "Of course I'm this way; my parents were so cold and critical. I never learned how to be intimate." Again, the influence of our past is profound and undeniable. It shapes our fears, our desires, our patterns of relating to others. A responsible life requires us to understand and grapple with our history. But the deterministic flight from responsibility occurs when our past is transformed from an explanation into a permanent alibi. It becomes a life sentence that excuses us from the ongoing, moment-to-moment choice of how to act *now*. The existential perspective insists that while we are never responsible for the hand we were dealt, we are always and completely responsible for how we choose to play that hand. To live in a state of authentic responsibility is to acknowledge the wounds of the past without allowing them to become the definitive script for the future.

We also engage in this avoidance on a societal level, appealing to a form of systemic determinism. We point to the very real injustices and constraints of our economic, political, and social systems as proof of our own powerlessness. The refrain becomes, "What's the point of trying when the system is rigged?" or "It's impossible for someone like me to get ahead in this economy." This is perhaps the most difficult form of avoidance to parse, because it is rooted in a significant truth. Systemic barriers are real and can be profoundly limiting. But the flight from responsibility occurs when this truth is used not as a catalyst for strategic action or collective resistance, but as a justification for personal apathy and despair. It becomes a narrative that forecloses any and all possibility of individual agency, a comforting blanket of hopelessness that relieves us of the burden of even having to try. The responsible position is one that holds two seemingly contradictory ideas at once: the acknowledgment that the system is powerful and often unjust, and the simultaneous insistence that we are still free to choose our response to that system.

Finally, we see this impulse to avoid responsibility manifest in our behaviors, particularly in the adoption of a posture of compulsivity or helplessness. A person may flee from the terrifying openness of their freedom by immersing themselves in a life of obsessive busyness or workaholism. The constant, unrelenting demands of their schedule create a sense of necessity that masks their underlying freedom. They do not have to make difficult choices about the meaning and direction of their life because they are simply "too busy." Their exhaustion becomes a badge of honor and a convenient excuse for their unlived life. Another common strategy is a kind of weaponized incompetence or learned helplessness. By adopting the role of the person who is "just not good at" certain things—managing finances, having difficult conversations, making decisions—we can often successfully induce others to take on that responsibility for us. It is a subtle but powerful way of remaining in a childlike state of dependency, protected from the risks and burdens of full adult agency.

All of these strategies—blame, projection, determinism, compulsivity, helplessness—serve the same fundamental purpose. They are attempts to reduce the unbearable anxiety of our radical freedom by creating a world in which we are not the authors of our own lives. They offer the profound psychological comfort of the alibi. The comfort, however, is a poisoned chalice. While it may shield us from the acute anxiety of choice, it does so at the cost of our vitality, our growth, and our sense of personal dignity. To live in a state of perpetual avoidance is to live as a ghost in one's own life, a passive spectator to a story that is happening to someone else. The first and most courageous step toward a more authentic existence is the willingness to see these patterns in ourselves, to turn on the lights in our psychological hiding places, and to begin the difficult but liberating work of reclaiming the responsibility we have so eagerly given away.

Responsibility in Love, Work, and Moral Life

The concepts of existential responsibility, guilt, and avoidance are not confined to the philosopher's study or the therapist's office. They are potent, dynamic forces that shape the most significant and intimate spheres of our lives. The weight of our authorship is felt most acutely not in moments of abstract contemplation, but in the concrete, high-stakes domains of our relationships, our careers, and our moral choices. It is in these arenas that the theoretical becomes deeply personal, and the failure to take ownership of our existence moves from being a philosophical error to a source of profound, tangible suffering. To live an authentic life requires us to carry the burden of responsibility not just as a general principle, but as a daily practice within the specific roles we inhabit.

Nowhere is the flight from responsibility more common, or more destructive, than in our intimate relationships. We enter into love carrying a powerful, culturally-endorsed fantasy: the myth of completion. We seek a partner who will make us whole, a soulmate who will understand us perfectly, a love that will heal our wounds and provide a permanent sanctuary from our existential aloneness. This romantic ideal, while alluring, is a sophisticated and powerful setup for bad faith. It frames the other person not as a separate, free being, but as an object whose purpose is to fill our own inner void. It is a fundamental abdication of our own responsibility for creating our own sense of wholeness and meaning. When we place this impossible burden on a relationship, the dynamic of blame and disappointment becomes inevitable.

Consider a common relational pattern: one partner complains of feeling unheard and abandoned, while the other complains of feeling suffocated and controlled. The first partner, let us call her Anna, blames her unhappiness on what she perceives as her partner's emotional distance. "He never opens up to me," she says. "He's a closed book. I can't feel close to him." The second partner, Tom, blames his withdrawal on Anna's perceived neediness. "She's always probing, always demanding more from me than I can give. I have to pull back just to feel like I can breathe." Both are engaged in a classic flight from responsibility. Anna is refusing to own her choice to make her partner the sole source of her emotional well-being. She is abdicating her responsibility for her own feelings, outsourcing them to Tom, and then blaming him when he fails to manage them to her satisfaction. Her sense of abandonment is real, but it is fueled by her own refusal to confront her existential isolation and to cultivate her own sources of validation and security.

Tom, equally, is in bad faith. He experiences his withdrawal not as a choice, but as a necessary, defensive reaction. He is refusing to take responsibility for his fear of intimacy and his difficulty with emotional expression. He has chosen to retreat into silence rather than to engage in the difficult and courageous work of setting boundaries, communicating his needs, and learning to be present even when it feels uncomfortable. He blames Anna for his withdrawal, just as she blames him for her unhappiness. They are locked in a self-perpetuating cycle of blame, each seeing themselves as the victim of the other. An authentic, responsible love would require a radical shift from both. It would require Anna to own her feelings and needs without making Tom responsible for them, and it would require Tom to own his fear and his choice to withdraw. It requires both to face the terrifying truth that their partner cannot save them from their own existential givens. True intimacy is not a fusion of two incomplete halves into a whole; it is a relationship between two free and responsible individuals who choose, day after day, to create a shared world while never losing sight of their fundamental separateness.

This same dynamic unfolds with equal force in the domain of our professional lives. For many in the modern world, a career is far more than a means of earning a living; it is a primary vehicle for identity, purpose, and self-actualization. This elevates the stakes immensely and creates fertile ground for the avoidance of responsibility. The most common manifestation of this is the posture of the "disenchanted employee," the individual who experiences their work as a source of drudgery, frustration, and meaninglessness. Their narrative is typically one of external blame: the company is soulless, the boss is incompetent, the work is trivial, the system is broken. They feel like a powerless "cog in the machine," a victim of corporate circumstance.

This feeling of powerlessness, while often rooted in very real frustrations, is a defense against the anxiety of ownership. To be a cog in the machine is to be absolved of responsibility. A cog is not responsible for the machine's direction or purpose; it simply turns when it is told to turn. The employee who adopts this posture has made an unconscious trade: they have surrendered their agency in exchange for the comfort of not having to choose. To take responsibility would be to confront a series of difficult and unsettling truths. It would be to acknowledge, "I am not a cog; I am a free person who is *choosing* to stay in this job. I am choosing the financial security, the predictability, or the familiarity of this role over the uncertainty and risk of seeking something more fulfilling. This state of disenchantment is not something that is happening *to* me; it is a state I am actively perpetuating through my own daily choice to show up."

This acknowledgment does not magically transform a bad job into a good one. What it does is transform the individual from a passive object into an active subject. It reclaims the agency that had been projected onto the corporation. Once a person owns their choice to be there, they are also forced to confront their freedom to choose differently. This is the source of the anxiety they were avoiding. It opens up a range of terrifying but empowering questions: What values am I compromising by staying here? What steps, however small, can I take to find more meaning in my current role? What is preventing me from looking for something else? What am I truly afraid of? Purpose, from an existential perspective, is not a magical quality that some jobs have and others do not. It is not something to be "found." It is something to be *built*. It is constructed, day by day, through the responsible application of our freedom, through the conscious choice to commit our energies to tasks and projects that align with our deepest values, even in the face of constraints and imperfections.

Finally, the weight of responsibility finds its ultimate expression in our moral life. A mature moral existence is not simply a matter of adhering to a set of externally imposed rules, whether from a religious text, a legal code, or a social convention. To do the "right" thing simply because you are told to, or out of a fear of punishment, is to remain in a state of moral childhood. An authentic moral life is one in which we take full responsibility for the values we choose to live by and for the consequences of the actions we take. It is the move from a morality of compliance to a morality of authorship.

The flight from this responsibility is evident in many forms. It is present in unthinking conformity, the tendency to adopt the moral judgments of our peer group or political tribe without critical self-examination. By outsourcing our conscience to the group, we avoid the difficult and lonely work of forging our own moral convictions. It is also present in a kind of cynical disengagement, the posture that "nothing matters" and that all moral choices are meaningless. This nihilism is not a sophisticated philosophical position, but a defense against the anguish of having to care, of having to choose a set of values and bear the responsibility for them in a world that offers no guarantees.

The challenge of moral responsibility is felt most acutely not in clear-cut situations, but in ambiguous ones, where values are in conflict and the right path is not obvious. It is in these moments that we are forced to confront our freedom in its rawest form. Imagine witnessing a colleague being subtly bullied in a meeting by a powerful superior. The conventional rules are unclear. To speak up is to risk your own professional standing. To stay silent is to be complicit in an act of cruelty. There is no simple, risk-free answer. In this moment, you are completely responsible. Your choice is not just about what you will do, but about who you will be. To speak up is to affirm a value of courage and solidarity. To stay silent is to affirm a value of self-preservation. Whatever you choose, you are the author of that act, and you are responsible for the self it creates. A mature moral life is defined by the willingness to stand in the anxiety of such moments and to make a choice, to own it, and to bear its consequences without excuse.

In love, in work, and in our moral lives, the fundamental challenge remains the same. It is the challenge of moving from a passive to an active stance, from seeing oneself as a product of circumstance to seeing oneself as the creator of a life. True intimacy, authentic purpose, and a dignified moral existence are not possible without this foundational act of taking responsibility. It is the weight that gives our freedom its meaning. It is the burden that, when lifted willingly, becomes the very source of our strength and our humanity.

* * *

II

Part Two: The Modern Predicament

How has modern life transformed freedom from a gift into a burden? Part 2 confronts our contemporary predicament, exploring how the endless options of consumer culture, the curated realities of the digital age, and the profound uncertainty of our times create a unique and heavy form of existential weight.

3

The Paradox of Choice

I f there is a central, unquestioned creed of modern Western society, it is that the path to well-being is paved with choice. This belief is the bedrock of our economic system, the promise of our political ideologies, and the implicit assumption in our personal lives. We have been raised on the gospel of options: that to be free is to have the maximum possible number of alternatives available to us at all times. The good life, according to this creed, is a life of expansive possibility, one in which the individual is empowered to select, from a vast and ever-growing menu, the precise components that will constitute their unique and optimized existence. This logic seems unimpeachable. If freedom is good, and choice is the mechanism of freedom, then more choice must necessarily be better. Our entire consumer culture is built upon this simple, alluring equation. The grocery store with one hundred types of cereal is considered superior to the one with ten; the streaming service with an endless library is preferable to a curated selection; the career path with limitless flexibility is deemed more desirable than a stable, predictable trajectory.

Yet, as we have begun to see, the lived reality of the human condition is rarely so simple. A profound and unsettling disconnect has emerged between this official doctrine of choice and our actual, subjective experience of it. While our rational minds continue to pay tribute to the ideal of infinite options, our emotional and psychological lives are telling a different, more complicated story. It is the story of the diner who stares, paralyzed, at a twenty-page menu, unable to decide and feeling a growing sense of anxiety rather than liberation. It is the story of the online shopper who spends hours comparing dozens of functionally identical products, only to feel a wave of dissatisfaction and buyer's remorse the moment the purchase is made. It is the story of the young adult, scrolling through endless profiles on a dating app, who experiences not a sense of boundless romantic opportunity, but a wearying, cynical sense of human beings as interchangeable commodities. This is the paradox of choice: the fact that the very abundance we believe will make us free and happy is, in many cases, making us anxious, indecisive, and profoundly dissatisfied.

To understand why this is happening, we must first appreciate what a radical and historically anomalous situation we find ourselves in. For the vast majority of human history, the primary struggle of life was a struggle against scarcity. The challenge was not choosing from a wide array of options, but finding any viable option at all. Our ancestors were concerned with finding enough food, not with choosing between thirty varieties of artisanal olive oil. Their life paths were largely determined by the circumstances of their birth: their family, their village, their social class. The psychological and cognitive hardware we have inherited evolved over millennia in this environment of limited choice and high stakes. Our minds were shaped to be effective in a world where a few critical decisions could mean the difference between survival and extinction.

Suddenly, within the span of just a few generations, we have been thrust into a world of radical, unprecedented abundance. The external constraints that once so powerfully narrowed the field of human choice have, for many in the developed world, been dramatically loosened. We have moved from a world of scarcity to a world of overwhelming plenitude, but our inherited psychological machinery has not had time to adapt. We are, in effect, running ancient software on a brand-new, impossibly complex operating system. The result is a system crash. We are short-circuiting, overwhelmed by the sheer cognitive load of the choices we are now expected to make on a daily basis, from the trivial to the life-altering.

This chapter is an investigation into the nature of that system crash. We will explore the specific psychological mechanisms that transform the promise of abundant choice into the reality of a psychological burden. Our inquiry will begin by examining the illusion of infinite options, showing how the proliferation of alternatives, far from being empowering, often leads to a state of decision paralysis. We will then turn to the science of decision fatigue, exploring the robust psychological finding that our capacity for making wise, rational choices is a finite resource, one that is depleted by the constant barrage of minor decisions that characterize modern life. From there, we will delve into the corrosive emotional consequences of this overload, particularly the pervasive experience of regret. We will see how an abundance of choice makes it far easier to imagine the better alternatives we might have chosen, trapping us in a cycle of counterfactual thinking and second-guessing that poisons our satisfaction with the choices we actually make.

Finally, having diagnosed the problem, we will turn to a potential solution, one that seems deeply counterintuitive to the modern mind: the deliberate embrace of limits. We will explore the wisdom of traditions like minimalism and the power of routines and rituals, not as forms of restriction, but as sophisticated strategies for preserving our most valuable psychological resources. This is not a call for a return to a past of enforced scarcity, but an argument for a more intentional and conscious relationship with the choices we face. It is a recognition that true freedom may not lie in having the most options, but in having the wisdom to cultivate the right ones. By understanding the psychology of why more is often less, we can begin to move from a life of frantic, dissatisfied choosing to one of thoughtful, committed, and meaningful engagement. This is the crucial next step in our journey: to take the grand, existential burden of freedom and see how it is magnified and complicated by the seemingly mundane realities of our modern age of choice.

The Illusion of Infinite Options

The modern marketplace, in all its forms, is built on a single, seductive promise: the promise of infinity. It whispers to us from the glowing screen of a streaming service with its endless library of content, from the cavernous aisles of a superstore stocked with a hundred different kinds of pasta sauce, and from the digital cascade of profiles on a dating application. The message is consistent and clear: a greater number of options equates to a greater degree of freedom, and therefore, a greater potential for happiness. We have been so thoroughly conditioned by this logic that we rarely pause to question it. The ability to choose is, after all, a core component of human dignity and self-determination. It seems only natural to conclude that maximizing the field of choice is the most direct path to maximizing a life. Yet, a growing body of psychological evidence, and a deeper look into our own lived experience, reveals a profound and unsettling truth: this promise of infinity is an illusion, and one that often delivers the very opposite of what it offers. Instead of liberation, it brings paralysis; instead of satisfaction, it fosters a quiet but persistent anxiety.

The classic demonstration of this phenomenon comes from a now-famous experiment conducted by the psychologists Sheena Iyengar and Mark Lepper. In a series of studies, they set up a tasting booth for high-quality jams in a gourmet food store. In one condition, they offered an extensive selection of twenty-four different varieties of jam. In another, they offered a much smaller, curated selection of just six. The results were a direct and stunning refutation of the "more is better" creed. The larger display, with its vibrant array of choices, was more effective at attracting shoppers to the table; people were drawn to the appearance of abundance. However, when it came to the crucial act of making a choice—actually buying a jar of jam—the dynamic flipped dramatically. Of the shoppers who stopped at the large display, only three percent ended up making a purchase. Of those who stopped at the small display, a remarkable thirty percent bought a jar of jam.

What this simple but elegant experiment revealed is a fundamental mismatch between our desires and our cognitive capacities. We are attracted to the idea of abundant choice, but we are psychologically overwhelmed by the reality of it. The shoppers at the large display were confronted with a task that was, on a subconscious level, simply too demanding. To make a truly rational choice from among twenty-four options would require them to compare and contrast dozens of variables: flavor profiles, sugar content, price points, personal preferences. The cognitive effort required to perform this analysis became a barrier, and the easiest choice, the one that required no effort at all, was to simply walk away. The shoppers at the smaller display, however, were faced with a manageable task. They could realistically compare the six options, make a decision with a reasonable degree of confidence, and feel good about their choice. The very limits that were placed on their selection paradoxically empowered them to act. They were, in a very real sense, freed by the restriction.

This dynamic, the paralysis that results from an overabundance of choice, extends far beyond the grocery aisle. It is a defining feature of our most significant and emotionally charged life domains. Consider the world of modern romance as it is mediated by technology. Dating applications present us with what appears to be a paradise of possibility. At our fingertips is a seemingly inexhaustible supply of potential partners, each one a swipe away. This system is explicitly designed to maximize our options. The promise is that with such a large pool to choose from, we are statistically more likely to find a perfect match. The psychological reality for many users, however, is not one of joyful discovery, but of a wearying, cyclical, and ultimately paralyzing experience.

The endless scroll of profiles transforms the deeply human act of seeking connection into a form of high-stakes comparison shopping. Each individual profile ceases to be a representation of a whole, complex person and becomes, instead, a collection of data points to be quickly evaluated and sorted. The sheer volume devalues each individual option. It fosters a pervasive "what if" mentality, a nagging sense that a better, more attractive, more interesting option might be just one more swipe away. This mentality is the enemy of commitment, not just to another person, but to the process itself. It becomes difficult to invest genuine attention and energy in any one conversation when dozens of other potential conversations are waiting in the wings. This is the jam study on a profound, existential scale. The abundance of choice does not lead to a greater likelihood of forming a meaningful connection; it often leads to a state of perpetual, low-grade shopping, a cycle of superficial engagement and quick dismissal that protects us from the risk and responsibility of making a real, committed choice.

The paralysis we experience in these situations is a direct, modern manifestation of the "dizziness of freedom" that Kierkegaard described. The superstore aisle and the dating app are our modern-day cliff edges. We look down into an abyss not of nothingness, but of an overwhelming everythingness. Each of the twenty-four jars of jam, each of the hundreds of potential partners, represents a different possible future, a different version of the self we might become. The freedom to choose becomes the oppressive necessity of having to choose, and the sheer number of options makes the act of choosing feel impossibly weighty. The dread we feel is the anxiety of our own authorship, magnified to an almost unbearable degree by the number of stories we could potentially write.

There are several distinct psychological mechanisms that contribute to this feeling of being overwhelmed. The first is a simple matter of cognitive overload, as demonstrated in the jam study. Our working memory, the mental dashboard where we process information and make decisions, has a very limited capacity. When we try to consciously compare too many options, we simply exceed that capacity. Our brains short-circuit, and we default to simplifying strategies, such as avoiding the decision altogether or making an arbitrary choice based on a single, superficial attribute.

The second mechanism is the escalation of expectations. When the world presents us with only a few options, our expectations are modest. We aim to find a choice that is "good enough." But when the world presents us with hundreds of options, our expectations escalate dramatically. We begin to believe that a "perfect" option must exist, and the goal of our search shifts from finding a good fit to finding the single best possible one. This raises the bar for what constitutes an acceptable choice to an impossibly high level. The jam has to be the perfect balance of sweet and tart; the potential partner has to be the perfect combination of witty, attractive, and emotionally available; the career path has to be the perfect blend of passion, prestige, and financial security. This search for the Platonic ideal of a choice makes it almost impossible to commit to any of the real, imperfect options that are actually available to us.

Finally, and perhaps most powerfully, the proliferation of options dramatically increases the potential for regret. When we choose one option out of three, we are forgoing only two alternatives. It is relatively easy to convince ourselves that we made the right choice. But when we choose one option out of two hundred, we are forgoing one hundred and ninety-nine alternatives. It becomes almost certain that some of those forgone options would have been better than the one we chose in some way. We anticipate this future regret even before we make the choice, and that anticipation can be paralyzing. The stakes of the decision feel too high, because a "wrong" choice carries with it the burden of all the other, better lives we might have lived. We are trapped not by a lack of freedom, but by a surplus of it. The illusion of infinite options promises to empower us, but in reality, it often holds us captive in a state of anxious indecision, unable to make the very choices that would allow us to move forward and live our lives. True freedom, it seems, requires not an endless horizon of possibility, but a landscape with enough definition to allow for a meaningful path.

Decision Fatigue and Psychological Overload

The paralysis that grips us in the face of overwhelming choice is only the most visible symptom of a deeper, more insidious problem. The illusion of infinite options creates an external landscape of cognitive overload, but this landscape, in turn, exacts a real and measurable internal cost. Every choice we make, from the most trivial to the most profound, is not a frictionless act of pure reason. It is a psychological exertion, a flexing of a mental muscle. And like any muscle, our capacity for self-regulation—the very faculty that allows us to weigh options, resist temptation, and make deliberate, thoughtful choices—is a finite and depletable resource. The architecture of modern life, with its relentless cascade of decisions, is placing this resource under a state of chronic strain, leading to a condition known as decision fatigue. This is the quiet, creeping exhaustion of the will, a depletion that degrades the quality of our choices and undermines our ability to live an intentional life.

For decades, the dominant model in economics and cognitive science was that of the rational actor. This model presumed that human beings make decisions based on a logical and consistent assessment of their self-interest. The emotional and physiological state of the decider was largely considered irrelevant noise. It took the pioneering work of the social psychologist Roy Baumeister and his colleagues to systematically dismantle this view and to demonstrate that our capacity for self-control is not a stable character trait, but a limited resource that operates much like a form of energy. Baumeister termed this phenomenon "ego depletion." The core idea is simple but revolutionary: every act of self-regulation, whether it's resisting a tempting dessert, forcing yourself to concentrate on a difficult task, or choosing between two job offers, draws from the same, single reservoir of mental energy. When this reservoir is low, our ability to self-regulate across the board is impaired.

The classic experiment that first illustrated this principle is both elegant and telling. Baumeister invited a group of hungry college students into a laboratory room that had been filled with the enticing aroma of freshly baked chocolate chip cookies. On a table in the center of the room were two bowls: one filled with the warm cookies and another filled with a far less appealing option, radishes. Some of the students were assigned to the "cookie" group and were invited to eat the cookies. Others were assigned to the "radish" group; they were instructed to eat the radishes and to completely ignore the cookies. A third, control group was presented with no food at all. The real experiment, however, was what happened next. After the food portion of the study was over, all the participants were taken to another room and given a series of difficult, in fact unsolvable, geometric puzzles to work on.

The results were remarkable. The students in the cookie group and the control group, who had not had to exert any willpower, worked on the puzzles for an average of about twenty minutes before giving up. The students in the radish group, however, gave up in less than half that time, averaging only eight minutes of effort. The conclusion was clear: the students in the radish group had used up a significant portion of their self-regulatory energy in the simple but difficult act of resisting the temptation of the cookies. This depleted mental resource was then no longer available to them when it came time to persist on the frustrating puzzle task. Their "willpower muscle" was already tired. They had not become lazier or less intelligent; they were simply cognitively fatigued.

This finding has been replicated in hundreds of studies and extended to a wide range of human behaviors. It turns out that the same limited resource that is used to resist cookies is also used to control our emotional responses, to manage our attention, to perform complex cognitive tasks, and, most importantly for our purposes, to make decisions. Every choice, no matter how small, is a rep for this muscle. The decision of what to wear in the morning, which route to take to work, which email to answer first, what to have for lunch—each one of these seemingly insignificant acts makes a small withdrawal from our finite daily account of self-regulatory strength. For most of human history, a typical day involved very few such choices. In our modern lives, we are often forced to make hundreds of them before we even sit down to our most important work. We are starting our days with a willpower muscle that is already halfway to exhaustion.

The consequences of this decision fatigue are both predictable and profound. As our self-regulatory strength wanes, two things begin to happen. First, we become more cognitively lazy. Our brains, seeking to conserve their remaining energy, begin to look for shortcuts. We become more susceptible to biases, more likely to make impulsive choices, and more likely to simply go with the default option. This is why supermarkets are designed to be minefields of decision fatigue. After an hour of making dozens of choices throughout the aisles—which brand of yogurt, which type of bread, which cut of meat—our willpower is at a low ebb. The store designers know this, which is why the checkout aisle, the final gauntlet we must run, is lined with the most impulsive, low-consideration items like candy, gum, and magazines. We are, at that moment, at our least capable of resisting them.

Second, when faced with a difficult choice, a fatigued mind is far more likely to simply avoid the decision altogether. Procrastination, in this light, is often not a sign of laziness but a symptom of genuine cognitive depletion. The thought of engaging in a complex decision, such as planning a major project or making a significant financial choice, feels so overwhelmingly taxing that we defer it, opting for the short-term relief of engaging in a less demanding activity instead.

Perhaps the most sobering real-world demonstration of decision fatigue comes from a study of parole board judges in Israel. Researchers analyzed over a thousand parole hearings and looked for a relationship between the time of day a case was heard and the verdict that was rendered. The judges' task was to decide whether to grant a prisoner parole, a complex decision requiring a careful review of files and a thoughtful consideration of risk. The default, and cognitively easier, option was to deny parole and maintain the status quo. The more demanding choice was to grant it, which required a greater leap of faith and a more thorough justification. The findings were staggering. At the beginning of the day, the judges granted parole in about sixty-five percent of cases. As the morning wore on, that number steadily declined, dropping to nearly zero just before their mid-morning food break. After the break, their favorable ruling rate shot back up to sixty-five percent, only to decline steadily again toward zero before their lunch break. The single best predictor of whether a prisoner would be granted freedom was not their crime, their sentence, or their ethnicity; it was the time of day their case happened to be heard. The judges were not consciously biased or cruel. They were simply human. They were suffering from decision fatigue, and as their cognitive resources were depleted, they defaulted to the simplest, safest option: no.

This is the hidden cost of our modern age of choice. The relentless demand to choose is not making us better choosers; it is making us worse ones. The psychological overload we experience is not just a feeling of being overwhelmed; it is a measurable degradation of our most essential cognitive faculty. We are making poorer decisions about our finances, our health, and our relationships, not because we lack information, but because we lack the mental energy to process it effectively. We snap at our partners, not because we are angry people, but because we have used up our capacity for emotional regulation in a day filled with a thousand trivial choices. We abandon our New Year's resolutions, not because we lack character, but because our willpower has been systematically exhausted by the very structure of our daily lives. The paradox is that the society that has given us more freedom of choice than any in history has simultaneously created an environment that is perfectly designed to undermine our ability to use that freedom wisely.

Regret and the Shadow of "What Might Have Been"

The paralysis induced by infinite options and the cognitive drain of decision fatigue are the immediate, practical consequences of our modern age of choice. They are the breakdowns that happen in the moment of decision. But even after a choice has been successfully made, the psychological assault is not over. In fact, for many of us, the most difficult phase is the one that comes next. It is the quiet, persistent, and often corrosive emotional state of regret. Regret is the tax that an abundance of choice levies on our satisfaction. It is the painful awareness that the path we have chosen is haunted by the ghosts of all the other paths we might have taken, and the gnawing suspicion that one of those other paths might have been better. In a world of limited options, satisfaction is easier to achieve. But in a world of seemingly endless alternatives, the spectre of the "road not taken" becomes a constant and unwelcome companion, undermining our ability to find peace and contentment in the lives we are actually living.

At the heart of regret is a powerful and quintessentially human cognitive process known as counterfactual thinking. The term, which literally means "contrary to the facts," describes our tendency to mentally simulate alternative realities, to constantly ask the question, "What if?" We are not creatures who live solely in the present; our minds are perpetual storytellers, constantly editing and rewriting the past. When we experience a negative outcome, we almost automatically generate upward counterfactuals, imagining how things could have turned out better. "If only I had left for the airport ten minutes earlier, I wouldn't have missed my flight." "If only I had studied harder, I would have passed the exam." This mental simulation can be a useful tool for learning and future planning, but when it becomes a chronic habit applied to the vast landscape of modern choice, it becomes a powerful engine for self-torment.

The architecture of abundant choice is perfectly designed to fuel this engine. When we make a choice from a very small set of options, the number of potential counterfactuals is limited and manageable. If you grew up in a small town with only two potential employers and you chose one, you only have one alternative reality to contend with. But when you choose a job from a global marketplace of thousands of potential employers, you are faced with a near-infinity of "what ifs." This proliferation of forgone alternatives makes it a statistical certainty that some of the options you rejected would have been superior to the one you chose in at least some respect. The job you took has a great salary, but the one you turned down had a better work-life balance. The car you bought is reliable, but a different model has a more stylish interior. The partner you committed to is kind and supportive, but an ex-partner was more adventurous. The abundance of options makes it almost impossible for any single choice to be perfect on all dimensions, and this imperfection is the fertile ground in which regret takes root.

Furthermore, an abundance of choice dramatically increases our sense of personal responsibility for the outcome, which is the very essence of regret's sting. If you buy the only brand of phone available and it turns out to be a disappointment, you can comfortably blame the manufacturer. The responsibility is external. But if you spend weeks researching two hundred different models, reading reviews, and comparing features, and the phone you ultimately select disappoints you, there is no one to blame but yourself.

The sheer number of options created the illusion that a perfect choice was possible, and your failure to find it is perceived not as a matter of bad luck, but as a personal failing. You feel you *should have* known better, that you *could have* chosen more wisely. This self-blame is the difference between simple disappointment and the deep, personal pain of regret.

The psychologist Barry Schwartz, in his seminal work on this topic, has provided a useful framework for understanding who is most susceptible to this cycle of regret. He distinguishes between two fundamental decision-making styles: "maximizers" and "satisficers." Maximizers are those who feel compelled to find the absolute best possible option in any given situation. They are exhaustive in their research, driven by a fear of making a suboptimal choice. They will read every review, compare every feature, and delay their decision until they are convinced they have examined every alternative. Satisficers, in contrast, operate on the principle of "good enough." They have a set of core criteria in mind, and once they find an option that meets those criteria, they make their choice and stop looking.

In a world of limited choice, the maximizing strategy can be effective. But in our modern world of abundance, it is a recipe for misery. The maximizer's quest for the "best" is an endless, anxiety-provoking task that rarely ends in a feeling of satisfaction. Even after making a choice, their mind continues to scan the horizon for evidence that they have erred. They are exquisitely sensitive to post-purchase dissonance, the feeling of anxiety that arises after a significant commitment. They are the ones who, after buying a new television, will continue to read reviews of other models, torturing themselves with the possibility that they missed out on a slightly better feature or a slightly lower price. Research has consistently shown that while maximizers may, on some objective measures, end up with slightly better outcomes, they are consistently less happy with those outcomes. They report higher levels of stress during the decision process and higher levels of regret after it. Satisficers, on the other hand, by virtue of their refusal to engage in the fantasy of the "perfect" choice, are far more content with the lives they build. Their ability to embrace "good enough" is a powerful psychological shield against the corrosive effects of regret.

This dynamic is now supercharged by the architecture of social media, which functions as a global, real-time counterfactual generator. We are no longer just haunted by the lives we can imagine; we are now constantly presented with highly curated, idealized images of the lives others are apparently living. We see a friend's perfectly filtered vacation photos from a destination we considered but did not choose, and we feel a pang of regret. We see a former colleague's announcement of a promotion at a company we once interviewed with, and we question our own career path. Social media creates an environment of perpetual social comparison, a constant stream of evidence that other people's choices may have been better than our own. It transforms the private, internal world of "what might have been" into a public, inescapable spectacle, making it harder than ever to find contentment in the imperfect, uncurated reality of our own lives.

The ultimate cost of this chronic, choice-fueled regret is that it prevents us from fully inhabiting the life we have actually chosen. To live with regret is to live with a divided mind, with one foot in the present and one foot in a fantasy world of idealized alternatives. This psychic division makes it impossible to bring our full attention and commitment to our current reality. The relationship, the job, the home we have chosen can never be fully satisfying because it is constantly being judged against a legion of perfect, imaginary competitors. The joy of the present moment is stolen by the ghost of a better past. The shadow of "what might have been" becomes so large that it blots out the sun of what actually is. This is the ultimate paradox: the pursuit of the best possible life, enabled by an unprecedented abundance of choice, is the very thing that prevents us from finding and enjoying a good one.

Minimalism and the Freedom of Limits

Having journeyed through the disorienting landscape of the modern choice paradox—from the paralysis of infinite options to the exhaustion of decision fatigue and the corrosive acid of regret—we arrive at a conclusion that feels deeply heretical to the modern mind. If the relentless pursuit of maximum choice is a primary source of our anxiety and dissatisfaction, then the path to a freer, more intentional life may lie not in a further expansion of our options, but in their deliberate and thoughtful restriction. This is the wisdom of the limit, the liberating power of the chosen constraint. It is an argument not for a life of deprivation, but for a life of intention, one in which we reclaim our most valuable psychological resources from the tyranny of the trivial so that we can apply them to what truly matters.

This approach is best understood as a form of strategic surrender. It is the recognition that our willpower, our attention, and our capacity for deep thought are our most precious and finite assets. The architecture of modern life is designed to wage a constant war of attrition against these assets, bombarding us with an endless stream of low-stakes decisions that drain our reserves. To consciously embrace limits is to declare a kind of strategic ceasefire in this war. It is to decide in advance which battles are not worth fighting. By creating structures, routines, and systems in our lives, we are effectively pre-making hundreds of future decisions, automating the mundane so that we can liberate our cognitive and emotional energy for the choices that give our lives shape and meaning.

The most visible and culturally resonant expression of this philosophy is the modern movement of minimalism. At its core, minimalism is a direct rebellion against the consumerist creed that a better life is always just one more purchase away. It is not, as it is often caricatured, simply about owning as few things as possible or living in a stark, white-walled apartment. It is the active, ongoing process of consciously curating one's life, of discerning what is essential and eliminating everything that is not. The minimalist asks not, "What can I acquire?" but, "What can I let go of?" The goal is not emptiness, but clarity. It is to remove the distracting clutter from our physical and mental environments so that we can focus on the people, the experiences, and the work that we have deemed to be of the highest value.

Consider the simple but profound example of the minimalist wardrobe. The individual who chooses to own only a small collection of versatile, high-quality clothes—or who, like Steve Jobs or Albert Einstein, adopts a personal "uniform"—is not sacrificing freedom. They are purchasing it. They have made a single, high-level decision that eliminates a whole category of recurring, low-value choices from their daily life. They are no longer required to expend mental energy each morning on the questions of what to wear, whether it matches, or what it says about them. This conserved energy is then available for more important tasks: for creative thought, for being present with their family, for tackling a difficult problem at work. They have freed themselves from the tyranny of the closet, and in doing so, have created more space for a life of purpose. This same logic can be applied to our homes, our digital lives, and our commitments. Each act of intentional subtraction is an act of addition, adding back time, focus, and energy.

Beyond the curation of our possessions, this philosophy finds its expression in the cultivation of routines and rituals. A routine is simply a pre-decided course of action for a recurring situation. A consistent morning routine, for example, in which one wakes at the same time, exercises, meditates, and eats the same healthy breakfast, automates a series of decisions that would otherwise drain our willpower before the day has even truly begun. A weekly meal plan eliminates the nightly, fatigue-drenched question of "What's for dinner?" These structures are not cages that restrict our freedom; they are the sturdy tracks that allow the train of our lives to move forward with power and direction, rather than constantly derailing into the weeds of trivial choice.

Rituals are a more soulful and meaning-infused version of routines. While a routine is about efficiency, a ritual is about significance. It is a way of embedding our deepest values into the rhythm of our daily lives. The act of sitting down for a family dinner with all devices put away, of writing in a journal for ten minutes each evening, of taking a solitary walk in nature every Sunday—these are not just habits. They are chosen constraints that create a sacred space for what we have deemed to be important: connection, reflection, or communion with the natural world. In a world that feels increasingly chaotic, fragmented, and devoid of shared meaning, the creation of personal rituals is a powerful act of existential authorship. It is a way of imposing a meaningful, self-chosen order onto the indifferent flow of time, a way of building a private cathedral of purpose in which to live our lives.

The embrace of limits is also a powerful antidote to the corrosive power of regret. As we have seen, the maximizer's endless search for the "best" is a primary driver of dissatisfaction. The deliberate choice to limit our options is an act of rebellion against this mindset. It is the conscious adoption of a "satisficer's" approach. By deciding in advance that we will only consider three options for a major purchase, or by committing to a particular path and refusing to constantly look over our shoulder at the alternatives, we are giving ourselves the psychological gift of closure. We are drawing a frame around our choices, and in doing so, we are making it possible to appreciate the picture within it.

This is perhaps the most profound freedom that limits can offer: the freedom from the haunting world of "what might have been." Commitment, which is the ultimate chosen constraint, is the only force powerful enough to slay the dragon of infinite possibility. To commit to a partner, a career, a craft, or a community is to voluntarily close a thousand other doors. This act of closure is not a loss of freedom, but its highest and most meaningful expression. It is the decision to stop being a frantic consumer of shallow experiences and to become a dedicated cultivator of a deep and substantive life. It is the understanding that a life of infinite breadth is, by necessity, a life of no depth. The paradox is that by accepting our finitude, by choosing our constraints, by embracing our limits, we finally give ourselves the permission to fully inhabit the one life we actually have. It is here, in this seemingly restrictive space, that the weight of choice is transformed from a burden to be endured into a tool to be wielded with purpose, clarity, and grace.

* * *

4

Freedom in the Digital Age

The existential predicaments we have been exploring—the anxiety of possibility, the weight of responsibility, the paradox of choice— are not new. They are fundamental features of the human condition, baked into the very structure of our self-aware consciousness. Yet, at the dawn of the 21st century, we have introduced a novel and impossibly powerful variable into this ancient equation: the digital world. The internet, and the ecosystem of platforms and devices it has spawned, arrived with a promise that spoke directly to our deepest aspirations for freedom. It was heralded as the ultimate tool of liberation, a technology that would democratize information, connect humanity, and offer each individual an unprecedented and near-infinite canvas for self-expression. It was to be the final, triumphant answer to the constraints of geography, social hierarchy, and limited choice. The digital world was supposed to make us, in a word, freer.

For a time, it felt as though the promise was being fulfilled. The early internet was a sprawling, chaotic, and often wondrous frontier, a space where one could explore niche communities, encounter radically new ideas, and begin to craft an identity separate from the confines of one's immediate physical world. But as this frontier has been tamed, commercialized, and consolidated, a profound and deeply unsettling irony has taken root. The very technologies that promised to expand our freedom have, in many crucial ways, begun to constrain it, creating new and uniquely modern forms of existential weight. The open field has been replaced by a series of exquisitely designed, walled gardens. The promise of authentic connection has been supplanted by the pressure of relentless self-performance. The dream of a limitless future has been tethered to the reality of a permanent, searchable past. The digital age has not resolved our existential burdens; it has simply given them a new and far more complex operating system.

This chapter is an investigation into this new digital condition. It is an exploration of how the architecture of our online lives is fundamentally reshaping our relationship with choice, identity, and responsibility. We have moved from the relatively straightforward overload of the consumer marketplace, as discussed in the previous chapter, to a far more subtle and psychologically invasive environment. The choices we face online are not just about which product to buy; they are about who to be, what to believe, and how to present our very existence to the world. And critically, these choices are being made within an ecosystem that is not a neutral platform, but an active participant, a powerful and invisible force that is constantly shaping the very options we are presented with and the very self we are trying to become.

Our inquiry will begin by dissecting the quiet and pervasive influence of the algorithm. We will explore how the recommendation engines that govern our social media feeds, our entertainment choices, and our access to information create what we will call the "algorithmic self." These systems operate under the guise of ultimate personalization, promising to deliver a world perfectly tailored to our individual tastes and preferences. Yet, we will argue that this is a hollow form of freedom. By relentlessly feeding us more of what we have already liked, the algorithm systematically narrows our horizons of possibility. It creates a comfortable but claustrophobic echo chamber that protects us from challenging encounters and genuine discovery, all while creating the illusion that we are in complete control of our choices. This is a new and technologically sophisticated form of bad faith, a system that encourages us to abdicate our responsibility for self-creation and to passively accept the curated, predictable self that the machine reflects back to us.

From there, we will turn our attention to the immense psychological pressure of the curated identity. The social media platform is not just a place for connection; it is a stage. It is a space in which we are all, to varying degrees, engaged in the constant and demanding performance of a particular version of ourselves. We are not just living our lives; we are producing, directing, and starring in a continuous documentary about them. This creates a new and heavy form of existential responsibility: the responsibility for maintaining a consistent, admirable, and seemingly "authentic" personal brand. We will examine the paralysis that this performance can induce, the split that emerges between our messy, private, and often contradictory inner lives and the polished, coherent narrative we present to the public. The freedom to be anyone online has, for many, collapsed into the oppressive duty to be someone impressive.

Next, we will confront one of the most novel and anxiety-provoking features of our digital age: the burden of a permanent record. For all of human history, the past was a fluid, malleable thing, subject to the gentle erosion of memory. Reinvention was possible because our former selves could, to a large extent, be forgotten. The internet has changed this forever. Our youthful indiscretions, our poorly-formed opinions, our past relationships—all are now preserved with crystalline fidelity in a vast, searchable archive. This digital panopticon creates a unique and modern form of dread. It forecloses future possibilities by tethering us irrevocably to our past choices. We will explore how this constant surveillance by our own history makes the Sartrean condemnation to freedom feel more acute than ever, creating a world in which we are not just the sum of our choices, but are haunted by a perfect, unerasable record of them.

Finally, having mapped the contours of these new burdens, we will ask the crucial question: what is to be done? This chapter is not an argument for a Luddite retreat from the digital world, an act that is for most of us neither possible nor desirable. It is, instead, a call for a more conscious and intentional form of digital citizenship. In our final section, we will explore practical and philosophical approaches for reclaiming our agency from the machine. We will discuss strategies for resisting algorithmic determinism, for cultivating a more authentic and less performative online presence, and for living with the reality of our digital footprint. The goal is not to escape technology, but to learn to use it as a tool for our own, freely-chosen projects of self-creation, rather than allowing ourselves to become a tool for its project of prediction and control. To be truly free in the digital age requires a new kind of literacy, a new set of critical faculties, and a renewed commitment to the difficult, analogue work of being a human being.

The Algorithmic Self

The guiding principle of the modern internet is personalization. It is a promise whispered to us from every corner of our digital lives, from the customized news headlines that greet us in the morning to the targeted advertisements that follow us across the web and the endless scroll of a social media feed that purports to be a perfect mirror of our unique interests. The architects of this digital world, the massive technology platforms that mediate our experience of it, have positioned themselves as the ultimate servants of our individuality. Their stated goal is to cut through the noise of an information-saturated world and to deliver to us a bespoke reality, a universe of content, products, and connections perfectly tailored to our pre-existing tastes and desires. This is a powerful and deeply alluring proposition. It feels like the ultimate evolution of freedom: a world in which we are no longer required to sift through the irrelevant, a world that anticipates our needs and presents us with a continuous stream of things we are virtually guaranteed to like. It is freedom frictionlessly delivered.

This curated reality is made possible by the most powerful and pervasive force in our digital lives: the algorithm. In this context, an algorithm is simply a complex set of rules and calculations that takes the data we provide—our clicks, our likes, our shares, our search queries, our viewing history, the amount of time we linger on a particular image—and uses it to make predictions about what we will want to see next. The recommendation engine of a video streaming platform, the news feed of a social network, the product suggestions on an e-commerce site—all are driven by this same basic logic. The system learns from our past behavior in order to shape our future experience. On the surface, this appears to be a neutral and helpful service. Yet, beneath this veneer of benign personalization lies a mechanism that is fundamentally altering our relationship with choice and, in a very real sense, with our own selves. The algorithm is not just a tool we use; it is an environment we inhabit, and like any environment, it subtly but powerfully shapes what we can become.

The central problem is that the primary goal of these commercial algorithms is not our personal growth, our intellectual expansion, or our self-actualization. Their goal is engagement. They are designed to do one thing with maximum efficiency: to capture and hold our attention for as long as possible, because our attention is the commodity they sell to advertisers. The most effective way to keep us engaged is not to challenge us, to surprise us, or to present us with ideas that might require difficult and effortful consideration. The most effective way is to show us more of what we have already demonstrated we like. The logic is one of reinforcement, not of discovery. If you watch a video about baking sourdough bread, the algorithm will not conclude that you might be interested in the broader world of culinary arts; it will conclude that you must be shown an endless succession of sourdough videos. If you express a mild political preference by liking a few posts, the algorithm will not present you with a range of nuanced viewpoints; it will push you deeper and deeper into the most extreme and emotionally resonant versions of that preference. The result is the creation of a sophisticated and highly personalized echo chamber.

This is a new and technologically sophisticated form of confinement that masquerades as freedom. We are living in what the activist Eli Pariser has called a "filter bubble," a unique and invisible universe of information that is created for us by our algorithmic curators. We feel like we are freely exploring a vast and open landscape, but we are, in reality, walking in a circle within a carefully constructed, invisible fence. The algorithm systematically prunes away the possibility of serendipity, the chance encounter with a book, a piece of music, an idea, or a person that could fundamentally change our perspective and alter the trajectory of our lives. These are the very experiences that are essential for genuine growth and the expansion of the self. Instead, we are offered a comfortable, predictable, and ever-narrowing version of the world, a world that constantly reassures us that our existing tastes are perfect, our current beliefs are correct, and we never have to stray outside the comfortable confines of what we already know.

This creates a technologically-enabled form of bad faith that is particularly seductive because it feels so good. We are given the constant, pleasant frisson of "choice" as we click and like our way through our feeds, and this illusion of active selection masks the profound passivity of our consumption. We are not truly choosing; we are simply ratifying the options that the machine has already chosen for us. This allows for a massive abdication of the responsibility of self-creation. The difficult, effortful, and often anxiety-provoking work of seeking out new experiences, of grappling with challenging ideas, of consciously cultivating new tastes, and of defining our own values is outsourced to the algorithm. We are relieved of the burden of our own freedom, and we do not even notice it has been taken.

Over time, this dynamic gives rise to what can be called the "algorithmic self." The algorithm, in its relentless effort to predict us, creates a model of who we are: a simplified, flattened, and commercially viable caricature. It sees us not as the complex, contradictory, and constantly evolving beings we actually are, but as a stable bundle of predictable preferences. The danger is that we begin to mistake this reflection for our true self. The feed becomes a mirror, and we subtly begin to shape ourselves to fit the image it shows us. The person who is consistently fed content from a particular political tribe begins to identify more strongly with that tribe, adopting its slogans and its enemies as their own. The person whose music app has decided they are a fan of a specific sub-genre of electronic music begins to think of that as a core part of their identity, closing themselves off to the worlds of classical, jazz, or folk music.

This process is a form of psychic hardening. It takes our fluid, dynamic, and potential-filled "for-itself" and encourages us to treat it as a fixed, defined, and predictable "in-itself." We learn to perform the role of the self that the algorithm expects us to be, and our future choices become constrained by the need to be consistent with this simplified, curated identity. The algorithm offers us a self that is coherent, predictable, and constantly validated by the content it serves us. To accept this self is to find a powerful refuge from the anxiety of Kierkegaard's dizziness of freedom. It is to step out of the room of a thousand doors and into a comfortable, well-lit hallway with only one. The choice has been made for us. All we have to do is keep walking. The freedom that is lost in this transaction is the most important freedom of all: the freedom to become someone other than who we are right now.

The Paralysis of the Curated Identity

If the algorithm creates the invisible architecture of our digital confinement, then the social media profile is the stage upon which we are compelled to perform our freedom. The platforms that dominate our social lives—Instagram, Facebook, TikTok, LinkedIn—are not neutral conduits for communication. They are theaters of identity. They have transformed the quiet, often messy, and deeply private process of self-creation into a public, competitive, and relentlessly documented performance. We have all been handed a script, a camera, and a global audience, and we have been tacitly instructed to produce a continuous documentary titled "My Life." The central paradox of this new reality is that the primary theme of this documentary is meant to be "authenticity." We are tasked with performing, for the consumption of others, a version of ourselves that appears effortlessly genuine, free, and living a life of purpose and joy. This is the existential weight of the curated identity: the immense and exhausting labor of manufacturing an "authentic" self, a process that often leaves us feeling more inauthentic, anxious, and paralyzed than ever before.

To understand the novelty of this predicament, we must distinguish it from the normal social roles we have always played. In our pre-digital lives, we have always presented different facets of ourselves in different contexts. The self we present to a prospective employer is different from the self we present to our children, which is different from the self we share with our most trusted friend. But these roles were compartmentalized and context-dependent. They were partial performances. The digital world, and the social media profile in particular, demands something far more totalizing. It demands the creation of a single, coherent, and continuous personal brand. It collapses all our different audiences—our boss, our grandmother, our ex-partner, our childhood friends, our future employers—into a single, undifferentiated mass of "followers." We are forced to construct a version of ourselves that is palatable and impressive to all of them simultaneously.

This turns the act of living into a form of content creation. Our experiences are no longer valued solely for their intrinsic worth, but for their "post-worthiness." A beautiful sunset is not just a moment of quiet awe; it is a potential story. A well-prepared meal is not just for nourishment and pleasure; it is a potential photo. A difficult personal struggle is not just a private trial to be endured; it is a potential narrative of resilience and growth to be shared. We begin to live with a divided consciousness, inhabited by both an "experiencing self" and an "observing self." The experiencing self is the one who is actually on the vacation, tasting the food, feeling the emotion. But the observing self is always present, hovering just behind, functioning as a kind of inner director, asking, "How does this look? How can this be framed? What is the most compelling way to tell this story?" This split is the source of a profound sense of alienation from our own lives. We become spectators of our own experience, and in the process, the experience itself is hollowed out, stripped of its immediacy and its un-self-conscious reality.

The pressure is not simply to document our lives, but to curate them into a narrative that is both admirable and, crucially, "authentic." This is the tyranny of the curated self. Authenticity, which in an existential sense means living in alignment with one's own freely chosen values and accepting the totality of one's being, is co-opted and transformed into a marketable aesthetic. The online performance of authenticity has its own set of unwritten rules. It requires a careful balance of aspirational content (the beautiful vacation, the professional achievement) and relatable vulnerability (the post about mental health struggles, the photo without makeup). Even the moments of supposed "realness" are often carefully staged and framed to fit the overall brand narrative. The post about anxiety is rarely a raw, unfiltered cry for help; it is more often a beautifully written, reflective piece that concludes with a message of hope and resilience. It is a performance of vulnerability, designed to elicit engagement and to signal a kind of admirable self-awareness.

This constant, high-stakes performance induces a unique form of paralysis. The weight of maintaining the curated identity becomes so heavy that it can stifle the very freedom it is meant to represent. This paralysis manifests in several ways. First, there is the paralysis of creation. The pressure to post something that is witty, beautiful, or profound can be so intense that we end up posting nothing at all. The blank status update box becomes a terrifying void, a final exam for which we feel perpetually unprepared. We scroll through the polished perfection of other people's feeds and conclude that our own messy, uncurated reality is simply not good enough to be seen. Our silence is not a choice for privacy, but a retreat born of inadequacy.

I recall a moment, standing at the edge of a stunning canyon at sunset, the light painting the cliffs in hues of orange and purple. It was a moment of pure, unadulterated awe. And my first, instinctive thought was not to breathe it in, but to frame the perfect photograph for Instagram. I spent minutes adjusting the angle, filtering the light, and crafting a caption that sounded suitably profound and spontaneous. By the time I posted it, the moment had passed. The real experience—the chill of the air, the scent of desert sage, the silent immensity of the geologic time before me—had been traded for a digital artifact. The likes and comments rolled in, a wave of validation for a performance that had cost me the very experience it was meant to document. That small, quiet emptiness was the price of the curated self. It was the distance between the person having an experience and the brand managing a story.

More consequentially, this can lead to a paralysis of action in our actual, offline lives. The pressure to live a "post-worthy" life can prevent us from engaging in activities where the outcome is uncertain or the aesthetic is not guaranteed. We might avoid trying a new hobby for fear of not being immediately good at it and therefore having nothing impressive to show for it. We might choose the restaurant with the more photogenic food over the one with the better-tasting but less visually appealing dishes. The desire to produce a good story about our life can begin to take precedence over the desire to live a good life. We become trapped in a prison of our own design, where our freedom is constrained by the need to maintain the illusion of the free, interesting, and successful person we are pretending to be online.

The emotional fallout from this constant performance is immense. The first and most common consequence is a pervasive feeling of being a fraud, a form of what is often called imposter syndrome. The greater the gap between our curated public self and our private, unedited reality, the more we live with a low-grade fear of being exposed. We feel that if people knew the truth—the truth of our anxieties, our failures, our petty jealousies, our boring moments—they would see that we are not the person we claim to be. This feeling is a direct consequence of a life lived in bad faith. We have identified so strongly with the object we have created (our profile) that we have become alienated from our true, subjective, and constantly fluctuating self.

This, in turn, fosters a profound sense of loneliness. Social media promises connection, but the connection it offers is often illusory. When we present a polished, invulnerable, and highly curated version of ourselves to the world, we prevent the possibility of true, authentic connection. Real intimacy is forged in the sharing of our imperfections, our vulnerabilities, and our unedited truths. When we hide these parts of ourselves, we may receive validation in the form of likes and positive comments, but we do not receive the deeper, more nourishing experience of being truly seen and accepted for who we are. We can be surrounded by a thousand "friends" online and yet feel utterly, existentially alone, because we know, on some level, that the person they are applauding is not the real us.

The freedom of the digital age, in this sense, has revealed itself to be a kind of trap. The freedom to be anyone has collapsed into the oppressive and demanding responsibility to be someone impressive, coherent, and consistently "on-brand." We have taken on a second, unpaid, and deeply demanding job: that of being the marketing director for our own lives. The weight of this role is immense. It depletes our psychological resources, alienates us from our own experience, and isolates us from genuine connection. It is a flight from the messy, unpredictable, and often difficult reality of an authentic existence into the controlled, predictable, but ultimately hollow world of a performance. To reclaim our freedom in this new environment requires a courageous act of rebellion: the willingness to be imperfect, inconsistent, and occasionally unimpressive in public, and in doing so, to make space for the possibility of being real.

The Burden of a Permanent Record

For the vast expanse of human history, the past was a soft and malleable thing. It existed primarily in the fallible and fluid medium of human memory, subject to the gentle, and often merciful, erosions of time. Stories would change in the telling, details would fade, and youthful indiscretions would soften into amusing anecdotes. The person you were ten or twenty years ago existed mostly as a series of disconnected images and feelings, a ghost accessible only through the unreliable archives of the mind. This impermanence was a form of grace. It was the foundation of reinvention, the necessary condition for a second act. The possibility of moving to a new town and starting over was not just a geographical shift, but a psychological one. It was the freedom to become someone new, unburdened by the constant, literal presence of who you used to be. The digital age has brought this era of forgetting to an abrupt and decisive end.

We now inhabit a world in which the past is no longer a fading memory but a high-fidelity, permanent, and instantly searchable archive. Our digital lives create an ever-expanding, indestructible data trail: every ill-conceived comment on a social media platform, every embarrassing photo from a college party, every half-formed opinion shared on a long-forgotten forum, every digital interaction is meticulously recorded, timestamped, and stored indefinitely on a server somewhere. The internet, in its quiet, computational way, has become the world's most diligent and unforgiving historian, and its primary subject is us. This creates a new and uniquely modern form of existential dread. The Sartrean pronouncement that we are the sum of our choices has been given a terrifying technological update: we are now the *searchable* sum of our choices, and this permanent record tethers us to our past selves in a way that profoundly constrains our freedom to become.

This burden is felt most acutely in the foreclosure of future possibilities. The very nature of growth, both personal and professional, requires the freedom to be a work in progress, the freedom to be wrong, to be naive, to be foolish. We learn by making mistakes. Yet, in an environment of total recall, these necessary mistakes are no longer ephemeral learning experiences; they are permanent stains on our record. The most obvious and widely discussed consequence is in our professional lives. A thoughtless joke tweeted as a teenager can be unearthed by a potential employer a decade later, costing a person a job opportunity without them ever knowing why. An old photograph depicting a moment of youthful irresponsibility can derail a career. The possibility of professional evolution is hindered by the digital ghost of a past self, a ghost that can be summoned at any time to cast judgment on the person we are today.

This dynamic extends into our personal lives with equal, if more subtle, force. The digital archive makes clean breaks and fresh starts nearly impossible. Past relationships exist not as memories, but as tangible, clickable collections of photos, comments, and tags, a shared history that can be revisited with a few keystrokes, making the difficult emotional work of moving on even harder. Old arguments, preserved with perfect fidelity in a text message or email chain, can be resurrected years later, preventing the healing that a fading memory once allowed. We are forced into a constant relationship with our former selves and our past connections, unable to achieve the psychological distance necessary for genuine change. The person who wishes to reinvent themselves, to leave behind a past identity, finds that their old self is always just a search query away, ready to be presented as evidence that their transformation is inauthentic or incomplete.

This creates a pervasive form of low-grade surveillance, a condition that has been described as a digital panopticon. The original panopticon was a prison design in which a single guard could observe all the inmates without them knowing if they were being watched at any given moment. The result was that the prisoners, under the assumption of constant potential observation, began to police their own behavior. The digital world has created a similar dynamic, but the guard in the tower is not some external authority; it is the collective, and eternal, memory of the network itself, including our own past selves. We live with the background awareness that anything we say or do online can and will be recorded and potentially used against us at a future date.

The psychological effect of this is a powerful pressure toward a rigid and performative consistency. It stifles our willingness to be intellectually and emotionally adventurous. We become afraid to try out a new idea, to ask a "stupid" question, or to change our mind on an important issue, because our past statements exist in the archive as a permanent record that can be used to accuse us of hypocrisy or foolishness. This is profoundly damaging to the process of personal and intellectual growth, which is, by its very nature, a process of trial, error, and evolution. To grow is to be inconsistent. It is to hold an opinion on Tuesday that contradicts the one you held on Monday. The digital archive, with its demand for a stable and consistent personal brand, creates an environment that is hostile to this necessary and messy process of becoming.

This gives rise to a distinctly modern form of anxiety, one born of what is known as "context collapse." In our analogue lives, our communication is naturally segmented. We speak differently to our close friends than we do to our boss or our grandparents. The context dictates the appropriate tone and content. Online, these distinct social contexts collapse into one. A sarcastic comment intended for a small group of friends can be screenshot, stripped of its original context, and presented to a global audience as a literal statement of belief. The result is a new form of social paralysis, a fear of being misunderstood on a massive scale. We self-censor, defaulting to the blandest, most inoffensive forms of expression in an attempt to produce content that is safe for all possible audiences, both present and future. This is a profound constraint on our freedom of expression, a cage built not of overt censorship, but of the fear of a permanent, context-free judgment.

The burden of the permanent record, then, is that it makes the weight of our authorship feel heavier than ever before. Every choice, every statement, every interaction is imbued with a new and terrifying sense of permanence. We are creating not just a life, but a permanent, searchable monument to that life, a monument we can never fully edit or demolish. This is the ultimate realization of Kierkegaard's dizziness of freedom, amplified for the digital age. We are not just standing at the edge of a cliff, contemplating our freedom to jump; we are doing so with the knowledge that our every hesitation, our every thought, is being live-streamed and recorded for all time. This creates an almost unbearable pressure to get it right the first time, a pressure that is antithetical to the messy, imperfect, and beautiful reality of a human life in the process of becoming. The grace of forgetting has been replaced by the tyranny of the archive, and learning to live with this new, heavy form of responsibility is one of the central existential challenges of our time.

Reclaiming Agency from the Machine

To have surveyed the landscape of our digital lives—the invisible fences of the algorithm, the exhausting performance of the curated self, and the unforgiving permanence of the archive—is to risk falling into a state of technological despair. The forces arrayed against our individual agency can seem so vast, so subtle, and so deeply embedded in the fabric of modern life that any act of resistance feels futile. A complete withdrawal, a Luddite retreat into an analogue world, is a fantasy for all but a very few. We are, for the most part, inextricably linked to this digital ecosystem for our work, our social connections, and our access to the world. The path forward, then, is not one of escape, but of conscious and courageous engagement. If the digital world is the new territory in which we must live our lives, then our existential task is to learn how to inhabit it as free subjects rather than as passive, predictable objects. Reclaiming our agency requires a new set of skills, a kind of digital mindfulness, and a series of deliberate, often counter-cultural, choices.

The first and most fundamental act of resistance is to declare independence from the tyranny of the algorithm. This means actively working to dismantle the filter bubbles and echo chambers that have been constructed for us. If the algorithm's primary function is to eliminate friction and surprise, then our task is to consciously reintroduce them into our intellectual and cultural lives. This is an act of reclaiming the responsibility for our own curiosity. Instead of passively consuming the feed that is served to us, we must become active foragers of information. This can take many forms. It might mean curating a list of thinkers, writers, and publications from a wide range of perspectives—especially those with whom we disagree—and making the deliberate choice to read them directly, rather than waiting for their content to find us through a social media feed. It might mean using tools like RSS feeds to create a personalized, algorithm-free stream of information.

On a simpler level, it means cultivating the habit of serendipity. It is the choice to occasionally wander into a section of the library or bookstore you would normally ignore, to listen to a genre of music that is outside your usual taste, to follow a link deep into a Wikipedia rabbit hole on a topic you know nothing about. These small acts of intellectual exploration are the digital equivalent of taking a different route home from work just to see what is there. They are tiny ruptures in the seamless, predictable world the algorithm wants to build for us. They keep our minds flexible, open to surprise, and remind us that the world is infinitely larger, stranger, and more interesting than the version presented in our personalized feeds. It is the conscious choice for a diet of discovery over a diet of reinforcement.

The second crucial practice is the de-escalation of the curated self. We must find ways to lower the stakes of our online performance and to reconnect with the messy, unedited reality of our own lives. This requires a rebellion against the pressure to be a brand and a return to the desire to be a person. A powerful first step is to shift our digital communication from a model of public broadcasting to one of private connection. It is to consciously invest more of our online time and energy in direct messages, small group chats, and video calls—forums where the audience is known, the context is shared, and the pressure to perform is significantly lower. These are the digital spaces where genuine, uncurated connection is still possible, where we can share our uncertainties and imperfections without fear of a public verdict.

This also involves a conscious choice to embrace and even to share our imperfections. It is the courage to occasionally post the un-flattering photo, to admit to not knowing something, to share a story of a small, un-cinematic failure. These are not acts of self-deprecation, but acts of liberation. Each small performance of imperfection is a crack in the polished facade of the curated identity, a moment of authenticity that not only frees us from the burden of our own performance but also gives others permission to be more real. Perhaps the most powerful tool in this fight is the deliberate and scheduled withdrawal from the stage altogether. The practice of a "digital Sabbath"—a day, or even just a few hours, each week where we put away our screens—is not an act of deprivation. It is an act of restoration. It is a dedicated time to re-ground ourselves in the unmediated world, to reconnect with our own thoughts and feelings without the lens of a potential audience, and to remember that the most valuable parts of our lives are often the ones that are not, and cannot be, documented.

Finally, we must learn to live with the reality of the permanent record without being paralyzed by it. This requires a dual strategy: a new prudence in our present actions and a new form of grace toward our past selves. The prudence is a simple, practical form of self-preservation. It is the adoption of a personal policy of thoughtful posting, the understanding that the internet is not a private diary but a public square. A useful heuristic is the "front porch" rule: do not say anything online that you would not be comfortable saying out loud on your front porch for your family, friends, and neighbors to hear. This is not about self-censorship, but about cultivating an awareness of context and consequence. It is a way of taking responsibility for our words and recognizing their enduring power.

The second part of the strategy, the cultivation of grace, is more of a philosophical and psychological challenge. We must learn to practice a form of cognitive and emotional forgiveness toward our past digital selves. We have to accept that the person who wrote that naive comment ten years ago is not the person we are today. We must learn to see our digital trail not as a fixed and final verdict on our character, but as the fossil record of our own evolution. To do this requires that we extend this same charity to others, that we resist the impulse to engage in the digital mob justice that so often erupts when someone's past words are stripped of their context and judged by the standards of the present. To live responsibly with a permanent record is to become an advocate for a culture of forgiveness, to recognize that a society without the possibility of growth and reinvention is a society without humanity.

Reclaiming our agency from the machine is not a single event, but a continuous practice. It is a form of existential resistance, a daily assertion of our desire to live a life of conscious, self-directed choice rather than one of passive, predictable consumption. It is the understanding that our attention is our most sacred resource, and that where we choose to place it is, in the end, the thing that constitutes our life. The ultimate act of freedom in the digital age is to choose to be the user, not the used; to be the artist, not just a color in someone else's paint-by-numbers canvas. It is to look at the powerful, alluring, and often demanding machine and to say, quietly but firmly, "You will be a tool for my project, not the other way around."

* * *

5

Freedom Without Guarantees

Our journey thus far has been an excavation of the complex and often paradoxical nature of modern freedom. We began with its profound discovery, the dizzying awakening to our own agency as described by the existentialists. We then felt its immense weight in the form of a total responsibility for the self we are creating. We have seen how this burden is magnified by the overwhelming abundance of the modern marketplace of choice, and how it is further complicated by the novel pressures of the digital age, with its algorithmic selves and its demand for a curated identity. Yet, woven through all of these explorations is a single, unspoken, and deeply unsettling thread. It is the fundamental context in which all our freedom is exercised, the invisible stage upon which the entire drama of our choosing unfolds: the profound and inescapable reality of uncertainty.

Every choice we make, from the most trivial to the most life-altering, is a step into an unknown future. We are free to choose our actions, but we are not free to choose the consequences of those actions. We can act with the best of intentions, with the most careful planning, with the most rigorous analysis, but we can never, not with absolute certainty, control the outcome. The world is a vast, complex, and chaotic system of interacting variables, a system far too intricate to be fully predicted or mastered by any single human mind. The arrow of our intention is always shot into a fog. This is perhaps the most difficult and humbling truth of the human condition: our freedom to act is absolute, but our power over the future is profoundly limited. We are the authors of our choices, but we are only the co-authors of our results.

This reality places us in a state of profound existential tension. As conscious, self-aware beings, we are wired with a deep and primal craving for certainty. Predictability is a form of safety. We want to know that our efforts will be rewarded, that our sacrifices will be meaningful, that the love we give will be returned, that the path we choose is the "right" one. We yearn for guarantees. We look to the world for a contract, a set of stable "if-then" propositions that will allow us to navigate our lives with a sense of confidence and security. If I work hard, then I will be successful. If I am a good person, then I will be happy. If I love my child well, then they will thrive. We seek a world that is fundamentally just, rational, and predictable.

The universe, however, has signed no such contract. It remains stubbornly, and often cruelly, indifferent to our need for guarantees. The hardworking employee is laid off due to a market downturn. The virtuous person is struck by a random illness. The loving parent watches their child struggle with forces beyond their control. The carefully planned business fails due to an unforeseen shift in technology. To be alive is to be in a constant, dynamic relationship with this radical uncertainty. To be free is to be compelled to act, to choose, to commit, and to invest our very selves in a future that offers no promise of a particular return. If we knew the outcome of our choices in advance, the act of choosing would be a simple exercise in calculation. It is the lack of guarantees that transforms choice from a mathematical problem into a human drama, one that requires not just intellect, but courage, faith, and the capacity to endure ambiguity.

This chapter is an exploration of our profound and often difficult relationship with this fundamental uncertainty. We will examine the deep-seated psychological resistance we have to a world without guarantees and the various strategies, both personal and cultural, that we employ in our desperate search for solid ground in a constantly shifting world. Our investigation will begin by establishing uncertainty not as a temporary problem to be solved, but as the natural and unavoidable context of a human life. We will explore the crucial distinction between our actions, which we control, and our outcomes, which we can only ever influence.

From there, we will turn to the psychological reasons why we find this reality so difficult to accept. We will delve into the robust scientific findings on risk and ambiguity aversion, exploring the deep-seated cognitive biases that lead us to prefer a known, even if negative, certainty over an unknown possibility. We will see why the human mind is so powerfully drawn to the illusion of control and why we so often make choices that are designed not to achieve the best possible outcome, but to minimize the discomfort of not knowing.

Next, we will broaden our focus to examine the large-scale cultural systems we have constructed as massive, collective defenses against uncertainty. We will analyze the powerful psychological pull of rigid religious doctrines, totalizing political ideologies, and fervent nationalism, not primarily as systems of belief, but as sophisticated and often effective mechanisms for providing their adherents with a sense of certainty, purpose, and order in a chaotic world. We will explore how these systems offer a kind of existential comfort, a release from the burden of having to navigate life without a map.

This heroic embrace of a difficult and uncertain reality has deep roots in the ancient world, most notably in the practical philosophy of Stoicism. For Stoic thinkers like Epictetus and Marcus Aurelius, the primary task of a human life was to achieve a state of inner tranquility and moral virtue in a world that is fundamentally outside our control. The foundational practice for this was the "dichotomy of control," the rigorous and constant mental discipline of distinguishing between what is within our power (our judgments, our intentions, our choices, our character) and what is not (our health, our reputation, the actions of others, the outcome of our efforts). This is a direct and powerful echo of the distinction between our actions, which we control, and our outcomes, which we can only influence. For the Stoic, true freedom is found not in changing the world, but in mastering our inner response to it. This mastery culminates in the ideal of *amor fati*, the "love of one's fate." This is not a passive resignation, but an active, and even joyful, acceptance of all that happens, seeing it as the necessary and unavoidable material from which we must forge our character. One can imagine Sisyphus as the ultimate Stoic sage, a man who has learned not just to bear his rock, but to love it, for it is the very instrument of his own hard-won integrity.

Finally, having understood our deep-seated aversion to uncertainty and the elaborate defenses we build against it, we will explore an alternative and more courageous path. Drawing on the parallel wisdom of existential philosophy and Buddhist psychology, we will consider the radical proposition that the acceptance of uncertainty and impermanence, far from being a source of despair, can in fact be the key to a more profound form of liberation. This is the path of learning to act with full commitment in the face of an unknowable future, of finding our meaning not in the final destination, but in the integrity of the journey itself. It is the path of discovering that the only true ground we have is the groundlessness of our own freedom, and that the only guarantee we need is the one we give to ourselves: the promise to live our lives with courage, responsibility, and an open heart, come what may.

Uncertainty as the Natural Context of Human Life

At the very core of the human psyche lies a deep and persistent longing for solid ground. We are, by our nature, creatures who seek patterns, who crave causality, who yearn for a predictable and orderly world. We want to believe that we are living in a fundamentally rational universe, one that operates according to a clear and comprehensible set of rules. This desire is the engine of science, the comfort of tradition, and the implicit promise of much of our educational and economic systems. It is the belief that if we can just gather enough information, formulate the right strategy, and execute our plans with sufficient discipline, we can effectively control the course of our lives and guarantee a desirable outcome. We want, in short, a contract with reality, a signed and notarized agreement that our good-faith efforts will be met with predictable and just rewards.

This longing, however noble and deeply felt, is based on a fundamental misreading of our situation. The natural context of a human life is not certainty; it is a profound and unceasing uncertainty. The universe has not signed our contract. The world we inhabit is not a predictable machine to be engineered, but a vast, chaotic, and endlessly complex ecosystem in which our own actions are but one variable among an infinity of others. To be a free, choosing being is to be constantly acting into a future that is, by its very nature, unknowable. This is the ultimate existential predicament, the stark and humbling truth that underpins every other challenge we face: we have absolute control over our actions, but only a fragile and partial influence over their outcomes.

This distinction between actions and outcomes is the single most important and most difficult lesson for a mature and responsible life. The sphere of our actions is our home. It is the domain of our freedom, our will, our character, and our responsibility. It encompasses our intentions, our efforts, the values we choose to embody, the words we speak, and the deeds we perform. In this sphere, our power is, in a very real sense, total. No external force can, without our consent, make us choose something we believe to be wrong or prevent us from acting with integrity. This is the inviolable core of our agency, the ground upon which we can and must stand.

The sphere of outcomes, however, is a different territory entirely. It is a wild and unpredictable landscape that lies outside the borders of our direct control. The outcome of any endeavor is a complex product, a synthesis of our own actions and a host of other forces: the free and unpredictable choices of other people, the hidden complexities of social and economic systems, the brute realities of biology and physics, and the simple, irreducible element of chance. To believe that we can unilaterally determine the results of our efforts is a form of hubris, a denial of the fundamental structure of reality. It is to mistake our role as a participant in the world for the role of its author.

Consider the act of parenting, perhaps the most profound and responsibility-laden of all human endeavors. A parent has the freedom and the responsibility to create a certain kind of environment for their child.

They can choose to be present, loving, and supportive. They can read to their child, provide them with nutritious food, set clear and consistent boundaries, and model a life of integrity and compassion. These are their actions, and in this, their responsibility is total. But the parent cannot, through these actions, *guarantee* a particular outcome. They cannot ensure that their child will be happy, that they will be free from suffering, that they will make wise choices, or that they will become a successful adult. The child is a separate, free being with their own consciousness, their own choices to make. And the world is a complex place that will present that child with its own set of unpredictable challenges and opportunities. The parent's sacred responsibility lies in the quality of their own actions, in the integrity of their effort, not in the impossible task of controlling the final shape of another human life.

This same dynamic holds true in every other domain. An entrepreneur can pour their life's savings and years of tireless work into a new business. They can have a brilliant idea, a meticulous business plan, and a superior product. These are their actions. But the success of that business—the outcome—depends on a thousand factors beyond their control: a sudden shift in consumer tastes, the emergence of a powerful competitor, a change in government regulations, a global economic downturn. To equate the failure of the business with a failure of the person is to misunderstand the nature of the world. The responsibility of the entrepreneur was to act with vision, courage, and diligence. The outcome was never solely theirs to command.

The implications of this distinction are profound and deeply challenging to our most cherished notions of fairness and control. It means that we must abandon the comforting "if-then" logic that we so desperately want to believe in. It is simply not true that if you are a good and virtuous person, then you will be rewarded with a happy and painless life. It is not true that if you work harder than everyone else, then you are guaranteed to succeed. And it is not true that if you love someone with all your heart, then they are guaranteed to love you back. These are the bargains of a child's world, a world of magical thinking where our desires are meant to shape reality. A mature, adult consciousness requires us to face the world as it is: a place where our best efforts can and sometimes do fail, where tragedy can strike without reason, and where the outcomes are never, ever guaranteed.

To truly accept this is to undergo a fundamental shift in our understanding of what it means to be a responsible person. It is a shift from an ethics of outcomes to an ethics of process. A life of responsibility is not one that is defined by its successes or failures, its victories or defeats. It is one that is defined by the quality and integrity of its choices, regardless of where they lead. The measure of a life becomes not "What did I achieve?" but "How did I choose to act? What values did I embody in the face of uncertainty? Did I act with courage, with compassion, with integrity?" This is the only ground we have to stand on. In a world without guarantees, the character of our own actions becomes the only thing that is truly ours. To take full responsibility for this, and to let go of the illusion that we can control the rest, is the beginning of a profound and difficult form of freedom.

The Weaponization of Uncertainty: The Age of Precarity

The universal uncertainty of human life has been compounded in the 21st century by a socially engineered condition: precarity. This is not the metaphysical uncertainty of whether our efforts will succeed, but a deliberate, systemic insecurity built into the foundations of modern work, housing, and social life. It is the gig economy worker who cannot predict next week's income, the contractor without health insurance, the renter facing skyrocketing leases and the constant threat of displacement.

Precarity is uncertainty weaponized. It takes the natural anxiety of an unknown future and transforms it into a chronic, managed state of economic and psychological vulnerability. This creates a unique and heavy form of the burden of freedom. When one's basic survival—shelter, food, healthcare—is perpetually in question, the "dizziness of possibility" is replaced by the sheer exhaustion of constant calculation and fear. The cognitive resources needed for long-term planning, creative risk-taking, and the kind of deep self-reflection we have explored are depleted by the relentless demands of navigating daily instability.

In this state, the freedom to "choose your attitude" can feel like a cruel joke. The existential call to authorship is drowned out by the more immediate need to secure the next paycheck, the next meal, the next month's rent. This systemic precarity forces a kind of existential bad faith, but from the outside in. Individuals are pushed into a position where they must tell themselves, "I am free and independent," while their material reality is one of profound dependency on volatile market forces and the whims of opaque algorithms that assign their work. It is much harder to embrace the abstract burden of cosmic freedom when you are crushed by the concrete burden of systemic insecurity. Understanding precarity is not to let the individual off the hook of their responsibility, but to recognize that the weight of that responsibility is not distributed equally, and for many, the load is already at the breaking point before they have even lifted the first stone of their own choosing.

The Psychology of Risk and Ambiguity Aversion

To state that we live in a world without guarantees is to describe the objective nature of reality. To understand why this reality causes us such profound and persistent distress, however, we must turn inward, from the structure of the world to the structure of the human mind. Our discomfort with uncertainty is not a philosophical preference or a failure of character; it is a deep-seated and powerful psychological bias, a product of cognitive wiring that has been shaped by millennia of evolutionary pressures. Our brains are, in a very real sense, certainty-seeking machines. We are programmed to detect patterns, to predict threats, and to value the known over the unknown. This ancient programming, while once essential for our survival in a world of immediate physical dangers, now operates as a kind of cognitive reflex that often leads us to make irrational and self-limiting choices in the complex, probabilistic world we now inhabit.

The scientific exploration of this phenomenon has revealed two distinct but related biases that govern our relationship with the unknown: risk aversion and ambiguity aversion. The first of these, risk aversion, is a concept well-understood in economics and psychology. It describes the general human tendency to prefer a certain, guaranteed outcome over a probabilistic one, even when the probabilistic outcome has a higher expected value. The choice is a simple one: would you rather accept a guaranteed payment of forty dollars, or flip a coin for a chance to win one hundred dollars? A purely rational calculation would favor the coin flip; its expected value is fifty dollars (a 50% chance of $100), which is higher than the certain forty. Yet, a significant majority of people, when faced with this choice, will take the guaranteed forty dollars. The small but real possibility of getting nothing is so psychologically aversive that we are willing to pay a ten-dollar premium, in the form of a lower expected value, just to eliminate it. We prefer the comfort of a sure thing, even if it is a lesser thing.

This preference for certainty is driven by one of the most powerful forces in human psychology: loss aversion, a concept first systematically described by the groundbreaking psychologists Daniel Kahneman and Amos Tversky. Their work on Prospect Theory demonstrated that, for most people, the psychological pain of losing a certain amount of money is roughly twice as powerful as the psychological pleasure of gaining the same amount. Our minds are not neutral accountants; they are exquisitely sensitive to potential loss. An uncertain future always contains the possibility of loss—the loss of our investment, our effort, our hopes. The prospect of this loss looms so large in our mental calculus that it often outweighs even a high probability of a significant gain. We are wired not to optimize our outcomes, but to protect ourselves from the sting of a negative result.

As powerful as risk aversion is, however, it is the second of these biases, ambiguity aversion, that reveals the true depth of our existential discomfort with the unknown. Ambiguity aversion is our preference for known risks over unknown risks. It is a fear not just of a bad outcome, but of not knowing the odds in the first place. The classic illustration of this is the Ellsberg Paradox, named for the economist who first described it. Imagine two urns, each containing one hundred balls. You are told that Urn A contains exactly fifty red balls and fifty black balls. For Urn B, you are told only that it contains a mix of red and black balls, but the exact ratio is unknown. Now, you are offered a bet: you will win one hundred dollars if you draw a red ball. From which urn do you prefer to draw? The overwhelming majority of people will choose to bet on Urn A.

This choice is, from a standpoint of pure logic, irrational. The probability of drawing a red ball from Urn A is exactly 50%. The probability of drawing a red ball from Urn B is unknown; it could be anything from 1% to 99%. But because we have no information, the rational assumption should be that there is a 50% chance it is in our favor. The expected value of the bet is the same for both urns. Yet, we are powerfully drawn to the one where the risk is quantifiable. We prefer the known devil to the unknown one. The anxiety of not knowing the odds is so uncomfortable that we will choose a known 50% chance of success over a situation that might, for all we know, offer us a 99% chance. It is the ambiguity itself that we find intolerable.

This aversion to ambiguity is a direct flight from the groundlessness of our existential condition. Urn A represents a world of manageable risk, a world we feel we can navigate with strategy and calculation. Urn B represents the world as it actually is: a place where the odds are often unknown, where the rules are unclear, and where the future is fundamentally opaque. Our preference for Urn A is a preference for a fantasy of control. This deep-seated need to feel in control, even in situations that are entirely random, has been termed the "illusion of control" by the psychologist Ellen Langer. Her research showed that people will, for example, place a higher value on a lottery ticket if they have chosen the numbers themselves rather than having them randomly assigned. The act of choosing gives them a spurious sense of agency over a purely chance event. In the same way, we cling to rituals, superstitions, and rigid plans not because they actually influence outcomes, but because they provide a comforting, if illusory, sense of participation in our own fate. They are our attempts to impose a knowable order onto a fundamentally ambiguous reality.

The real-world consequences of these cognitive biases are profound and pervasive. They are the invisible forces that shape our most significant life decisions, often trapping us in suboptimal situations simply because those situations are known. Consider the person who stays for years in a predictably miserable but stable job. They are choosing a bad certainty (the known misery of their current role) over an uncertain possibility (the potential, but not guaranteed, happiness of a new one). The ambiguity of the job search—the unknown odds of success, the possibility of rejection, the risk of ending up in an even worse position—is so psychologically taxing that the known awfulness of the present feels like the safer option.

We see this same logic in our health decisions. A person who is experiencing a worrisome medical symptom may put off going to the doctor for months. They are choosing to live in a state of ambiguity rather than risk the possibility of a bad certainty in the form of a diagnosis. The ambiguity, as frightening as it is, allows for a sliver of hope and denial; the certainty of a diagnosis, even if it would allow for treatment, feels like a verdict too terrible to face. The known risk of a disease is often less frightening to us than the ambiguous process of confronting it.

Our aversion to ambiguity is the psychological engine of our resistance to a world without guarantees. It is the reason we cling to rigid ideologies, why we seek out gurus who claim to have all the answers, and why we are so susceptible to conspiracy theories that offer a simple, clear, and certain explanation for a complex and chaotic world. These are all attempts to transform the terrifying ambiguity of Urn B into the comforting, manageable risk of Urn A. To be a free and responsible person in a world without guarantees requires us to do something that runs contrary to our deepest psychological programming: it requires us to learn to tolerate ambiguity, to act with courage even when we do not know the odds, and to find our security not in the illusion of a certain outcome, but in the integrity of our own choices.

Cultural Attempts to Remove Uncertainty

The deep-seated human aversion to ambiguity is not merely a private, individual struggle. It is a powerful collective force that has shaped the grand course of human history, giving rise to our most elaborate and enduring cultural creations. When the anxiety of living in a world without guarantees becomes too heavy for the individual to bear alone, we instinctively seek refuge in the arms of a group, in a shared story that is larger and more certain than our own. Our most powerful systems of meaning—our religions, our political ideologies, our national identities—can be understood not just as sets of beliefs or social structures, but as massive, sophisticated, and often magnificent psychological defense mechanisms. They are humanity's collective attempt to build a permanent, stable fortress of certainty in the midst of a fundamentally uncertain and chaotic universe.

The most ancient and arguably most powerful of these systems is religion. At its psychological core, organized religion is a profound and comprehensive answer to the problem of existential dread. It addresses each of the ultimate concerns with a direct and deeply comforting promise. Against the terror of a meaningless universe, it posits a transcendent order, a divine consciousness, and a sacred plan. The random, often cruel, events of a human life are reframed as meaningful chapters in a larger, purposeful narrative written by an ultimate author. This instantly transforms a chaotic world into a coherent cosmos, providing a sense of ultimate safety and significance.

Against the heavy burden of moral responsibility—the Sartrean anguish of having to create our own values—religion offers a clear and absolute ethical framework. The rules for a good life are not to be agonized over and invented; they are revealed. A divine lawgiver provides a set of commandments, a clear distinction between right and wrong, that relieves the individual of the terrifying freedom of moral authorship. The path is not to be chosen, but to be followed. This provides immense psychological relief and a clear guide for action. And against the ultimate uncertainty of death, religion offers the most powerful guarantee of all: the promise of an afterlife, a continuation of consciousness, and a final reckoning in which the injustices of this world will be rectified. The finite, uncertain story of our earthly life is recast as a mere prelude to an eternal and certain existence.

The psychological "bargain" of religious faith, from this perspective, is a trade of a certain kind of freedom for a profound sense of security. It is a willing surrender of the burden of ultimate authorship in exchange for the comfort and clarity of living within a pre-written, divinely sanctioned script. To the existentialist, this might appear as a form of bad faith, a flight from freedom. But to the person suffering under the weight of a world without guarantees, it can feel like a life-saving grace, a solid rock in a turbulent sea.

In the more secular landscape of the modern world, political and economic ideologies have often come to serve the same psychological function. A powerful, totalizing ideology like Marxism or fascism is not just a theory of history or a program for governance; it is a secular religion that offers a comprehensive and certain explanation for the chaos of the world. It provides a clear, simple narrative of history, identifying a single, overarching cause for all societal problems—be it class struggle, racial impurity, or state oppression. This narrative instantly simplifies a complex and ambiguous social reality into a clear-cut battle between good and evil.

Furthermore, these ideologies provide a clear object for our devotion and a clear direction for our actions. They identify an unambiguous enemy (the bourgeoisie, the foreign power, the entrenched elite) and offer a vision of a guaranteed utopia that will be achieved once this enemy is vanquished. This transforms the vague, anxious energy of modern life into a focused and purposeful mission. The individual is no longer an isolated, insignificant actor in a confusing world; they are a soldier in a grand, historic struggle, a member of a vanguard marching toward a certain and glorious future. This sense of belonging, of shared purpose, and of historical certainty is a powerful antidote to the feelings of isolation, meaninglessness, and powerlessness that plague the individual in an age of uncertainty. The ideology provides a map, a compass, and a tribe, and in doing so, it relieves its adherents of the disorienting freedom of having to find their own way.

A more diffuse but equally potent form of this collective defense is nationalism. Nationalism is the powerful and often unconscious belief in the specialness and enduring nature of one's own nation or people. It creates what the historian Benedict Anderson called an "imagined community," a deep, horizontal comradeship that allows millions of strangers to feel a profound sense of connection and shared destiny. This identity provides a powerful buffer against existential dread. While the individual life is fragile, finite, and uncertain, the nation is imagined as a vast, powerful, and quasi-eternal entity. To identify with the nation, to devote oneself to its glory and preservation, is to participate in a project that will outlive one's own small existence. It is a powerful source of symbolic immortality.

Like religion and ideology, nationalism also simplifies the moral landscape. It often creates a clear in-group/out-group dynamic, a simple framework of "us versus them" that can provide a powerful, if often dangerous, sense of moral clarity and collective purpose. In times of national crisis or war, the ambiguous and complex choices of an individual life can be subsumed into the single, overriding, and certain goal of defending the nation. The burden of individual freedom is willingly surrendered for the security and righteousness of the collective cause.

All of these cultural systems—religion, ideology, nationalism—function as powerful "existential anxiety buffers." They are elaborate, collective narratives that we construct to make an uncertain and often terrifying world feel safe, meaningful, and predictable. They provide what the theologian Paul Tillich called the "courage to be as a part," the courage that comes from grounding one's individual existence in a reality larger than oneself. This is not to dismiss the genuine truths, the profound beauty, or the social cohesion that these systems can provide. It is, however, to recognize their deep psychological function. They are humanity's most powerful and enduring attempts to manage the terror of living in a world without guarantees. The comfort they offer is real, but it almost always comes at a price: a willing constriction of individual freedom, a surrender of the burden of doubt, and an embrace of a certainty that the universe itself has never promised to provide.

110

Embracing Impermanence

Our exploration of the human relationship with uncertainty has, up to this point, been a story of evasion. We have seen how our own psychological wiring makes us averse to ambiguity and how we have constructed elaborate and powerful cultural systems—religions, ideologies, and nationalisms—to provide a comforting, if often illusory, sense of certainty and permanence. This flight from the fundamental groundlessness of our existence is a deeply understandable, and perhaps even necessary, part of the human drama. But it is not the only possible response. Woven through some of the world's most profound philosophical and contemplative traditions is a different, more courageous, and ultimately more liberating path: the path of turning toward uncertainty and embracing it not as a curse to be endured, but as a fundamental truth to be understood and even welcomed. This is the wisdom that teaches that true freedom is found not in securing a guarantee from the universe, but in letting go of our need for one.

This perspective finds one of its most powerful expressions in the existential philosophy of Albert Camus, particularly in his famous essay "The Myth of Sisyphus." Camus begins by acknowledging the fundamental absurdity of the human condition. The absurd, for Camus, is the clash, the divorce, between two things: our profound and passionate human need for meaning, reason, and order, and the universe's silent, irrational, and indifferent refusal to provide it. We are meaning-seeking creatures living in a meaningless world. To confront this reality is to stand at a precipice of potential despair. The ancient myth of Sisyphus, the king condemned by the gods for all eternity to roll a massive boulder up a hill only to watch it roll back down again, is for Camus the perfect metaphor for this absurd existence. His labor is futile, repetitive, and without ultimate purpose.

Yet, it is at the very moment of greatest despair—the moment Sisyphus watches the rock thunder back down into the valley—that Camus locates the possibility of a unique and heroic form of freedom. This moment, when Sisyphus walks back down the hill to begin his task anew, is a moment of consciousness. In this moment, he is fully aware of the futility of his fate. He is without hope in the conventional sense. And it is precisely this lucidity, this clear-eyed view of his condition without illusion, that makes him superior to his rock. Camus concludes with a stunning and paradoxical assertion: "One must imagine Sisyphus happy." Sisyphus's happiness is not the happiness of a guaranteed outcome; it is the happiness of scornful rebellion. His freedom lies in his conscious choice to embrace his fate and to find his meaning not in the arrival at the summit, but in the integrity and the passion of the struggle itself. His victory is in the act of rolling the stone, not in the hope that it will one day stay at the top. This is the existential embrace of uncertainty: to act, to love, to create, and to live with full-throated passion, all the while knowing that there are no ultimate guarantees and no final victories. It is to find our purpose in the process, not the product.

A remarkably similar, though methodologically different, path is found in the core teachings of Buddhist psychology. The central diagnosis of the human condition in Buddhism is encapsulated in the concept of *dukkha*, a term often translated as "suffering" or "dissatisfaction." The root cause of this suffering, the Buddha taught, is not the world itself, but our resistance to its fundamental nature. And the most fundamental aspect of its nature is *anicca*, or impermanence. Everything, without exception, is in a constant state of flux: our thoughts, our emotions, our bodies, our relationships, our world. There is no solid, stable, enduring ground to be found anywhere. Suffering arises from our craving (*tanha*) for permanence in an impermanent world. We try to grasp onto pleasant experiences, to hold onto a fixed sense of self, to secure a permanent state of safety and happiness. This struggle is, by its very nature, doomed to failure, and it is this constant, futile grasping that is the source of our chronic dissatisfaction.

The path to liberation, in this view, is not to somehow achieve a state of permanence, but to see, with radical clarity and acceptance, the truth of impermanence. The goal of mindfulness practice is precisely this: to train the mind to observe the ceaseless arising and passing away of all phenomena without judgment and without grasping. It is to learn to rest in the groundlessness, to become comfortable with the constant flow of experience. This is not a state of passive resignation; it is a state of profound and dynamic engagement with life as it actually is, moment by moment. To accept impermanence is to let go of our war with reality. And in that surrender, we find a new and unexpected kind of freedom.

When we are no longer desperately trying to secure a future outcome, we are liberated to act with full presence and compassion in the here and now. When we are no longer clinging to a fixed and rigid idea of who we are, we are free to be fluid, to grow, and to change. The acceptance of uncertainty becomes the ultimate security. The knowledge that everything changes, that both pain and pleasure are transient, allows us to navigate the vicissitudes of life with a sense of equanimity and grace. It is the understanding that the only true refuge we can find is in our own clear-sighted, open-hearted awareness.

Though they arise from vastly different traditions, the resonance between the existential and Buddhist perspectives is profound. Both diagnose our fundamental problem as a clash between our desires and the unyielding nature of reality. Both see our attempts to find permanent security in a world without guarantees as the primary source of our anguish. And both propose a form of radical acceptance as the path to a deeper, more authentic freedom. They teach us that the only way to truly live is to let go of our demand that life be something other than what it is.

To embrace this wisdom in our own lives is to begin the difficult but liberating work of reframing our relationship with the future. It is to learn to hold our goals and plans with a lighter touch, to see them as guiding stars rather than as fixed destinations. It is to shift our focus from controlling the outcome to taking full responsibility for the quality of our input. The measure of success becomes not whether we achieved what we set out to, but whether we acted with courage, integrity, and kindness along the way. It is to find our meaning not in the hypothetical rewards of a guaranteed future, but in the rich, tangible, and undeniable reality of the present moment. This is the ultimate liberation that an acceptance of uncertainty can offer. It frees us from the exhausting and futile project of trying to control the uncontrollable, and in doing so, it returns us to the only thing we ever truly have: the freedom to choose how we will inhabit this one, precious, and profoundly uncertain life.

* * *

III

Part Three: The Psychology of Avoidance

Why do we so often flee from our own freedom? Part 3 enters the heart of our psychological defenses. We will dissect the common strategies of avoidance—blame, denial, conformity, procrastination—and reveal the powerful, unconscious ways we hide from the immense weight of responsibility.

6

The Flight from Freedom

Our journey thus far has been a descent into the profound and often uncomfortable realities of our own agency. We have confronted the dizzying anxiety that awakens with the discovery of our freedom, the immense and unshakeable weight of responsibility for our own existence, and the disorienting paradoxes of a modern world that offers us both infinite choice and a future without guarantees. We have, in essence, laid the full burden of freedom on the table for examination. It is a weight that is heavy, relentless, and for many, ultimately unbearable. The logical, and perhaps most human, question that arises from this examination is: what do we do when a burden becomes too heavy to carry? While one possible answer is to build the strength to bear it, another, far more common response is to simply find a way to put it down.

This chapter is an investigation into this second path: the path of escape. It is an exploration of the powerful, pervasive, and often unconscious impulse to flee from the very freedom our culture so ardently celebrates. This is not a passive drifting or a simple failure of courage. The flight from freedom is an active, motivated, and psychologically complex process. It is a voluntary, if often unacknowledged, surrender of our autonomy in exchange for the promise of security, belonging, and the sweet, intoxicating relief from the anguish of having to choose. It is the story of how and why human beings, both individually and collectively, will often choose the comforting certainty of a cage over the terrifying openness of the wild.

The thinker who most brilliantly and presciently diagnosed this phenomenon was the German-American psychoanalyst and social philosopher Erich Fromm. Writing in the shadow of the Second World War, Fromm was haunted by a question that defied easy explanation: why had the people of a modern, cultured, and seemingly advanced nation like Germany so eagerly and enthusiastically surrendered their freedom to the totalitarian authority of Nazism? The conventional explanations—economic hardship, political manipulation, mass psychosis—seemed to him incomplete. They described the external conditions, but they failed to capture the inner, psychological dynamic, the deep human need that fascism had so successfully, and catastrophically, promised to fulfill. In his landmark 1941 work, *Escape from Freedom*, Fromm proposed a radical and enduring thesis: the primary psychological driver behind the rise of totalitarianism was the unbearable weight of modern freedom itself.

Fromm's analysis begins with a historical arc. For the individual in the Middle Ages, he argued, freedom in the modern sense did not exist. A person's identity was fixed, predetermined by their rigid role in a stable and hierarchical social order. They were a peasant, a craftsman, a nobleman. Their life was not their own to create; it was a path to be followed, one laid out by the church, the guild, and the lord of the manor. This life was profoundly un-free, but it was also psychologically secure. The individual was never alone; they were a clearly defined part of a meaningful, coherent, and stable whole. The great project of the modern era—the Renaissance, the Reformation, the rise of capitalism and democracy—was the project of liberating the individual from these traditional bonds. This was the birth of "freedom *from*"—freedom from the dictates of the church, from the constraints of a feudal economy, from the arbitrary power of a monarch.

But this liberation, Fromm argued, came at a tremendous psychological cost. In breaking the chains that had once bound them, modern human beings had also severed the ties that had given them a sense of security and belonging. The newly liberated individual was now a newly isolated one. Standing alone in a vast and indifferent universe, stripped of a fixed place in a stable order, the individual was now solely responsible for creating their own meaning, their own values, and their own identity. This condition of "negative freedom"—the freedom *from* external constraints—is the very condition of anxiety and powerlessness that we have been exploring. Without a corresponding development of what Fromm called "positive freedom"—the freedom *to* spontaneously connect with others in love and to create meaningful work—this isolated freedom becomes an unbearable burden.

It is from this state of unbearable isolation and anxiety, Fromm concluded, that the flight from freedom begins. The individual seeks to escape the terror of their own aloneness by finding a way to submerge their individual self into something larger and more powerful. This is the desire for a new set of chains, but this time, they are chains that are voluntarily put on. This chapter will take Fromm's foundational analysis as its starting point and apply it to the unique pressures of our contemporary world. The specific mechanisms of escape have mutated since Fromm's time; the authorities we submit to and the groups we conform to look different today. But the underlying psychological impulse remains remarkably, and disturbingly, the same.

We will begin by revisiting Fromm's three primary "escape routes"—authoritarianism, destructiveness, and automaton conformity—and explore how these classic patterns manifest in our 21st-century lives, from the appeal of populist political movements and charismatic gurus to the cynical negativity of online trolling. From there, we will examine the uniquely modern variants of this escape, the new and technologically sophisticated ways we outsource our identity to social media algorithms, brand affiliations, and the endless, demanding project of curating a public persona. We will then delve deeper, beneath these observable behaviors, to analyze the underlying psychological defense mechanisms—projection, repression, splitting—that make this flight from responsibility possible. Finally, we will ground this entire inquiry in a series of concrete, intimate case studies, looking at the real-world vignettes of individuals who, in various ways, sabotage their own freedom to avoid the weight of its consequences. This chapter, then, is a journey into the heart of our own resistance, an attempt to understand the powerful and seductive pull of the un-free life, so that we might be better equipped to recognize it, to confront it, and ultimately, to choose a different, more courageous path.

Erich Fromm's Escape Routes

To understand the modern flight from freedom, we must first turn to the thinker who wrote its definitive field guide. Erich Fromm, witnessing the catastrophic surrender of an entire nation to the promises of fascism, proposed that the mechanisms of escape from freedom are not aberrations of a sick society, but are, in fact, morbid solutions to a problem that is endemic to the modern human condition: the unbearable feeling of aloneness and powerlessness that follows our liberation from traditional bonds. He identified three primary psychological strategies, or "escape routes," that individuals and societies use to alleviate this existential anxiety. Though Fromm was diagnosing the ills of the mid-20th century, his framework remains a startlingly prescient and powerful tool for understanding the psychological currents of our own time. The costumes and the technologies have changed, but the fundamental drama of escape remains the same.

The first and most dramatic of these escape routes is authoritarianism. This is the tendency to abandon the independence of one's own self and to fuse one's existence with something larger and more powerful. Fromm astutely observed that this dynamic has two symbiotic forms, which he termed the masochistic and the sadistic. The masochistic impulse is the drive to submit, to become a part of a larger, overwhelming power, be it a charismatic leader, a political movement, a nation, or a divine being. In doing so, the individual is relieved of the crushing burden of their own freedom. The agonizing responsibility of choice, of creating one's own values, is joyfully handed over to the authority. The individual's feeling of powerlessness is overcome by participating in the perceived omnipotence of the leader or the group. They find their security and their identity not in their own strength, but in the strength of the whole to which they now belong.

The sadistic impulse is the other side of this coin: the drive to dominate, to control, and to possess others. The sadist, like the masochist, is driven by an inability to tolerate their own aloneness and insignificance. They seek to overcome this feeling by making other people extensions of themselves. By controlling others, by making them dependent, the sadist gains a sense of power and purpose that they cannot generate from within. The masochist and the sadist are locked in a perfect, if pathological, embrace; both are fleeing from the intolerable burden of an isolated, individual self.

In our contemporary world, this authoritarian dynamic is alive and well, most visibly in the political sphere. The global rise of populist and authoritarian leaders is a testament to the enduring power of this escape route. These leaders typically offer their followers a seductive bargain: in exchange for your critical thought, your individual judgment, and your tolerance for ambiguity, I will give you certainty, strength, and a powerful, simplified identity. The complexities of global economics, social change, and political compromise are brushed aside in favor of a clear, simple narrative of national greatness, a defined external enemy, and the promise of decisive, powerful action. For the individual feeling adrift and powerless in a confusing world, the appeal of submitting to such a figure is immense. It is a profound relief to no longer have to grapple with difficult questions, but to simply trust in the strength and wisdom of the leader who claims to embody the will of the people. It is the classic flight from the anxiety of freedom into the secure arms of a powerful authority.

The second escape mechanism Fromm identified is destructiveness. This is a darker, more desperate response to the feeling of overwhelming powerlessness. While the authoritarian seeks to escape their insignificance by becoming part of a larger whole, the destructive personality seeks to escape it by eliminating the world that makes them feel so small. If the world is a constant source of threat and anxiety, a constant reminder of one's own impotence, then the ultimate act of self-assertion is to destroy it. This drive is not born of sadism, which seeks to control; it is born of a nihilistic rage, which seeks to annihilate. The act of destruction, Fromm argued, is a last, tragic attempt to prove that one exists, to make a mark on the world, even if that mark is a scar.

We can see this destructive impulse at play in the more toxic corners of our digital world. The phenomenon of anonymous internet trolling, the organized harassment campaigns, the gleeful "doxxing" and reputational destruction of public figures—all are manifestations of this dynamic. The individual, often feeling powerless and insignificant in their own life, discovers that they can wield a tremendous, albeit negative, power from behind a screen. The act of tearing someone else down, of spoiling a conversation, of destroying a person's peace of mind, provides a potent, if fleeting, sense of agency. It is a desperate attempt to matter, to have an effect on the world. This is not about reasoned critique or debate; it is about the raw, nihilistic pleasure of demolition. It is the cry of an isolated self that can only feel its own existence by negating the existence of others.

The third, and according to Fromm, by far the most common escape route in modern democratic societies, is automaton conformity. This is a less dramatic but more pervasive form of escape. It is the process by which the individual ceases to be an authentic self and becomes a perfect reflection of the personality type offered by their culture. They adopt the thoughts, the feelings, the desires, and the values that are expected of them, and they do so so completely that they are no longer aware that they are conforming. Their genuine, spontaneous self—with all its doubts, anxieties, and unique desires—is replaced by a kind of pseudo-self, a social construct designed for maximum acceptance and minimum friction. The goal is to eliminate the painful feeling of being different, of being alone, by becoming indistinguishable from everyone else. As Fromm put it, "The discrepancy between 'I' and the world disappears and with it the conscious fear of aloneness and powerlessness."

This is the dominant mode of escape in our consumerist and social-media-driven culture. We are constantly presented with pre-packaged identities, lifestyles that can be purchased and performed. We conform not to the dictates of an authoritarian state, but to the more subtle but equally powerful pressures of the market and the trend. We become an "Apple person" or a "CrossFit person," adopting the entire suite of aesthetic and behavioral traits that come with the brand. Our choices in clothing, music, and even food become less an expression of a genuine, internal preference and more a performance of a particular social identity, a signal that we belong to the right tribe.

Social media has accelerated this process to an unprecedented degree. The constant, ambient awareness of what others are doing, thinking, and liking creates an immense pressure to align oneself with the prevailing consensus of one's chosen in-group. To deviate is to risk social friction, disapproval, or even ostracism. It is far easier and safer to adopt the correct opinions, to use the correct slang, to perform the correct emotional responses. We become automatons of the zeitgeist, smoothly and efficiently reflecting the cultural patterns we are fed. This is perhaps the most insidious flight from freedom because it feels so natural. We do not feel like we are surrendering our freedom; we feel like we are simply being a normal person. But the cost is immense. In our quest to eliminate the anxiety of being alone, we risk erasing the very self that makes our life our own.

Modern Variants of Escape

While Erich Fromm's classic framework of authoritarianism, destructiveness, and conformity provides a timeless map of our psychological escape routes, the landscape of our modern world has been dramatically reshaped by the forces of digital technology and consumer capitalism. The fundamental desire to escape the burden of an isolated, free self remains the same, but the mechanisms for doing so have become more personalized, more seductive, and far more seamlessly integrated into the fabric of our daily lives. The new forms of escape are often so effective because they do not feel like acts of surrender; they feel like acts of self-expression and individual choice. We have not eliminated the flight from freedom; we have simply rebranded it, optimized it, and turned it into a consumer product.

The most powerful of these new variants is the outsourcing of the self to the algorithm. As we have explored, the recommendation engines that govern our digital experience are designed to create a frictionless and highly predictable world, tailored to our pre-existing tastes. This system functions as a new and profoundly subtle form of authority. It is not the jackbooted, overt authority of a totalitarian state, but a soft, personalized authority that presents itself as our ultimate servant. It is an authority that whispers, "I know you. I know what you like. Let me take care of the difficult work of choosing for you." This is an offer that is almost impossible to refuse. The algorithm becomes our trusted guide, our personal curator for life, relieving us of the anxiety-provoking responsibility of forging our own path of discovery.

The act of surrendering to this algorithmic authority is a modern form of the masochistic impulse Fromm described. We willingly submit to a power that is larger, more knowledgeable, and more capable than ourselves. We allow its logic to shape our cultural diet, our political opinions, and even our social connections. We trust the streaming service to tell us what movies to watch, the social network to tell us what news is important, and the e-commerce site to tell us what to desire. Each act of passive acceptance is a small abdication of our freedom, a small release from the burden of having to be an active, discerning, and self-directed individual. The result is a slow, almost imperceptible atrophy of our capacity for genuine, autonomous choice. We have not been forced into a prison; we have been offered a personalized, all-inclusive resort, and we have willingly handed over our passports at the gate.

A second, and closely related, modern escape is the flight into brand affiliation. This is a contemporary and highly commercialized version of Fromm's automaton conformity. In a world where traditional sources of identity like religion, community, and stable careers have become increasingly fluid, consumer brands have stepped into the void, offering powerful, pre-packaged identities that can be purchased and performed. We no longer just buy products for their utility; we buy them for the sense of self they confer. To be an "Apple person" is not just to own a particular set of electronic devices; it is to adopt a whole aesthetic of minimalist design, creative professionalism, and quiet innovation. To be a "Patagonia person" is to signal a commitment to environmentalism, outdoor adventure, and anti-corporate values, all while participating in a corporate ecosystem.

These brand identities function as powerful social signifiers, providing a cognitive shortcut to belonging. They offer a ready-made script and a set of props that allow us to instantly communicate who we are—or who we want to be—to the world. This is a profound relief from the existential labor of having to construct an identity from scratch. The brand provides the values, the aesthetic, and the community of fellow conformists. All we have to do is consume. This is a flight from freedom into a curated and market-tested form of belonging. We avoid the anxiety of being a unique, and therefore potentially isolated, individual by becoming a recognizable, and therefore acceptable, archetype. We become a walking, talking billboard for a chosen lifestyle, and in the clarity and simplicity of that role, we find a refuge from the messy, undefined nature of an authentic self.

The most sophisticated and psychologically demanding of these modern escapes, however, is the flight into the curated persona. This is the endless and exhausting project of constructing and maintaining an idealized version of ourselves, primarily on social media platforms. The curated self is the ultimate pseudo-self for the digital age. It is a carefully edited, beautifully filtered, and narratively coherent avatar that we create and then, in a profound act of self-deception, begin to identify with. We flee from the chaotic, contradictory, and often disappointing reality of our inner lives into the manageable and admirable world of our online profile.

This performance is a full-time job. It requires a constant monitoring of the self, a perpetual assessment of our experiences for their "post-worthiness." It is an escape from the freedom to be inconsistent, to be boring, to be un-photogenic, to be anything less than the optimized version of ourselves we are performing. The curated persona is a fortress we build to protect ourselves from the judgment of others, but it quickly becomes a prison that locks us out of our own real lives. The validation we receive for this performance—the likes, the shares, the positive comments—is a powerful but addictive anesthetic. It numbs the pain of our existential isolation, but it does so by replacing the possibility of genuine connection with the certainty of positive feedback for a fictional character. This is the ultimate escape: a flight not just from freedom, but from our very own being, into a digital effigy of our own creation.

Spiritual Bypassing: The Transcendent Escape

In our search for refuge from the anxieties of freedom, we have examined the flight into authority, the crowd, and the curated self. There is another, more subtle and often well-intentioned escape route that has flourished in the modern spiritual marketplace: the phenomenon of spiritual bypassing. Coined by psychologist John Welwood, spiritual bypassing is the use of spiritual ideas, beliefs, and practices to avoid facing unresolved emotional issues, psychological wounds, and the difficult, messy realities of human life. It is a form of existential avoidance dressed in the robes of enlightenment, a flight from the immanent responsibilities of the human condition into the illusion of transcendent detachment.

At its core, spiritual bypassing is a sophisticated mechanism of denial. It is the tendency to prematurely transcend the necessary, gritty work of being human. The individual engaged in spiritual bypassing does not consciously reject their freedom; they simply reframe it out of existence. The raw, anxious, and often painful feelings that accompany genuine freedom—dread, guilt, responsibility, grief—are not confronted and integrated. Instead, they are labeled as "low-vibration," "egoic," or "illusions" to be risen above.

Consider the common mantras of this bypassing mentality:

- Confronted with the profound responsibility of a life-altering choice, one might say, "There are no wrong paths; it's all a lesson from the universe." This sounds wise, but it can function as a way to sidestep the anguish of committing to a single, finite path and annihilating the others. It denies the real, consequential weight of choice.
- Faced with the legitimate pain of a personal failure or loss, one might

reflexively affirm, "Everything happens for a reason," or "I am grateful for this challenge." While gratitude and meaning-making are powerful, when used prematurely, they can be a defense against the necessary, human process of grieving, of feeling anger, of sitting in the void of meaninglessness before a new meaning can be authentically built.

- When called to account for a hurtful action, one might deflect with, "That's just your ego being triggered," or "You must release your attachment to that story." This is a profound abdication of interpersonal responsibility. It projects the cause of the conflict onto the other person's failure to be "evolved" enough, rather than owning one's own role in the dynamic.

In each case, the language of spirituality is weaponized to create a kind of psychological Teflon, allowing the individual to avoid the sticky, uncomfortable, and demanding realities of finite, embodied, and relational existence. This is bad faith in a new key. It is the attempt to be a pure, transcendent "for-itself" without the inconvenient facticity of a vulnerable, feeling, and sometimes flawed human being.

Spiritual bypassing is particularly seductive because it mimics genuine spiritual maturity. It offers a tantalizing shortcut. The hard work of psychotherapy—of confronting childhood wounds, of acknowledging shadow selves, of learning to tolerate painful emotions—is traded for the promise of an immediate, painless ascent to a higher plane. The burden of freedom is not carried; it is declared an illusion.

But as Welwood insists, "The path is not about rising above our humanity, but about embracing it fully." True spirituality does not bypass the human condition; it passes directly through its very heart. It requires the courage to feel the full force of existential anxiety without a metaphysical safety net. It demands that we take radical responsibility for our choices and their consequences, even—and especially—when we can find no cosmic reason for them. It calls us to be fully present with our own suffering and the suffering of others, without rushing to a transcendent explanation that would explain it away.

The person who is genuinely working with their freedom might sit with the "dizziness" of a decision, acknowledging the terror and the potential for regret. The spiritual bypasser, in contrast, will quickly invoke "divine guidance" or "surrendering to the flow" to escape that same dizziness. One is building the muscle to bear the weight; the other is seeking to disintegrate the weight through a trick of perception.

To overcome spiritual bypassing is to realize that enlightenment, if it means anything, is not an escape from the human condition, but a profound and compassionate intimacy with it. It is to understand that the spiritual and the psychological are not separate paths, but intertwined dimensions of a single journey toward wholeness. We cannot transcend what we have not first fully faced. The courage to be free, therefore, includes the courage to descend from the abstract heights of spiritual bypassing and to stand, naked and responsible, on the solid, difficult, and sacred ground of our own imperfect, choosing, and beautifully human lives.

Psychological Defense Mechanisms

The observable flights from freedom we have discussed—the submission to authority, the conformity to the crowd, the curation of a digital persona— are not, for the most part, conscious and deliberate choices. They are the visible symptoms of a much deeper, more subtle, and largely unconscious process. To truly understand why we so readily surrender our autonomy, we must move from the external world of behavior into the internal world of the psyche. Here, we find a complex and powerful set of operations, first systematically charted by Sigmund Freud and later elaborated by his daughter Anna Freud, known as psychological defense mechanisms. These are not signs of pathology; they are the universal and necessary tools the human ego uses to protect itself from anxiety that is too overwhelming to bear. In our context, the most overwhelming anxiety of all is the one that springs from our direct confrontation with our own radical freedom and the total responsibility it entails. Defense mechanisms are the unconscious mind's brilliant, intricate, and ultimately costly strategies for softening the terror of this truth, for constructing a version of reality that is more manageable, more predictable, and less demanding than the raw, unvarnished facts of our existence.

These mechanisms operate like an internal diplomatic corps, constantly negotiating between the demands of our inner world and the pressures of external reality. They work automatically, outside of our conscious awareness, and their primary function is to distort reality in some way so that we can avoid a painful feeling or a threatening thought. While they are essential for navigating the inevitable pains and disappointments of life, they become problematic when they become our primary and most rigid way of engaging with the world. A life lived in the grip of its defenses is a life lived in a state of self-deception, a flight from the very truths that are necessary for genuine growth and authentic living. To understand the flight from freedom, we must understand the primary tools that make it possible: the psychic maneuvers of projection, repression, and splitting. These are the engines that power our escape.

The first of these, and perhaps the most crucial for offloading the burden of responsibility, is projection. In its simplest form, projection is the unconscious act of taking an unacceptable or undesirable part of ourselves— a thought, a feeling, an impulse, a character trait—and attributing it to someone else. It is a way of disowning a piece of our own inner landscape and seeing it as if it were coming at us from the outside world. The process is a form of psychic laundering; we take our own internal "dirt" and perceive it as a stain on another person. The person who is struggling with their own unacknowledged anger, for instance, does not experience themselves as an angry person; instead, they experience the world as a hostile and aggressive place, constantly perceiving slights and ill-intent in the neutral actions of others. The internal threat ("I am full of rage") is converted into an external one ("The world is full of angry people attacking me"), which is a far more comfortable and manageable reality.

The existential function of projection is to provide a powerful and immediate release from the burden of self-ownership. The responsibility for managing our own inner conflicts is a heavy one. It requires self-awareness, discipline, and the courage to confront the less admirable parts of our own character. Projection offers a seductive shortcut. Instead of engaging in this difficult internal work, we can simply locate the problem "out there." This transforms us from a conflicted individual into a righteous victim. We are no longer responsible for our own feelings; we are simply reacting to the provocations of a flawed and hostile world. This dynamic is a primary fuel for almost all forms of interpersonal and group conflict. Consider the manager who is deeply insecure about their own competence and terrified of making a mistake. This internal anxiety is profoundly uncomfortable. Through projection, the manager disowns their own insecurity and instead perceives their highly competent team as being untrustworthy, lazy, or constantly on the verge of error. This allows the manager to convert their internal anxiety into an external problem: the "problem" of their team's performance. They can now engage in controlling behaviors like micromanagement not as an expression of their own fear, but as a "necessary" response to the perceived flaws of their subordinates. They have successfully fled from the responsibility for their own professional insecurity by creating a drama of external control.

In the political sphere, projection operates on a massive scale. It is the engine of tribalism and polarization. We take the undesirable qualities of our own political group—the internal contradictions, the moral compromises, the moments of hypocrisy—and project them onto the opposing party. The other side becomes the pure embodiment of all that is evil, stupid, and corrupt, while our own side is perceived as virtuous and well-intentioned. This allows us to avoid the agonizingly difficult and responsible task of grappling with moral and political ambiguity. We are relieved of the burden of critical thought and complex judgment and are free to indulge in the simple, satisfying righteousness of a world clearly divided into saints and sinners. Projection, then, is a profound abdication of responsibility. It is a refusal to own the totality of our own being, and in doing so, it keeps us in a state of perpetual conflict with a world that is, in many ways, just a mirror of our own disowned self.

If projection is the act of casting out what is unacceptable within us, repression is the act of burying it deep within our own psyche. Repression is the foundational defense mechanism, the unconscious process of pushing threatening or painful thoughts, memories, desires, and feelings out of our conscious awareness. It is not a conscious decision to "not think about something"; it is an automatic and powerful mechanism that prevents the threatening material from ever reaching the light of day. While Freud was primarily concerned with the repression of traumatic memories or forbidden sexual and aggressive impulses, from an existential perspective, one of the things we most consistently and powerfully repress is the awareness of our own freedom.

The full, unvarnished knowledge of our total responsibility for our lives is, for most of us, a thought too terrifying to hold in our conscious minds for very long. The awareness that we are choosing our unfulfilling job, that we are choosing our unhappy marriage, that we are choosing our life of quiet desperation—this knowledge is the source of profound existential guilt and anxiety. Repression is the mind's way of protecting us from this pain. We do not consciously deny our freedom; we simply arrange our mental lives in such a way that the question of our own agency never fully arises. We bury the knowledge of our own authorship under a thick layer of routine, distraction, and rationalization.

This repression often manifests as a pervasive sense of apathy or numbness. The person who feels emotionally dead, who claims to have no strong passions or desires, may in fact be engaged in a massive act of repression. To feel a genuine desire—a desire for a different life, a different career, a different way of being—is to be confronted with the terrifying freedom and responsibility to act on that desire. It is far safer to feel nothing at all. The emotional numbness is a defense against the vitality that would make the burden of choice unavoidable. Similarly, the person who lives in a state of chronic, frantic busyness, the workaholic who fills every waking moment with tasks and obligations, is often repressing the quiet, empty spaces in which the terrifying questions of meaning and purpose might arise. The noise of their activity is a shield against the silent call of their own unlived life. They have repressed their freedom by simply making no room for it in their consciousness.

A third, and particularly primitive, defense mechanism that serves as a powerful escape from freedom is splitting. Also known as all-or-nothing thinking, splitting is the failure to integrate the positive and negative qualities of the self and others into a cohesive and realistic whole. The world, through the lens of splitting, is not a complex and ambiguous place filled with flawed but decent people; it is a stark, black-and-white landscape of angels and demons, saints and sinners, heroes and villains. Splitting is the ultimate defense against the anxiety of ambiguity. It simplifies a complex reality into a manageable cartoon, and in doing so, it makes the act of choosing feel much easier.

We see this most clearly in our relationships, particularly in the cycle of idealization and devaluation. When we first fall in love, we often engage in splitting by idealizing our new partner. We see them as "all good"—perfect, flawless, the answer to all our problems. This is a profound flight from the responsibility of engaging with a real, complex, and imperfect human being. It allows us to surrender to the fantasy that this person will save us from our own existential burdens. Inevitably, however, the real, flawed person emerges. They have annoying habits, they disappoint us, they fail to meet our unspoken needs. For the person who relies on splitting, this emergence of imperfection is intolerable. The psyche cannot hold the tension of someone being both good and bad, loving and frustrating, supportive and flawed. And so, the pendulum swings. The partner is devalued; they are now seen as "all bad," selfish, narcissistic, and fundamentally flawed. This makes the choice simple: the relationship must end. Splitting protects us from the difficult, mature, and responsible work of loving a whole person. It allows us to live in a world of romantic fantasies and righteous dismissals, forever avoiding the messy, ambiguous reality of real intimacy.

We also use splitting to manage our own self-concept. We may split ourselves into an "all good" public persona—the curated self we present online—and a secret, hidden, "all bad" self that we believe to be our true, shameful reality. This allows us to avoid the difficult work of integrating the light and shadow of our own character. Or, conversely, we may fall into a state of global self-loathing, seeing ourselves as entirely and irredeemably flawed. This, paradoxically, can also be a flight from responsibility. If we are "all bad," then nothing good can be expected of us. We are absolved of the responsibility to live up to our own potential, to share our gifts, and to make a positive impact on the world. The declaration of our own worthlessness is a comforting, if miserable, excuse.

These defenses—projection, repression, and splitting—are the silent, invisible engines of our flight from freedom. They are the unconscious tricks of the mind that allow us to construct a reality in which we are not the authors of our own lives. They allow us to blame others for our inner conflicts, to bury the terrifying knowledge of our own potential, and to simplify a complex world into a manageable but distorted caricature. The first and most courageous step toward a more authentic life is not to try to eliminate these defenses, which is an impossible task, but to begin to cultivate the self-awareness to notice them in action. It is to begin to ask ourselves, with compassion and curiosity, "Is it possible that the frustration I feel toward this person is a disowned part of myself? Is it possible that my emotional numbness is a shield against a desire I am afraid to feel? Is it possible that my need to see this situation in black and white is a defense against its uncomfortable complexity?" This act of questioning is the beginning of the return journey. It is the first, hesitant step out of the shadows of avoidance and back into the difficult, demanding, but ultimately life-giving light of our own freedom.

Procrastination: The Sabotage of Potential

Among the many strategies we employ to lighten the burden of freedom, procrastination is perhaps the most mundane, the most universal, and the most misunderstood. It is typically dismissed as a simple failure of time management, a character flaw of laziness, or a lack of discipline. But from the existential perspective, chronic procrastination, especially on projects that matter deeply to us, is rarely about time at all. It is a sophisticated form of self-sabotage, a covert operation launched by the psyche to avoid the existential risks inherent in genuine action. It is a silent strike against our own potential.

To understand this, we must see the procrastinator not as lazy, but as paralyzed by the dizzying height of the cliff they are being asked to jump from. Every significant project—writing a book, starting a business, pursuing a degree, creating a work of art—is a vessel for our freedom. It is a concrete path through which we attempt to turn our boundless potential into a finite, tangible reality. And this is precisely what terrifies us.

When we procrastinate on a meaningful task, we are engaging in a form of "magical thinking" that keeps us safe in the realm of pure potential. As long as the book remains unwritten, the business plan un-executed, the canvas blank, we can still cling to the fantasy of its perfection. We are the brilliant, unrecognized novelist; the visionary entrepreneur; the master artist in waiting. Our potential is intact, pristine, and unassailable.

To act is to murder this perfect phantom. The moment we write the first sentence, we are no longer a person who *could* write a masterpiece; we are a person who *is writing a flawed first draft*. The gap between our glorious self-image and our imperfect, stumbling efforts is suddenly, painfully revealed. Procrastination is a defense against this inevitable humiliation, this confrontation with our own finitude and fallibility. It is a protective mechanism that prioritizes the preservation of a perfect self-image over the risky, and often disappointing, work of bringing a real self into the world.

In this light, procrastination is a direct manifestation of Kierkegaard's "dizziness of freedom." The procrastinator is frozen in the room with a thousand doors, not out of laziness, but out of a terror of choosing the wrong one and discovering that they are not the person they hoped to be. The anxiety of possibility is so acute that the only safe choice is to make no choice at all—to remain in the limbo of preparation, research, and minor, peripheral tasks. This is the "waiting" that the playwright Samuel Beckett so brilliantly captured—a life deferred in order to avoid the responsibility of living it.

Furthermore, procrastination serves as a perverse, self-administered alibi for failure. By delaying until the last possible moment, the procrastinator creates a ready-made excuse. If the project turns out poorly, the cause was not a lack of talent or worth, but a simple lack of time. "I could have done great work if I'd only started sooner," becomes the comforting refrain. This is bad faith in its most common form: the construction of a narrative in which we are not responsible for the outcome because we were not truly, fully engaged. We choose to fail on our own terms—through delay—rather than risk the more devastating possibility of failing despite our best efforts.

The emotional texture of procrastination confirms its existential nature. It is not a state of relaxed idleness, but one of intense, mounting anxiety and self-loathing. The procrastinator is acutely aware of the freedom they are failing to exercise—the unwritten pages, the unmade decisions, the passing time. This awareness generates what we earlier identified as **existential guilt**: the guilt of the unlived life, of the potential being squandered. The frantic, last-minute effort to meet a deadline is often a desperate attempt to silence this guilt, to prove to ourselves that we are, in fact, capable of action, even if it is rushed and imperfect.

To overcome chronic procrastination, therefore, requires more than a new app or a time-management system. It requires an existential intervention. It demands the courage to accept that our creations will be flawed, that our efforts will sometimes fall short, and that our finite, real-world self will never fully match the infinite potential of our imagination. It means embracing the "good enough" and understanding that a finished, imperfect project is infinitely more valuable—and more real—than a perfect, unwritten one. It is to choose, moment by moment, the difficult dignity of being a flawed author of a real life over the comfortable misery of being the brilliant, potential author of an imaginary one.

Case Studies of Flight

The complex machinery of our psychological defenses and the powerful allure of our escape routes from freedom are not distant, theoretical concepts. They are the invisible scripts that govern the most pivotal moments of our lives. The flight from freedom is not a grand, dramatic event, but a series of small, quiet, and often unconscious decisions: the missed deadline, the avoided conversation, the cynical shrug. To see this dynamic clearly, we must move from the general to the specific, from the abstract principle to the lived story. The following case studies are drawn from the common struggles of ordinary life, each one a portrait of an individual standing at a crossroads, faced with the anxiety of a meaningful choice, who ultimately chooses the deceptive comfort of escape.

First, consider the case of Mark, a talented and highly competent senior software engineer at a thriving tech company. For years, Mark has been the go-to person on his team. He is a brilliant problem-solver, respected by his peers, and consistently praised by his superiors. His manager has made it clear that a promotion to a team lead position is the next logical step, a role that would come with a significant raise, more influence, and the chance to shape the direction of new projects. Mark, on a conscious level, wants this promotion. He speaks about it with his wife, plans for the increased income, and feels a sense of pride in his well-earned reputation. Yet, as the time for the formal promotion review approaches, a subtle but distinct pattern of self-sabotage begins to emerge.

An important project deadline, which he would normally meet with ease, is suddenly in jeopardy. He finds himself procrastinating, getting lost in minor details, and feeling an uncharacteristic sense of mental fog. In a crucial presentation to senior leadership, he makes a series of unforced errors, misrepresenting a key data point and appearing flustered and unprepared. His communication in team meetings, once clear and confident, becomes more passive and withdrawn. When his manager, disappointed but still supportive, postpones the promotion discussion, citing the need for Mark to get "back on track," Mark's reaction is a strange and contradictory mixture of righteous indignation and a quiet, unacknowledged wave of profound relief.

What is happening here? Mark is engaged in a classic flight from the responsibility of a new and more demanding form of freedom. The role of a senior engineer, while challenging, is a well-defined one. His tasks are clear, his success is measurable, and his responsibility is primarily to his own excellent work. The role of a team lead, however, is a step into a world of profound ambiguity. It is a role that requires not just technical skill, but the messy, unpredictable, and emotionally demanding work of managing other people. He would be responsible for their careers, for their conflicts, for their failures. He would have to make difficult decisions with incomplete information, choices that would affect the livelihoods of his team members. The open-ended nature of leadership, the lack of a clear "right answer" in many situations, represents the very "dizziness of freedom" that Kierkegaard described. The promotion is not just a new job; it is a demand to become a new, more responsible, and more existentially exposed version of himself.

His self-sabotage is an unconscious but highly effective strategy for avoiding this demand. It allows him to fail without having to take responsibility for his fear of success. He has created a situation in which the choice is seemingly taken away from him. He can now tell himself, and his wife, a comforting story of victimhood: "This company is too political. They don't truly appreciate my contributions. They've exploited my talents and then pulled the rug out from under me." This narrative, a product of projection and rationalization, is a powerful shield. It protects him from the far more terrifying and authentic truth: "I was offered a new level of freedom and responsibility, and I was so afraid of it that I chose to fail." The relief he feels is the relief of a prisoner who, having been offered parole, commits a small crime to ensure he can remain within the familiar and predictable confines of his cell.

Next, let us turn to Chloe, a vibrant and successful graphic designer in her early thirties. Chloe is in a loving, stable, and deeply supportive relationship with her partner, Ben, a man she genuinely adores. They have been together for three years, have built a shared life, and by all external measures, are a perfect match. Ben is ready to take the next step: marriage, a house, a future. But as the topic of commitment becomes more explicit, Chloe is gripped by a growing sense of panic, a kind of existential claustrophobia that she cannot articulate. The thought of a lifelong commitment, of a final and irreversible choice, feels less like a joyful beginning and more like an ending.

Her mind becomes a relentless counterfactual generator. She finds herself thinking about the adventurous life of travel she might be sacrificing. She scrolls through dating apps, not with any intention of cheating, but with a kind of compulsive curiosity, a need to reassure herself that other possibilities still exist. She begins to engage in a process of devaluation, a form of splitting. Ben's small, endearing quirks, which she once found charming, now begin to grate on her as major character flaws. His stability, which once felt like a source of security, now feels like a sign of a boring and predictable future. She is unconsciously building a case against the relationship, seeking a justifiable reason to flee. Eventually, she picks a fight over a minor issue, escalates it into a major conflict, and ends the relationship, telling a heartbroken Ben, and herself, that "something just doesn't feel right."

Chloe's flight is a direct escape from the responsibility of commitment in a world of infinite options. She is a victim of the paradox of choice in its most intimate form. To choose Ben, definitively and forever, is to accept the necessary and painful loss of all the other lives she could live, with all the other people she could love. It is to accept the responsibility of building a real, imperfect life with a real, imperfect person, rather than living in the exciting but imaginary world of pure potential. Her escape is disguised as a noble quest for the perfect "feeling," for a romantic certainty that the world simply does not offer. Her rationalization that "something was missing" is a defense against the terrifying truth that nothing is ever perfect, and that a good life is not found, but built, through the courageous and difficult act of choosing to close doors. She has chosen the shallow freedom of endless possibility over the deep, demanding, and ultimately more meaningful freedom of a committed love.

Finally, consider David, an intelligent and well-informed man in his fifties who is completely disengaged from political and civic life. He prides himself on being "above the fray." He follows the news with an air of ironic detachment, speaks of all politicians with a sweeping and dismissive cynicism, and has not voted in over two decades. His mantra, repeated at dinner parties, is, "They're all corrupt. The whole system is broken. It makes no difference what you do." His friends see him as a sophisticated, if somewhat jaded, observer of the political scene. But his cynicism is not a sign of intellectual superiority; it is a carefully constructed fortress, a defense against the heavy burden of civic responsibility.

To truly engage in the democratic process would be to accept a series of uncomfortable realities. It would mean acknowledging that the world is a complex, ambiguous place with no easy answers. It would require him to grapple with difficult trade-offs, to tolerate moral compromises, and to accept the frustratingly slow and imperfect nature of incremental change. It would mean taking a side, making a choice, and accepting his own small but real complicity in the outcome. It would, in short, require him to care, and to care is to be vulnerable to disappointment. David's cynical detachment is a form of Fromm's destructiveness, albeit a passive one. Unable to face the overwhelming responsibility of being a co-creator of his society, he opts to mentally annihilate it, to declare the entire project a sham. His posture of being "above it all" is a flight from the anxiety of being *in* it all.

This abdication allows him to maintain a sense of pristine, detached innocence. By never participating, he can never be wrong. He can sit on the sidelines and offer critiques of the players on the field without ever having to risk making a play himself. It is a profound escape from the messy, demanding, and often frustrating responsibility of being a citizen. He has traded the difficult freedom of a participant for the safe, simple, and ultimately sterile role of a spectator.

In Mark, Chloe, and David, we see the same fundamental drama unfold in different costumes. Each is faced with a choice that demands a new level of responsibility, a new degree of authorship over their own life. And each, in their own way, flees from that demand, constructing a narrative of victimhood or cynical detachment that allows them to avoid the terrifying and magnificent burden of their own freedom.

* * *

7

Existential Avoidance and Distortions

I n our previous chapter, we explored the grand, macro-level strategies of our flight from freedom: the willing submission to an authoritarian power, the nihilistic release of destructiveness, and the comforting camouflage of automaton conformity. These are the large-scale social and behavioral dramas that unfold when the burden of an isolated, individual existence becomes too heavy to bear. But the flight from freedom is not always so dramatic. It does not always involve joining a political movement or curating a public persona. More often, and for most of us, the escape is a quieter, more intimate, and more persistent affair. It is a war waged not on the grand stage of society, but in the subtle, subterranean corridors of our own minds. It is a war of attrition, fought with the mundane but powerful weapons of our everyday habits, our interpersonal dynamics, and our most cherished beliefs.

This chapter is a journey into that internal battlefield. It is an examination of the specific psychological mechanisms of existential avoidance and the cognitive distortions we employ to make that avoidance possible. If the flight from freedom is the strategic goal, then these mechanisms are the tactical maneuvers. Avoidance, in this context, is not just the act of putting off an unpleasant task; it is the systemic, often unconscious, refusal to make contact with the raw, anxiety-provoking realities of our condition: our freedom, our responsibility, our finitude, our ultimate aloneness. Distortion is the essential tool that makes this avoidance palatable. It is the mind's remarkable ability to bend, twist, and reframe reality so that its sharpest, most terrifying edges are softened and its most demanding truths are obscured. We look at the world not through a clear pane of glass, but through a lens that has been warped by our own need for comfort and security.

It is crucial to understand that these patterns are not, in themselves, signs of pathology or weakness. They are, in a profound sense, creative and meaningful strategies. They are the psyche's best attempt to protect us from what it perceives as an overwhelming, and potentially annihilating, level of anxiety. The mind that blames another person for its own unhappiness has found an ingenious, if ultimately self-defeating, solution to the problem of existential guilt. The mind that clings to an absolute, unshakeable certainty has discovered a powerful anesthetic for the chronic pain of living in an ambiguous world. These are not malfunctions; they are distorted solutions to the fundamental problems of being human. Our task is not to condemn them, but to understand them, to see them for what they are, and to begin to recognize the immense price we pay for the comfort they provide. The price, in almost every case, is a piece of our own authentic life.

To illuminate these patterns, we will begin our inquiry with one of the most common and universally experienced forms of avoidance: procrastination. We will reframe this familiar struggle not as a simple failure of time management or a lack of discipline, but as a profound and often unconscious act of resistance against the finality of choice. Procrastination, we will see, is a way of lingering in the seductive, pre-committal world of pure potential, a refusal to perform the irreversible act of closing doors that every meaningful choice requires. It is a rebellion against the tyranny of a linear, finite life, an attempt to remain in the dizzying but strangely comforting state of not yet having to be anyone in particular.

From this internal struggle, we will move to the interpersonal domain and revisit the powerful dynamics of blame and projection. Here, we will dissect the psychological calculus that makes it feel so much easier to locate the source of our problems in the external world rather than within ourselves.

We will explore how blaming others, or projecting our own unwanted traits onto them, serves as a powerful defense against the heavy responsibility of self-ownership. It is a strategy that turns the difficult, ambiguous work of introspection into a simple, righteous drama of external conflict, allowing us to maintain a sense of our own innocence at the cost of genuine self-knowledge and mature relationships.

Next, we will broaden our scope to the level of our belief systems and examine the profound psychological comfort of certainty. In a world without guarantees, the appeal of a system of thought—be it religious, political, or even scientific—that offers absolute, black-and-white answers can be nearly irresistible. We will analyze how fundamentalism, in all its forms, functions as a powerful psychological anesthetic, numbing the anxiety of doubt, the burden of moral ambiguity, and the responsibility of having to think for oneself. It is the ultimate intellectual and spiritual flight from freedom into a pre-fabricated, perfectly ordered, and deeply secure reality.

Finally, we will trace these patterns of avoidance and distortion to their most extreme and crystallized forms: the clinical manifestations that are diagnosed as psychological disorders. We will explore how a chronic and rigid pattern of existential avoidance can be understood as a central feature of many common struggles. We will look at how generalized anxiety disorders can be seen as the state of a person overwhelmed by an unacknowledged and unused freedom; how specific phobias can be understood as the process of taking a diffuse, free-floating existential dread and concentrating it onto a single, concrete, and avoidable object; and how an avoidant attachment style is, at its core, a relational strategy for never having to face the profound risks and responsibilities of genuine, committed intimacy.

This chapter, then, is a deep dive into the shadowlands of our own minds. It is an attempt to bring a compassionate, non-judgmental awareness to the ways we all, in our own unique styles, hide from the full and demanding truth of our existence. The goal is not to eliminate these defenses, for that would be an impossible and even undesirable task. The goal is to recognize them. For it is only in the act of recognition, in the moment we see a pattern for what it is, that a space is created. And in that space, a new choice becomes possible: the choice to continue the flight, or the choice to turn, with courage and with trepidation, and begin the difficult journey home to ourselves.

Procrastination as Resistance

Of all the forms of existential avoidance, procrastination is the most common, the most mundane, and perhaps the most misunderstood. We speak of it as a personal failing, a character flaw, a correctable habit on par with nail-biting or tardiness. The vast and ever-growing industry of self-help offers us an arsenal of tools to combat it: time-management systems, productivity apps, life hacks designed to trick ourselves into action. But these solutions, while occasionally effective in the short term, almost always fail to address the deeper source of the problem. They treat the symptom while ignoring the disease. For in a great many cases, procrastination is not simply a matter of poor discipline or a lack of motivation. It is a profound and deeply meaningful act of psychological resistance. It is an unconscious, and often desperate, refusal of the fundamental demands of our freedom.

To understand procrastination in this light, we must see it not as a failure to act, but as an active choice to remain in a particular state of being: the state of pure potential. Before a choice is made, before the work is begun, the world is a place of infinite possibility. The unwritten novel could still be a masterpiece. The un-started business could still be a wild success. The un-made decision could still be the perfect one. This realm of the "not yet" is a seductive and deeply comforting place. It is the world as Kierkegaard's dizzying abyss, but seen from a safe distance, where its terror is transmuted into a kind of thrilling potential energy. To procrastinate is to choose to linger in this shimmering, pre-committal world. It is to refuse to take the irreversible step from the boundless realm of what *could be* into the singular, finite, and often disappointing realm of what *actually is*.

Every meaningful choice is an act of creation, but it is also, simultaneously, an act of annihilation. To commit to one path is to kill all the other potential paths that were available in that moment. To write the first sentence of the novel is to destroy the possibility of the thousand other first sentences that might have been written. To accept the job offer is to close the door on all the other careers one might have pursued. This act of closure, of making a finite reality out of an infinite potential, is the very essence of what it means to live a life in time. Procrastination is a rebellion against this fundamental law. It is a desperate, unconscious attempt to keep all the doors open, to live in a state where no possibilities have yet been sacrificed. It is a refusal to accept the tragic and beautiful burden of having only one life to live. The procrastinator is a connoisseur of beginnings that never begin, a lover of potential who is terrified of the actuality.

At its core, then, procrastination is a direct flight from the responsibility of authorship. As long as the canvas is blank, the artist cannot be judged. As long as the decision is unmade, the choice cannot be wrong. By putting off the act of choosing, we are cleverly avoiding the burden of being the chooser. We are avoiding the moment of truth in which our abilities are tested, our judgments are rendered, and we are forced to become the definitive author of a specific, imperfect outcome. This allows us to preserve a fragile, idealized version of ourselves. The student who delays writing a term paper until the last possible minute is not just avoiding the tedium of the work; they are protecting themselves from the possibility of a mediocre result. As long as the paper is unwritten, their private self-image as a brilliant, insightful student remains intact and unchallenged. The panicked, caffeine-fueled rush to complete the assignment at the eleventh hour provides a ready-made alibi for any potential shortcomings. The resulting grade, if it is poor, can be attributed not to a lack of ability, but to a lack of time. "If only I had started sooner," the student can tell themselves, "it would have been a masterpiece." This narrative is a sophisticated defense mechanism, a way to fail without ever having to take full responsibility for the failure. It is an ingenious strategy for preserving the fantasy of our own potential at the expense of its actualization.

This dynamic creates a vicious and self-perpetuating cycle. The act of avoidance itself generates anxiety. The longer we put off a task, the larger and more intimidating it looms in our minds. The initial resistance to a small, manageable choice metastasizes into a full-blown dread of a massive, overwhelming undertaking. This mounting anxiety then serves as further justification for our inaction. We are no longer simply choosing not to act; we now feel that we *cannot* act, that we are paralyzed and "stuck." This feeling of being overwhelmed is the emotional consequence of our repressed freedom. We have denied our agency for so long that we have come to genuinely feel powerless. The procrastination, which began as an active (if unconscious) choice, has now successfully disguised itself as a passive state of being, a condition that is happening *to* us rather than a strategy we are employing. We have become the convincing victims of our own refusal to choose.

We see this pattern unfold in every domain of life. The person who delays a difficult but necessary conversation with their partner is not just avoiding an unpleasant conflict. They are resisting the finality of a choice that the conversation would force upon them. The conversation might lead to a breakup, a painful but definitive end to the relationship. By avoiding the conversation, they are able to keep the relationship in a state of ambiguous limbo, a kind of quantum superposition where it is both alive and dead at the same time. This state of uncertainty, while painful in its own way, can feel safer than the stark, irreversible clarity of a final decision. They are choosing the chronic ache of a problem deferred over the acute, and potentially catastrophic, pain of a choice made.

To truly understand and overcome procrastination, then, requires us to look beyond the surface-level behaviors and to engage with the deep existential anxieties that are driving them. It requires a shift from asking, "How can I force myself to do this?" to asking, "What am I so afraid of choosing?" To see our procrastination not as a sign of laziness but as a signal of our terror in the face of our own freedom is the first step toward a more compassionate and effective form of self-engagement. It reframes the problem from one of productivity to one of courage. The ultimate remedy for procrastination is not a better to-do list, but a cultivated willingness to bear the anxiety of being a finite, imperfect, and decisive author of our own one and only life. It is the courage to make a mark on the page, knowing it can never be erased, and to accept the profound and terrifying responsibility of saying, "This, for better or for worse, is what I have chosen to create."

Blame and Projection

If procrastination is the passive resistance to the demands of freedom, a quiet refusal to step onto the field of action, then blame is its active and aggressive counterpart. It is a powerful and immediate counter-offensive, a strategic maneuver designed to take the heavy, uncomfortable burden of our own authorship and forcefully place it onto the shoulders of another. Blame is the most common, the most reflexive, and the most socially infectious of all our existential avoidance strategies. It is the psychic equivalent of a magic trick: in one swift, almost imperceptible motion, we make our own responsibility disappear and reappear as someone else's fault. This act provides an instantaneous and deeply gratifying sense of relief, a release from the anxiety of self-examination and the difficult labor of personal change. It is, however, a relief that comes at a catastrophic long-term cost: the complete surrender of our own agency and the perpetual stagnation of our lives.

To understand the immense psychological appeal of blame, we must first appreciate the complex and demanding nature of its alternative: self-responsibility. To take responsibility for our own unhappiness, our own failures, or our own complicity in a difficult situation is an act of profound psychological and emotional maturity. It requires us to engage in the messy, ambiguous, and often painful work of introspection. We must be willing to confront our own limitations, our character defects, our hidden fears, and our poor choices. It demands that we sit with the uncomfortable feelings of guilt, regret, and disappointment in ourselves. And, most terrifyingly, it requires that we then do something about it. To accept responsibility is to be confronted with the freedom and the necessity to change. This is difficult work. It is slow, uncertain, and it offers no easy answers.

Blame, on the other hand, is wonderfully simple. It slices through the Gordian knot of internal complexity with a single, decisive cut. The problem is not a tangled web of my own making; the problem is *you*. This act of externalization performs several crucial psychological functions at once. First, it simplifies reality. The ambiguous, multi-causal nature of a personal failure—a failed project, a broken relationship, a stalled career—is reduced to a single, linear, and easily comprehensible narrative. "The project failed because my team was incompetent." "The relationship ended because my partner was emotionally unavailable." "My career is stuck because the economy is bad and my boss is a fool." These are simple stories. They have a clear villain, and in that clarity, there is a profound comfort. It is the comfort of a world that makes sense, a world where problems have a single, identifiable source that is located safely outside of ourselves.

Second, and most critically, blame preserves our sense of innocence. It is a powerful defense against the pain of existential guilt. If someone else is at fault, then by definition, I am the victim. The posture of the victim is, in many ways, the most comfortable and least demanding of all psychological roles. The victim is blameless. The victim is owed sympathy. And, most importantly, the victim is absolved of all responsibility for their own predicament. While it is a state of profound powerlessness, it is also a state of perfect, unassailable innocence. Many of us will unconsciously choose the righteousness of victimhood over the demanding and ambiguous work of being a free and responsible co-creator of our own lives. The momentary satisfaction of being "right" is often more appealing than the long-term, difficult project of actually *being* happy.

This brings us to a deeper, more unconscious mechanism that powers our most persistent and irrational forms of blame: the defense of projection. As we have seen, projection is not simply the conscious act of pointing a finger; it is the unconscious process of taking a part of ourselves that we find unacceptable—our own insecurity, our greed, our anger, our incompetence, our unacknowledged desires—and perceiving it as a quality in another person. We do not just say that another person is angry; we genuinely *experience* them as an aggressive and hostile force, all the while remaining completely oblivious to the rage simmering within ourselves. Projection is the engine that transforms simple blame into a deeply felt, and often unshakeable, conviction. We are not just making an accusation; we are, in our own minds, simply reporting on the objective facts of a hostile world.

The existential function of projection is to allow us to engage in our most pressing internal battles as if they were external conflicts. The fight against our own inner demons is a terrifying, lonely, and often losing proposition. It is far easier, and far more exciting, to fight a demon that has been conveniently located in another person. Consider a man who is deeply ambivalent about commitment. He consciously desires the comfort and stability of a long-term relationship, but he is unconsciously terrified of the loss of freedom that it entails. This internal conflict is a source of constant, low-grade anxiety. Through projection, he can escape this internal battle. He disowns his own fear of being trapped and instead begins to perceive his loving, committed partner as being "controlling" or "needy." Her every request for intimacy is interpreted as an attempt to suffocate him. Her desire for a shared future is seen as a cage being built around him.

He can now engage in a righteous fight for his freedom against his "controlling" partner. He can justify his emotional distance, his late nights out, his refusal to discuss the future, not as expressions of his own deep-seated ambivalence, but as necessary acts of self-preservation in the face of her tyranny. He has successfully transformed a difficult internal problem ("I am terrified of being trapped") into a simple external one ("My partner is trying to trap me"). He has fled from the responsibility of his own complex feelings and found refuge in the simple, blame-filled narrative of a relationship in which he is the heroic freedom-fighter and she is the villainous warden.

This dynamic is not confined to our intimate relationships. It is endemic in our professional lives. The employee who is secretly convinced of their own inadequacy and lives in constant fear of being exposed as a fraud may project this feeling onto their colleagues, perceiving them as hyper-critical, competitive, and constantly looking to undermine them. This allows the employee to convert their internal feeling of shame into an external experience of persecution. Their defensive and guarded behavior is now justified as a necessary response to a "toxic work environment." They have successfully avoided the terrifying responsibility of confronting their own imposter syndrome by creating a world in which everyone else is the source of the judgment they so deeply fear.

On a societal scale, projection is the psychological bedrock of prejudice, tribalism, and nearly all forms of group conflict. It is the mechanism by which a group takes its own "shadow"—its collective greed, violence, or hypocrisy—and projects it onto an "other," an enemy group who can then be seen as the pure embodiment of those negative traits. This allows the in-group to maintain a sense of its own righteousness and virtue, all while avoiding the difficult work of confronting its own internal contradictions. Blame, fueled by projection, is the ultimate simplification of a complex world. It is a powerful psychological tool that allows us to avoid the terrifying responsibility of seeing our own reflection, in all its complexity and imperfection, in the face of our enemies, our colleagues, and our partners.

The ultimate and tragic irony of blame is that in our attempt to flee from the responsibility of our freedom, we end up surrendering our agency entirely. As long as the source of our unhappiness is located outside of ourselves, we are, by definition, powerless to change it. The person who blames their misery on their partner can only be happy if their partner changes. The employee who blames their stagnation on their boss can only succeed if their boss is replaced. The citizen who blames their disempowerment on a broken system can only be empowered if the entire system is magically fixed. In every case, the locus of control has been placed in the hands of another. The act of blaming, which provides a momentary feeling of righteous power, ultimately reinforces a deep and pervasive sense of helplessness. It is a self-imposed prison. To live in a world of blame is to be a perpetual passenger in the vehicle of one's own life. The difficult but liberating truth is that the moment we stop blaming, the moment we ask the courageous question, "What is my part in this?", is the moment we take our hands, for the first time, and place them firmly on the steering wheel.

Excellent. Our previous discussions have centered on my understanding of our word count targets, and I will proceed with that in mind, ensuring this section is as substantive and detailed as the topic requires.

The Comfort of Certainty

The human mind is a meaning-making organ. In the face of a universe that is vast, indifferent, and fundamentally silent on the question of our purpose, we are cursed, or blessed, with a relentless cognitive imperative to find a pattern, to tell a story, to impose a coherent narrative onto the chaotic data of our experience. As we have seen, the raw, unfiltered reality of our existential condition—a condition of radical freedom, total responsibility, and profound uncertainty—is the source of our deepest and most persistent anxiety. This anxiety is the psychic equivalent of a constant, low-grade pain. And like any creature in pain, our most primal instinct is to seek relief, to find an anesthetic that can numb the ache and provide a measure of peace. While procrastination offers a temporary delay of this pain and blame offers a momentary release by externalizing it, the most powerful and long-lasting anesthetic of all is the embrace of an absolute and unshakeable certainty.

This is the profound psychological appeal of fundamentalism. The term is most often associated with rigid forms of religion, but its psychological structure can be found in any system of thought—be it religious, political, or even scientific—that offers a totalizing, inerrant, and closed explanation of reality. Fundamentalism, in this existential sense, is not defined by its specific content, but by its form and its function. Its function is to be a perfect and complete defense against the anxiety of doubt. It is a grand, elaborate, and internally consistent architecture built for a single purpose: to eliminate ambiguity. It offers a pre-fabricated and perfectly ordered reality, a psychological fortress designed to withstand the turbulent and unpredictable winds of an uncertain world. To enter this fortress is to find a profound and deeply seductive form of comfort, but the price of admission is the surrender of the one thing the existential tradition holds most sacred: the freedom and the responsibility of an authentic, individual inquiry.

The architecture of these fortresses of certainty is remarkably consistent across different domains. At the foundation, there is always an unimpeachable and absolute source of authority. In religious fundamentalism, this is typically a sacred text—the Bible, the Quran—which is held to be the literal, inerrant, and complete word of God. In political fundamentalism, it may be a foundational text like Marx's *Das Kapital* or a collection of the speeches of a charismatic national leader. This central authority serves a crucial psychological function: it outsources the agonizing burden of interpretation and judgment. The individual is no longer required to grapple with the messy, contradictory, and ambiguous nature of reality on their own; they are simply required to learn and to apply the definitive answers provided by the authority. The agonizing question, "What should I believe?" is replaced by the far simpler and more comforting task of understanding "What does the text/leader say I should believe?"

Upon this foundation, a clear and unambiguous moral framework is constructed. The world is rendered in stark, black-and-white terms. The complex, grey-scale nature of real-world ethical dilemmas is dissolved into a simple binary of good and evil, right and wrong, permissible and forbidden. This provides an immense relief from the weight of moral authorship. The individual is no longer a lonely legislator in a groundless world, forced to create their own values through the anguish of choice. Instead, they become a citizen in a well-ordered kingdom with a clear and divinely sanctioned legal code. Their responsibility is reduced from the terrifying task of *creating* the law to the far more manageable task of *obeying* it. This moral clarity is a powerful anesthetic for the anxiety of living in a world where good people suffer, bad people prosper, and our best intentions often lead to unforeseen and tragic consequences.

This moral simplification is almost always accompanied by a social one. Fundamentalist systems excel at creating a powerful and clearly defined sense of in-group identity ("us") by positing a clear and often demonized out-group ("them"). The world is neatly divided into the believers and the unbelievers, the saved and the damned, the patriots and the traitors, the enlightened vanguard and the ignorant masses. This dynamic provides a powerful antidote to the pain of existential isolation. The individual is no longer a solitary, adrift consciousness in a vast and indifferent universe. They are a member of a special and chosen community, a soldier in a righteous army, a part of a cosmic or historical drama that imbues their life with a powerful sense of belonging and shared purpose. The love and validation received from within the in-group is intensified by the shared animosity and sense of superiority directed toward the out-group. This provides a simple, clear, and deeply satisfying social map, a powerful refuge from the messy and demanding work of navigating a pluralistic world filled with people who hold different, and equally sincere, beliefs.

It is here, in this carefully constructed psychological environment, that the anesthetic properties of certainty begin their work. The first and most profound pain that is numbed is the pain of doubt itself. Within a fundamentalist system, doubt is not seen as a sign of intellectual curiosity or a necessary component of a sincere search for truth; it is reframed as a temptation, a moral failing, a sin. The act of questioning is seen as an act of disloyalty. This reframing is a brilliant psychological defense. It transforms the anxiety of not knowing into the guilt of disbelief. The individual learns to police their own mind, to treat their own critical faculties with suspicion, and to find a sense of virtue and strength in the act of unquestioning belief. The comfort of faith becomes a reward for the suppression of the very parts of the mind that produce existential dread.

With the anxiety of doubt successfully anesthetized, the system can then work on the deeper pain of freedom and responsibility. The life of a true believer is a life relieved of the burden of ultimate choice. The big questions—What is my purpose? How should I live? What happens when I die?—have all been answered. The path is laid out. The individual's task is to walk that path with diligence and fidelity. This is a profound and total release from the Sartrean condemnation to be free. The individual's life is no longer their own terrifying project of self-creation; it is a meaningful role in a pre-written divine or historical play. The relief this provides cannot be overstated. It is the relief of a soldier who no longer has to question the war, but can find their purpose in simply following orders. It is the relief of an actor who is handed a script and can finally stop agonizing over what to say next.

The ultimate comfort, of course, is the promise of a guaranteed outcome. The fundamental uncertainty of the human condition is vanquished by the promise of a final, triumphant, and absolutely certain conclusion. For the religious fundamentalist, this is the promise of eternal salvation, a final and perfect state of being that retroactively imbues all of the suffering and ambiguity of earthly life with a transcendent meaning. For the political fundamentalist, it is the promise of a future utopia, a perfect society that will be achieved once the historical struggle is won. This guarantee of a happy ending is the ultimate psychological balm. It allows the believer to endure the chaos and injustice of the present with a sense of calm and purpose, secure in the knowledge that it is all part of a larger plan that is heading toward a guaranteed and glorious destination.

This, then, is the immense comfort of certainty. It is a total and comprehensive solution to the fundamental problems of the human condition. It offers meaning in the face of meaninglessness, belonging in the face of isolation, moral clarity in the face of ambiguity, and a guaranteed future in the face of an uncertain world. But this comfort, as profound as it is, comes at an equally profound price. The price is the surrender of the authentic self. To enter the fortress of certainty, one must check their intellectual curiosity, their tolerance for complexity, and their capacity for independent moral judgment at the gate. The system demands the sacrifice of the individual's unique, questioning, and evolving consciousness in exchange for the security of a collective identity. The anesthetic that numbs the pain of freedom also, by necessity, numbs the very vitality, creativity, and courage that make a human life a work of art rather than a foregone conclusion. The flight into certainty is the ultimate escape, a journey from the difficult and demanding light of an open-ended existence into the comforting, peaceful, but ultimately lifeless dark of a closed and finished world.

The Quantified Self: The Illusion of a Calculated Life

Beyond the comfort of ideological certainty, our technological age offers a more intimate and seductive escape route: the promise of total self-mastery through data. This is the flight into the "Quantified Self." If fundamentalism is a flight from intellectual and moral freedom, the Quantified Self is a flight from the terrifying, ambiguous freedom of being an embodied, biological creature.

The logic is alluringly simple. By meticulously tracking our every input and output—every calorie consumed, every minute of sleep staged by a wearable, every heartbeat variability measured, every step counted—we believe we can transform the messy, unpredictable project of a human life into a clean engineering problem. The existential question "How should I live?" is reduced to the technical question "How can I optimize my metrics?" This is a sophisticated, 21st-century form of bad faith. We treat ourselves not as a mysterious and dynamic "for-itself," a being that is always in a process of becoming, but as an "in-itself," a complex machine whose optimal performance can be calculated and guaranteed if we just gather enough data points.

This creates the illusion of a calculated life, a life where risk, decay, and the inherent uncertainty of the flesh can be engineered away. The deep, existential anxiety we feel about our health, our aging, and our eventual death is numbed by the daily ritual of checking our data dashboard. The wearable on our wrist becomes a secular talisman, a technological rosary we finger to ward off the specters of chance, genetics, and time. It offers a comforting, if illusory, narrative of control. We are no longer passive victims of our biology; we are the CEOs of our own corporeal corporations, making data-driven decisions to maximize shareholder value.

But this flight, like all others, comes at a cost. The relentless pursuit of optimization creates a state of hyper-vigilance that is itself a source of profound anxiety, often termed "orthosomnia"—the inability to sleep due to the pressure to achieve perfect sleep scores. More importantly, it alienates us from the lived, subjective experience of our own bodies. We cease to feel hunger or fatigue; we instead read a "caloric deficit" or a "sub-optimal recovery score." We no longer go for a walk for the joy of movement and the smell of the air; we go to "close our activity ring." The body becomes a foreign object to be managed, a source of data to be corrected, rather than the very ground and medium of our existence.

The Quantified Self, in its extreme, is thus a rejection of the fundamental "given" of our embodied freedom. We are born into a specific body (facticity) with its unique strengths, vulnerabilities, and genetic lottery, but we have the freedom (transcendence) to choose how we live within it, what meaning we assign to its capacities and its limitations. The Quantified Seeker attempts to deny this dialectic. They seek to dissolve the facticity of the body into pure data and believe that perfect transcendence—total control—is possible. In doing so, they flee from the beautiful, tragic, and unquantifiable reality of being a human animal: a creature that gets sick for no reason, that ages in ways we cannot predict, that finds strength in moments of apparent weakness, and whose most meaningful states—love, joy, awe, creativity—are utterly unmeasurable. To reclaim this embodied freedom is to sometimes take off the watch, to eat the piece of cake without logging it, to listen to the wisdom of fatigue rather than the demand of a step goal, and to accept that a life well-lived is an art, not a science.

Clinical Manifestations

The human psyche is remarkably resilient. For most of us, most of the time, our strategies of existential avoidance—our procrastinations, our projections, our small conformities—function as a kind of psychological immune system, protecting us from overwhelming anxiety without completely shutting down our lives. They are the subtle, everyday compromises we make to navigate the difficult terrain of being human. But what happens when these defenses become too rigid, too absolute, too successful? What happens when the flight from freedom ceases to be a series of tactical retreats and becomes a permanent, all-encompassing state of being? It is here, at the far end of the spectrum of avoidance, that we enter the territory of clinical suffering. From an existential perspective, many of our recognized psychological disorders can be understood not as random biochemical malfunctions or simple learned behaviors, but as the logical and tragic endpoint of a life lived in a state of profound and chronic existential evasion. They are not a sign that the mind is broken, but rather a sign that the mind's heroic, if misguided, attempts to protect itself from the truth of its condition have become the very cage in which it is now trapped.

This perspective does not seek to replace or invalidate the invaluable insights of biological psychiatry, cognitive-behavioral therapy, or psychodynamic theory. Instead, it offers a deeper, complementary layer of meaning. It asks us to look beneath the surface-level symptoms and to inquire into the fundamental human struggle that these symptoms may be expressing in a distorted and painful form. To see a psychological disorder through an existential lens is to see it not just as a problem to be solved, but as a meaningful, albeit maladaptive, solution to the overwhelming anxiety of being a free, responsible, and mortal creature in a world without guarantees.

Consider, for example, the condition we call Generalized Anxiety Disorder (GAD). In conventional diagnostic terms, it is characterized by chronic, excessive, and uncontrollable worry about a wide range of everyday things: work, health, finances, relationships. The person with GAD lives in a state of perpetual, free-floating apprehension, their mind constantly scanning the horizon for potential threats and playing out catastrophic "what if" scenarios. It is a profoundly exhausting and debilitating state of being. From an existential viewpoint, however, this chronic worry is not the disease itself; it is the primary symptom of a deeper predicament. GAD can be understood as the state of a person who is drowning in their own unused freedom. The constant, frenetic activity of worrying is a tragic substitute for the courageous and decisive act of choosing.

The individual with GAD is living a life suspended in the terrifying abyss of Kierkegaard's pure possibility. Every potential action, every possible future, is perceived as being fraught with catastrophic risk. The mind, in an attempt to manage this overwhelming freedom, engages in a kind of magical thinking. It believes that if it can just worry enough, if it can just anticipate every possible negative outcome, it can somehow control the future and prevent disaster. The act of worrying feels like a form of responsible work; it feels like a necessary preparation for life. But it is, in fact, the ultimate evasion of the responsibility to *live*. It is a life lived entirely in the preface, a constant rehearsal for a play that is never performed. The anxiety is the psychic energy of their own un-actualized potential, which, having no outlet in decisive action, has turned inward and become a source of self-torment. They are not afraid of a specific thing in the world; they are terrified of the responsibility of having to be a specific person, of having to make a specific choice and to bear its uncertain consequences. The chronic worry is the noise they create to drown out the silent, terrifying demand of their own freedom.

If generalized anxiety is the result of a diffuse and uncontained dread, a specific phobia is the result of a mind that has performed a brilliant, if costly, piece of psychic surgery. A phobia is an intense, irrational, and debilitating fear of a specific object or situation: spiders, heights, enclosed spaces, public speaking. The object of the phobia is, on a rational level, disproportionate to the level of fear it inspires. From an existential perspective, a phobia is the product of a powerful psychological defense mechanism known as displacement. The mind takes the vast, formless, and intolerable anxiety of our existential condition—our dread of death, of meaninglessness, of groundlessness, of freedom itself—and concentrates all of that free-floating terror onto a single, concrete, and, most importantly, *avoidable* target.

The existential dread that haunts us is so terrifying precisely because it is inescapable. We cannot avoid our own mortality. We cannot avoid our own freedom. There is no place to hide. The phobia is the mind's ingenious solution to this problem. It takes the un-avoidable terror of being and transforms it into the avoidable fear of a thing. I cannot do anything about the fact that I am going to die, but I *can* do something about the spider in my bathroom. I cannot escape the groundlessness of my existence, but I *can* refuse to get on an airplane. The phobic object becomes a kind of scapegoat for all of our existential anxieties. By focusing all of our fear onto this one thing, and by then meticulously avoiding it, we create a powerful and deeply comforting illusion of control. The phobic's world becomes a much smaller, more constricted place, a landscape filled with no-go zones. But within the walls of this self-imposed prison, they feel a measure of safety. The tragedy is that the cage that protects them from their specific fear also cuts them off from the richness and possibility of a fully-lived life. The avoidance of the phobic object becomes the central organizing principle of their existence, a profound and life-limiting flight from a much larger, unacknowledged fear.

Finally, consider the set of relational patterns that attachment theory describes as an avoidant attachment style. The individual with this style is often characterized by a fierce and guarded independence, a discomfort with emotional intimacy, and a tendency to suppress their own needs for connection. They may be successful in their careers and have a wide circle of acquaintances, but they struggle to form deep, lasting, and vulnerable romantic bonds. From an existential viewpoint, this is not a simple fear of relationships; it is a fear of the profound responsibilities and the loss of autonomy that genuine intimacy entails. It is a strategic and systemic avoidance of the existential givens of love.

To truly love another person is to enter into a world of profound uncertainty and risk. It is to make oneself vulnerable to the possibility of loss, rejection, and heartbreak. It is to accept the responsibility of being a caretaker of another person's heart. And it is to confront, in the most direct and powerful way, the reality of our ultimate separateness. The avoidant individual's entire relational strategy is designed to defend against these existential demands. Their pseudo-independence is not a sign of strength, but a fortress built to protect them from the terrifying vulnerability of needing another person. They keep their partners at an emotional arm's length, never fully committing, never fully surrendering, because to do so would be to give that person the power to wound them. They often sabotage relationships just as they are about to become truly intimate, finding fault with their partner or complaining of feeling "suffocated." This feeling of suffocation is the allergic reaction of a self that is terrified of having its boundless, theoretical freedom constrained by the real, concrete needs and demands of another human being. It is a profound flight from the responsibility of love, a choice to live in the safe but lonely world of the self-sufficient individual, forever protected from the risks, and therefore the rewards, of a truly shared life.

In each of these clinical manifestations, we see the same tragic pattern: a life that has become organized around what it is trying to avoid rather than what it is trying to create. The anxious, the phobic, and the avoidant are all living in a state of profound self-constriction. They have traded the terrifying, open-ended freedom of an authentic existence for the predictable, if painful, security of a symptom. To see their suffering in this light is not to blame them, but to recognize the immense courage that a life of genuine engagement requires. It is to understand that the path out of this suffering is not just about managing symptoms, but about a gradual, supported, and courageous process of turning to face the very existential truths they have spent their lives trying to escape.

* * *

IV

Part Four: Freedom in the Real World

How do we carry the weight of freedom in our daily lives? Part 4 grounds our inquiry in the real world. We explore the burden of choice in our careers, relationships, and civic duties, across the human lifespan, and within the inescapable reality of our own bodies.

8

The Burden in Everyday Life

T he great questions of existence do not announce themselves with
philosophical fanfare. They do not arrive as abstract intellectual
puzzles to be solved in the quiet of a study or the solemnity of a
lecture hall. Instead, they ambush us in the most mundane and familiar
of settings. The weight of our freedom, the anxiety of our choices, and
the terror of a world without guarantees are not concepts to be debated;
they are the very texture of our lived reality. They are present in the sterile
quiet of a doctor's office, in the late-night tension of a conversation with
a partner, in the anxious scroll through a job board, and in the profound,
heart-stopping moment when we look at our own child and wonder if we
are doing enough. The burden of freedom is not an abstract noun; it is an
everyday verb, an active and persistent pressure that shapes the contours of
our most significant human projects.

Having explored the deep structure of this burden and the psychological
mechanisms we use to flee from it, our task now is to ground this inquiry
in the soil of the ordinary. This chapter is a journey into the primary arenas
where our existential condition is most acutely felt and our choices carry
the most tangible weight: our careers, our intimate relationships, our roles
as parents, and our relationship with our own physical bodies. These are
the domains where the stakes are highest, where our authorship is most
consequential, and where the lack of a pre-written script is most terrifyingly

apparent. It is here, in the messy, high-stakes drama of everyday life, that the flight from freedom ceases to be a psychological strategy and becomes a lived tragedy, and the embrace of responsibility ceases to be a philosophical ideal and becomes a daily, courageous practice.

The world of work, for many of us, is the primary stage upon which we are expected to construct a meaningful identity. Yet, the very nature of this stage has been radically and irrevocably altered. The stable, linear, and often lifelong careers that provided a sense of predictability and identity for previous generations have all but vanished. We now inhabit a fluid, globalized, and technologically volatile economy that demands constant adaptation, reinvention, and a kind of entrepreneurial vigilance. The modern worker is no longer a passenger on a well-defined corporate ladder; they are a solitary navigator in a perpetually shifting sea, solely responsible for charting their own course without a reliable map. In this section, we will explore the profound existential instability of this new reality. We will see how the pressure to be constantly choosing, pivoting, and branding ourselves creates a state of chronic, low-grade anxiety, a modern manifestation of the Sartrean condemnation to be perpetually creating our own professional essence.

If our careers are the stage for our public identity, our intimate relationships are the crucible of our private selves. It is here, in the presence of another, that our deepest needs for connection clash with our equally powerful fears of being trapped, and our desire for certainty collides with the irreducible mystery of another human being. The modern world, with its dating apps and its culture of infinite options, has transformed the search for love into a project of optimization, creating the illusion that a "perfect" partner exists and that the primary task is to find them. We will delve into the profound burden this places on our ability to commit. We will examine how choosing one partner is, in an age of perceived infinity, a more profound and anxiety-provoking act of renunciation than ever before. To build a life with one person is to actively and definitively close the door on a thousand other imagined lives, a sacrifice of possibility that the modern psyche is often unwilling, or unable, to make.

Perhaps no human endeavor brings us into more direct and humbling contact with the limits of our own control than the act of parenting. Our culture places an immense and often contradictory pressure on parents to be the perfect architects of their children's lives. We are expected to be the vigilant guardians of their safety, the meticulous curators of their experiences, the brilliant engineers of their future success. We are held responsible not just for our actions, but for the outcome: a happy, successful, well-adjusted adult. Yet, this entire project is built on an illusion. The child is not a block of clay to be molded, but a separate, free, and ultimately unknowable consciousness on their own journey. In this section, we will explore the profound existential challenge of parenting: the task of taking total responsibility for a process whose result we can never truly control. It is the ultimate exercise in acting with love and commitment in a world without guarantees.

Finally, we will turn to the most intimate and inescapable reality of our existence: our own bodies. For much of our lives, particularly when we are young and healthy, we are able to live with the comfortable illusion that we are a disembodied consciousness, a free-floating mind that happens to inhabit a physical form. The onset of a serious illness or a chronic condition shatters this illusion with brutal force. It is a stark and unwelcome reminder of our facticity, of the unchosen, biological realities that ground and constrain our freedom. An illness confronts us with our own mortality, our vulnerability, and the fundamental limits of our own agency. Yet, paradoxically, it also thrusts upon us a series of new and incredibly weighty choices regarding treatments, lifestyle changes, and how we will choose to live in the face of our own physical limitations. We will examine how the experience of illness is, for many, a compressed and intensified form of the entire existential journey: a sudden loss of certainty, a confrontation with finitude, and the demanding, inescapable responsibility of choosing a path forward in a world that has been irrevocably changed.

This chapter, then, is a journey through the heart of our most human concerns. It is an attempt to show that the insights of existential thought are not a separate, academic subject, but an essential lens for understanding the beauty, the difficulty, and the profound significance of our ordinary lives. The courage to be is not a quality reserved for philosophers or heroes; it is a quiet virtue that is demanded of us every day, in the simple but profound choices we make about how we will work, how we will love, how we will parent, and how we will inhabit the one and only body we have been given.

Career Decisions in a Fluid Economy

For the greater part of the last century, the concept of a "career" offered a powerful organizing principle for a human life. It was imagined as a ladder, a clear, linear, and largely predictable ascent within a stable institution. One started in the mailroom or as a junior associate and, through diligence, loyalty, and the steady accumulation of experience, climbed rung by rung toward a secure and respectable perch. This model, a cornerstone of the post-war industrial and corporate economy, provided more than just a paycheck; it provided an identity. To be a "company man," a tenured professor, a skilled tradesman with a union card—these were stable, legible roles. They offered a script. The choices were relatively few, the path was well-trodden, and the responsibility of the individual was primarily to play their assigned part with competence. This structure, for all its potential for conformity and tedium, served as a powerful buffer against existential anxiety. It provided a ready-made answer to the terrifyingly open-ended question, "What should I do with my life?"

That world, for the vast majority of us, is gone. The ladder has been dismantled, and in its place is not a new structure, but a kind of open, volatile, and perpetually shifting terrain. We now inhabit a fluid economy, one characterized by globalization, rapid technological disruption, the rise of the gig economy, and the decline of long-term institutional loyalty. The very language we use to describe our professional lives has changed. We no longer speak of climbing a ladder, but of navigating a landscape, of building a portfolio, of curating a personal brand. The script has been torn up, and the modern worker has been cast onto the stage without a director, without a clear role, and with the sole, stark instruction: improvise. The result is a profound and pervasive sense of instability, a state of chronic professional vertigo that is the defining existential condition of work in the 21st century.

This new reality represents the Sartrean condemnation to be free, translated into the language of the modern workplace. The modern worker is the ultimate embodiment of the being whose existence precedes their essence. There is no pre-defined professional self to inhabit. We are not simply a "banker" or a "teacher"; we are the perpetual, anxious entrepreneur of our own career, a startup of one that is never fully funded and is always just one pivot away from obsolescence. The responsibility is total and unceasing. We are responsible not just for performing our current job, but for constantly anticipating the next one. We are responsible for acquiring new skills on our own time, for cultivating a professional network, for maintaining a polished and consistent online presence, and for crafting a compelling personal narrative that can be sold to the next potential employer or client.

The burden of this constant self-creation is immense. It transforms the very nature of work from a set of tasks to be performed into an endless project of identity management. Consider the ubiquitous pressure to build a "personal brand." This is the explicit demand that we package and market our skills, our personality, and our life story as a coherent and desirable product. Our LinkedIn profile must be a perfect fusion of competence and relatability; our social media presence must reflect our values and our expertise; our professional interactions are all, on some level, a performance designed to enhance our brand equity. This is a profound and exhausting form of alienation. We are forced to split ourselves into two beings: the actual, fluctuating, and often insecure person who does the work, and the polished, confident, and highly curated avatar who sells the work. The pressure to maintain the integrity of this brand, to ensure that all our choices are "on-brand," is a powerful new constraint on our freedom, a cage built of our own marketing materials.

This dynamic creates a state of perpetual, low-grade anxiety. In the old model, security was found in stability. In the new model, security is found only in a state of constant, vigilant adaptability. The skills that are valuable today may be automated tomorrow. The industry that is thriving this year may be disrupted the next. This means that the modern worker can never truly rest. There is always another skill to learn, another certification to acquire, another networking event to attend. This is not the anxiety of a specific, identifiable threat; it is the diffuse, free-floating anxiety of a world without guarantees, a world in which professional survival is a matter of our own, unaided, and relentless effort. It is the anxiety of knowing that we are entirely responsible for a future that is entirely unpredictable.

This condition is acutely felt in the proliferation of choice that characterizes the modern career path. A young person today is not choosing a single profession, but is navigating a vast and bewildering sea of potential gigs, projects, and "side hustles." This is the paradox of choice writ large. The theoretical freedom to be anything often collapses into the practical paralysis of not knowing what to be. Each potential path is haunted by the ghosts of all the others. To commit to a career in marketing is to sacrifice the potential life of a coder, a designer, a non-profit worker. In an unstable world, this act of commitment feels riskier than ever. The fear of choosing the "wrong" path, a path that may become obsolete or unfulfilling, can lead to a state of protracted professional adolescence, a decade-long period of dabbling, interning, and exploring that is, at its core, a flight from the responsibility of a definitive choice.

The ultimate psychological cost of this fluid and demanding reality is often a deep and pervasive sense of burnout and disenchantment. The constant pressure to perform, to self-promote, and to adapt in the face of uncertainty is cognitively and emotionally exhausting. It can lead to a state of profound cynicism, a feeling that the entire professional world is an inauthentic and meaningless game. This is the posture of the "disenchanted employee" we have discussed before. Their apathy and withdrawal are not a sign of laziness, but a form of psychological self-preservation. It is a defense mechanism against a system that demands everything from them while offering very little in the way of genuine security or stability. By deciding that "it's all just a job" and that "none of it really matters," they are performing a kind of existential retreat. They are creating an inner sanctuary of indifference to protect themselves from the pain of a world that asks them to invest their whole selves into a project with no guaranteed return. It is a tragic but deeply understandable flight from the unbearable burden of being the sole, unsupported, and perpetually anxious author of one's own professional life.

Love and Commitment Under Uncertainty

If the modern economy has dismantled the stable structures of our professional lives, the cultural shifts of the last half-century have performed an even more radical demolition on the architecture of our intimate relationships. For most of human history, the choice of a life partner was a decision heavily constrained, and in many ways simplified, by a host of external forces: family alliances, religious edicts, social class, and geographical proximity. The primary purpose of marriage was often economic and social, a contract designed for stability and procreation rather than for personal fulfillment. The pool of potential partners was small and the script for a successful union was clearly written. The existential burden was, in this sense, relatively light. The question was not the terrifyingly open-ended, "Who, out of all the people in the world, should I be with?" but the far more manageable, "Who, among the few suitable options available to me, is the most viable choice?"

We now inhabit the precise inverse of this reality. We have been liberated from nearly all of these external constraints, and the choice of a partner is now considered the ultimate act of personal expression, the most significant decision in the project of a happy and authentic life. The cultural mandate is no longer to find a suitable partner, but to find a soulmate. We are searching not for a co-worker in the project of life, but for a perfect fusion of best friend, passionate lover, intellectual equal, and therapeutic guardian of our emotional well-being. This elevation of the stakes, combined with a technologically-enabled explosion of perceived options, has transformed the landscape of modern love. It has turned the quiet, hopeful search for connection into a frantic, high-stakes, and deeply anxiety-provoking marketplace, and in doing so, it has made the act of commitment—the free and willing choice to bind oneself to another—one of the most difficult and terrifying existential tasks of our time.

The engine of this new anxiety is the dating app, the ultimate symbol of the paradox of choice applied to the human heart. The app functions as a human catalogue, transforming the mysterious and nuanced process of getting to know another person into a rapid-fire, consumerist act of sorting and selection. It presents us with what appears to be an infinite supply of alternatives, a perpetual stream of new faces and new possibilities. This system, while promising to maximize our chances of finding the perfect match, is in fact psychologically engineered to make the act of choosing almost impossible. It actively cultivates a "maximizer" mindset, subtly training us to believe that the perfect option is always just one more swipe away.

This endless supply of perceived alternatives has a profoundly devaluing effect. It fosters a culture of disposability. Minor imperfections, disagreements, or moments of boredom—the inevitable and necessary friction of any real human relationship—are no longer seen as challenges to be worked through, but as signals that a "better" and more compatible option should be sought. The person in front of us is constantly being judged against the idealized, phantom competitor in our pocket. This creates a state of perpetual comparison shopping that is the very antithesis of the focused, patient, and generous attention that genuine intimacy requires. We become shoppers for people, and in a market of infinite supply, the incentive to ever truly leave the store and commit to a single purchase is vanishingly small.

This dynamic is a direct manifestation of the Kierkegaardian dread of closing doors. In a world of limited options, the choice of a partner was a significant but manageable act of renunciation. In our modern world, the choice to commit to one person feels like an act of almost unimaginable sacrifice. To say "yes" to one person, definitively and with the intention of permanence, is to say a conscious and final "no" to the thousands, perhaps millions, of other potential lives we could have lived with other people. It is to accept the profound and painful finitude of our own existence. The fear of making the "wrong" choice, the fear of future regret, the fear of missing out on a hypothetical better match—these anxieties become so overwhelming that they often lead to a state of relational paralysis.

This is the psychological root of what is often called "commitment phobia." It is not, in most cases, a fear of the other person, but a terror of the choice itself. The individual who flees from a good and loving relationship as it begins to deepen is not fleeing from their partner; they are fleeing from the irreversible act of their own freedom. The feeling of being "trapped" or "suffocated" is the allergic reaction of a self that has become addicted to the shallow, thrilling freedom of pure potential. To commit is to move from the exciting, imaginary world of "what could be" to the real, imperfect, and demanding world of "what is." It is to accept the responsibility of building a life, rather than perpetually browsing for one. This flight from commitment is often disguised, both to the self and to the partner, in a flurry of rationalizations: "The timing isn't right." "I need to work on myself first." "I'm just not sure if you're 'The One.'" These are the sophisticated alibis of a self that is in a state of terrified retreat from the weight of its own authorship.

Underneath this fear of commitment lies an even deeper existential avoidance: the flight from the given reality of our own aloneness. The cultural myth of the soulmate is a powerful defense against the truth of our existential isolation. It is the fantasy that another person can, and should, save us from ourselves. We seek a partner to "complete" us, to fill our inner emptiness, to be the source of our self-worth, and to provide a permanent refuge from the anxieties of the world. This is a profound act of bad faith. It is the attempt to outsource the fundamental responsibility of creating our own meaning and wholeness onto another human being. This places an impossible and deeply unfair burden on our partners and on our relationships. We are asking them to solve a problem that is not theirs to solve.

When the relationship inevitably fails to vanquish our inner demons, when we find that we still feel lonely, anxious, or incomplete even in the presence of a loving partner, the logic of blame takes over. We conclude that we have simply chosen the wrong person. The failure of the relationship to live up to its magical, therapeutic promise is seen not as evidence that the promise itself was an illusion, but as a sign of our partner's inadequacy. This can lead to a serially monogamous pattern of intense idealization followed by bitter devaluation, a constant search for the next person who will, this time, finally provide the existential salvation we crave.

An authentic and mature love, from an existential perspective, requires a radical dismantling of this entire framework. It begins with the courageous acceptance of our own aloneness. A healthy relationship is not a fusion of two incomplete halves, but a partnership between two whole, and wholly separate, individuals. It is a relationship in which we do not ask our partner to be the source of our meaning, but invite them to be a cherished companion and witness on our own individual journey. Authentic commitment, in this view, is not the end of freedom, but its most profound and meaningful expression. It is the free and conscious choice, made day after day in a world of infinite distractions, to create a shared reality with another person. It is an act of saying, "I see the thousand other lives I could live, and I choose this one, with you." It is an act that acknowledges the lack of all guarantees—the guarantee that we will always feel "in love," that we will not change, that we will be safe from suffering—and chooses to build something beautiful in that uncertain space. This is the difficult, demanding, and ultimately liberating responsibility of love in a world without a script.

Parenting Without Control

Of all the roles we inhabit, none is more saturated with the illusion of control, nor more ruthlessly exposed to the reality of its absence, than that of a parent. The contemporary culture of parenting, particularly in the Western middle class, is built upon a single, powerful, and deeply anxiety-provoking premise: that the child is a project to be managed, and that a "good" parent is an architect who, with the right combination of inputs, can and should engineer a successful and happy human being. This belief is the engine of a multi-billion-dollar industry of expert advice, educational toys, enrichment classes, and optimization strategies, all promising to give the conscientious parent a decisive edge in the competitive project of human development. We are told, implicitly and explicitly, that we are not just responsible *for* our children, but for the *outcomes* of their lives. Their failures are our failures; their successes are our successes.

This cultural mandate is a profound and sophisticated flight from the fundamental uncertainty of existence. It is an attempt to transform the wild, unpredictable, and mysterious process of a human life unfolding into a manageable, predictable, and controllable manufacturing process. The child becomes the ultimate existential product, the vessel into which we pour all of our own anxieties about the future and all of our hopes for a kind of vicarious immortality. Our own unfulfilled ambitions, our own unhealed wounds, our own deepest values—all are projected onto the small and vulnerable screen of our child's life. In their success, we seek the validation of our own life choices. In their happiness, we seek a balm for our own existential unease. This is perhaps the most common and socially sanctioned form of bad faith: the abdication of our own life project in favor of obsessively managing the life project of another.

The initial stages of a child's life do much to reinforce this illusion of control. An infant is a creature of almost total dependency, a being whose survival and comfort are directly and immediately tied to the parent's actions. This experience, of being the all-powerful center of another's universe, can be deeply gratifying. It provides a potent, if temporary, antidote to our own feelings of insignificance in a vast and indifferent world. But this state is, by its very nature, fleeting. For the central and sacred task of a child's development is a journey of separation, a slow, messy, and often defiant movement from a state of complete dependency to one of autonomous selfhood. And it is here, in the collision between the parent's need for control and the child's burgeoning freedom, that the central existential drama of parenting unfolds.

The parent's project inevitably and necessarily collides with the irreducible reality of the child as a separate and independent being. The child arrives in the world with their own unique facticity: their own innate temperament, their own genetic predispositions, their own mysterious and unchosen consciousness. The parent who dreamed of a calm, studious child may be faced with the reality of a wild, rambunctious, and spirited one. The parent who values athletic achievement may have a child who is drawn to the solitary world of art or music. This is the first and most humbling lesson of parenting: the child is not a blank slate upon which we can write our own story. They are a story that is already being written, and our role is not that of the author, but of a privileged and often perplexed first reader.

As the child grows, their own freedom begins to assert itself. They make choices that deviate from the parent's carefully constructed plan. They choose friends the parent dislikes, pursue interests the parent finds baffling, and develop values that may be in direct conflict with those of their family. Each of these small acts of self-creation is, from the child's perspective, a necessary step toward building an authentic self. But from the perspective of the parent invested in the illusion of control, each of these acts can feel like a betrayal, a failure, a terrifying loss of control. This is the source of so much of the conflict and anguish in family life. It is the friction generated when the parent's anxiety-driven need for a predictable outcome grinds against the child's existential imperative to become their own person.

The great and difficult task of a conscious parent is to perform a radical and ongoing act of recalibration, to shift their understanding of their role from that of an architect to that of a gardener. The architect designs a building and controls every aspect of its construction to ensure it matches the blueprint. The gardener, on the other hand, works in partnership with a force they cannot control. The gardener can choose the seeds, prepare the soil, provide water and sunlight, and protect the young plant from harm. But the gardener cannot *make* the plant grow. They cannot dictate the exact shape it will take, the number of blossoms it will produce, or the precise timing of its bloom. The gardener's role is one of stewardship, of creating the conditions for growth, and then stepping back with a mixture of hope, awe, and profound humility to witness what emerges. The outcome is not theirs to command.

This is the crucial distinction between responsibility and control that lies at the heart of an authentic parental love. A responsible parent is not one who produces a particular kind of child. A responsible parent is one who acts with love, integrity, and wisdom within the relationship, *regardless of the outcome*. The responsibility is for the process, not the product. The parent is responsible for creating a safe and loving environment, for setting clear and consistent boundaries, for modeling a life of compassion and courage, for listening with an open heart. But they are not, and cannot be, responsible for the choices their child will ultimately make. To accept this is to release both the parent and the child from an impossible and crippling burden. It frees the parent from the chronic anxiety of trying to control the uncontrollable, and it frees the child from the suffocating pressure of having to live out their parent's unlived life.

This act of letting go is not one of indifference; it is, in fact, the highest and most difficult expression of love. It is the love that honors the freedom and the mystery of the other. It is a love that says, "I will be the secure base from which you can explore the world. I will be the safe harbor to which you can always return. But your journey is your own. Your life is your masterpiece to create, and I will not try to hold the brush for you." To be a parent, in this sense, is to be in a constant, lifelong process of saying goodbye. It is a slow and gradual release, from the first day of kindergarten to the day they leave home for good. Each of these moments is a small death of the parent's illusion of control and a celebration of the child's emerging selfhood. To navigate this process with grace is to find our ultimate meaning not in the false promise of a guaranteed outcome, but in the profound, terrifying, and beautiful act of loving another free being into their own existence.

Health, Illness, and Agency

For the great majority of our lives, if we are fortunate, we are able to exist in a state of blissful ignorance. We inhabit our bodies as one might inhabit a well-built and unremarkable house, taking for granted the silent, ceaseless, and miraculous work of its internal machinery. We experience ourselves not primarily as physical beings, but as a kind of free-floating consciousness, a will, a personality, a mind that happens to be accompanied by a body. This body is treated largely as a tool, an instrument for carrying out the projects of the self: a vehicle for getting us to work, a machine for exercising, a vessel for experiencing pleasure. This comfortable and deeply ingrained mind-body dualism is a form of existential denial. It is a way of living as if we are pure transcendence, pure freedom, untethered to the messy, vulnerable, and ultimately mortal reality of our own biological facticity.

The onset of a serious illness, a chronic condition, or a significant injury is a violent and unwelcome end to this illusion. It is a brutal and undeniable confrontation with the truth that we are not, in fact, disembodied minds. We *are* our bodies. The diagnosis of a disease is a stark and terrifying reminder of our own contingency, of the fact that the house we inhabit is fragile, subject to decay, and ultimately temporary. It is a direct and often shocking encounter with the ultimate givens of our existence: our finitude and our mortality. The casual, taken-for-granted freedom of a healthy body—the freedom to walk, to work, to eat, to simply be without pain or thought—is suddenly revealed for the precious and precarious gift it always was. The illness appears as a hostile, invading force, a tyrant that constricts our freedom and holds our future hostage.

Yet, in this experience of profound powerlessness, a strange and demanding paradox emerges. The very event that so radically limits our freedom simultaneously thrusts upon us a new and incredibly weighty set of choices and responsibilities. The loss of bodily autonomy is immediately replaced by the urgent and inescapable burden of patienthood. While we did not choose the illness, we are now solely responsible for choosing how we will respond to it. The passive, unthinking state of being healthy is replaced by the active, demanding, and often terrifying work of being a patient. This is the central existential crisis of illness: it is a simultaneous experience of our ultimate powerlessness and our absolute responsibility.

The first and most overwhelming of these new burdens is the responsibility of knowledge. In the modern medical system, the patient is no longer expected to be a passive recipient of care, but an active and informed participant. This means we are suddenly tasked with becoming a reluctant expert in our own pathology. We are handed pamphlets, directed to websites, and presented with complex and often terrifying statistical probabilities. We must learn the language of a foreign country—the country of our own disease—with its arcane vocabulary of cell counts, tumor markers, and treatment protocols. We must learn to navigate the labyrinthine complexities of the healthcare system, to advocate for ourselves, and to make sense of often conflicting second opinions. This cognitive and emotional labor is immense. It is a full-time job that we did not apply for, a crash course in a subject we never wanted to study. The freedom of information, which in other contexts is so empowering, here feels like a crushing weight, a constant and anxiety-provoking reminder of the stakes of our situation.

Upon this foundation of information, we are then faced with the burden of choice. Modern medicine is rarely a world of singular, clear-cut answers. More often, it is a world of options, each with its own complex matrix of benefits, risks, side effects, and probabilities of success. Do you choose the aggressive chemotherapy that might offer a chance at a cure but will certainly devastate your quality of life, or do you choose the less aggressive treatment that offers better quality of life but a lower chance of long-term survival? Do you undergo the risky surgery, or do you opt for a strategy of watchful waiting? These are not abstract, philosophical dilemmas; they are real, high-stakes choices that must be made with incomplete information and no guarantee of a positive outcome. This is the ultimate confrontation with the reality of a world without guarantees, a situation where our choices have the most profound and irreversible consequences, and yet must be made in a state of profound and terrifying uncertainty.

Beyond the medical choices, illness forces upon us a series of deeply personal and existential ones. We are forced to confront the question of our own identity. How do we integrate the reality of this illness into our sense of self without being completely consumed by it? The world may begin to see us, and we may begin to see ourselves, primarily as a "cancer patient" or a "diabetic" or a "cardiac patient." To resist this totalizing label, to maintain a connection to the parts of ourselves that are not sick, to continue to be a partner, a parent, a friend, an artist, becomes a difficult and courageous act of existential authorship. We are responsible for telling a story about our life that is larger and more complex than the story of our disease.

This entire predicament is a compressed and intensified version of the flight from freedom versus the embrace of responsibility. The flight is a powerful and seductive option. It is the path of the passive patient, the one who completely surrenders their agency to the medical establishment. They adopt the posture, "Just tell me what to do, doctor." This is a form of authoritarian escape, a willing submission to the all-knowing authority of the physician. It is a profound relief from the burden of choice and the anxiety of uncertainty. The patient becomes a compliant object, a body to be treated, and in doing so, they are absolved of the terrifying responsibility of being a co-creator of their own medical destiny.

The alternative is the path of the responsible patient. This is not the path of rejecting medical expertise, but of choosing to be an active and engaged partner in one's own care. It is the path of doing the hard work of understanding the options, of asking difficult questions, and of making choices that are aligned with one's own deepest values, not just with statistical probabilities. It is the path of taking responsibility not just for the disease, but for the life that is being lived in the midst of it. It requires the courage to say, "This illness is a part of my reality, but it is not the whole of my reality. I will face the facts of my condition without being defined by them. I will make the best choices I can in the face of uncertainty, and I will own those choices, for better or for worse."

Illness, in this sense, is a brutal but powerful form of existential education. It is an unwelcome and often tragic catalyst that strips away the trivialities, the distractions, and the illusions of our everyday lives. It forces a direct confrontation with the fundamental truths we spend most of our healthy lives trying to avoid: that our time is finite, that our bodies are fragile, that our control over the world is profoundly limited, and that we are, in the end, solely responsible for the meaning we create in the one life we have. To navigate this terrain with agency and dignity, to choose to live a meaningful life within the new and often harsh limits that illness imposes, is not just a medical journey; it is a profound spiritual and existential achievement. It is the ultimate act of finding freedom not in the absence of constraints, but in the heart of them.

* * *

9

Freedom Across the Lifespan

Our exploration of the human condition has, until now, treated freedom and its burdens as a kind of static, universal predicament. We have spoken of the anxiety of choice, the weight of responsibility, and the flight from our own agency as if they are timeless features of a single, unchanging psychological landscape. Yet, this is a necessary simplification. The reality is that our relationship with freedom is not a fixed state, but a dynamic, unfolding, and lifelong drama. The existential terrain shifts beneath our feet as we age. The specific challenges, the dominant fears, and the potential triumphs of our freedom are profoundly shaped by the season of life in which we find ourselves. The burden of freedom feels different at twenty than it does at fifty, and different again at eighty. It is not a single, monolithic weight, but a living thing that changes its shape, its texture, and its demands as we journey from the open horizon of our youth to the reflective landscape of our later years.

This chapter is an attempt to map that journey. It is a developmental exploration of our existential condition, an inquiry into how the great themes of choice, responsibility, and uncertainty are re-negotiated and redefined at each major stage of the human lifespan. A mature and authentic life is not one that solves the problem of freedom once and for all, but one that learns to courageously re-engage with its evolving demands time and time again. To live well is to understand that our task is not to arrive at a final destination, but to learn to navigate the ever-changing territory of a life in time.

Our journey will begin where individual freedom first erupts with its full, untamed, and terrifying force: in youth. The period from late adolescence through young adulthood is the moment of maximum possibility. It is the time when the script of childhood has ended and the vast, blank page of a life is laid before us. This is the stage of what we might call "absolute freedom," a state of being defined more by what has not yet been chosen than by what has. The young person stands in Kierkegaard's room of a thousand doors, and the feeling is a volatile and overwhelming mixture of exhilaration and terror. In this section, we will explore the profound and often paralyzing burden of this initial, unstructured freedom. We will examine the core existential tasks of this era: the construction of an initial identity, the choice of a professional path, the search for a defining love, all undertaken without a map and with the paralyzing awareness that every choice is an act of profound and potentially irreversible self-creation.

From the boundless potential of youth, we will move into the dense, structured, and often demanding terrain of midlife. If youth is defined by the choices yet to be made, midlife is defined by the choices that have already been made. The commitments of our twenties and thirties—our careers, our marriages, our children, our homes—cease to be theoretical possibilities and become our lived reality, our Sartrean "facticity." Freedom, in this stage, undergoes a fundamental redefinition. It is no longer the "freedom *from*" the constraints of the past, but the "freedom *to*" act meaningfully within the structures we have consciously chosen. The central existential challenge of midlife is to live an authentic life not in a world of infinite options, but within the chosen limits of our own creation. We will explore how this stage is often marked by a confrontation with these limits, the classic "midlife crisis" being, at its core, a painful and necessary reckoning with the paths not taken and a renewed questioning of the meaning of the path we are on.

Next, our journey will take us into the unique and often misunderstood landscape of later life. This is a stage characterized by another profound shift in our relationship with freedom. On one hand, it is a period of new liberation. The heavy responsibilities of midlife—the demands of a career, the raising of children—often recede, creating a new and unprecedented spaciousness, a "freedom from" certain duties that can be a source of great creativity and peace. Yet, this newfound freedom is cast in the long shadow of the ultimate and inescapable limit: the finitude of our own time. The horizon of possibility, once seemingly infinite, is now clearly and visibly bounded by our own mortality. In this section, we will explore the unique existential paradox of old age: a time of maximum freedom from social obligation and maximum constraint by biological reality. The choices of later life are imbued with a new kind of urgency and poignancy, as the central question shifts from "What will I build?" to "What does it all mean?"

Finally, having charted the course of an individual life, we will zoom out to consider the broader, collective dimension of this temporal journey. Our individual lifespan does not unfold in a vacuum. It is a single link in a great, intergenerational chain. The freedoms we enjoy and the constraints we face were, in large part, created by the choices and sacrifices of the generations that came before us. And the choices we make in our own time—how we treat our planet, how we structure our societies, the values we instill in our children—create the very conditions of freedom for the generations that will follow. In our final section, we will explore this profound concept of intergenerational responsibility. We will see how our individual, existential authorship is not just a private affair, but a public trust. To live a fully responsible life is to recognize that our freedom is a temporary stewardship, a gift that we have received from the past and that we are obligated to pass on, hopefully enriched, to the future. This chapter, then, is a meditation on time and its relationship to our freedom, an attempt to understand that to be a human being is to be a creature in constant, dynamic, and lifelong negotiation with the beautiful, terrifying, and ever-shifting burden of our own becoming.

The Terror and Exhilaration of Youth

There is a moment in the life of every individual when the world cracks open. It is not a single, dramatic event, but a slow, dawning, and often disorienting realization that the script we have been following has abruptly run out. Childhood and adolescence are, for the most part, a life lived on rails. Our existence is structured by the timetables of school, the rules of our parents, the clear expectations of a well-defined social world. Our primary responsibility is to learn the lines and to play a role that has been largely written for us. But then, somewhere in the transition from the late teens to the early twenties, the rails disappear. The path forward is no longer a path at all, but a vast, uncharted, and intimidatingly open field. This is the moment of our anointing into existential freedom, a period of life defined by a sudden and shocking surplus of possibility. It is a state of being that is both profoundly exhilarating and, for a great many, almost unbearably terrifying.

The exhilaration is the first and most obvious sensation. It is a feeling of pure, intoxicating potential. The young person stands at the precipice of their own life and feels, for the first time, the full power of their own authorship. The great, defining questions are no longer hypothetical; they are immediate, urgent, and entirely their own to answer. Where will I live? What work will I do? Who will I love? What will I believe in? Who will I become? The sheer scale of this newfound sovereignty can feel like a superpower. It is the thrilling, vertiginous sense that "I can be anything," that the future is not a destination to be arrived at, but a raw material to be shaped. This feeling is the engine of youthful ambition, the fuel for the hopeful migration of young people to new cities, new countries, and new ventures. It is the beautiful, necessary, and heroic belief that one's own life can be a work of art, and that the canvas is, at last, completely blank.

But this exhilaration is almost always accompanied by its dark twin: a profound and paralyzing terror. This is the raw, undiluted anxiety of Kierkegaard's "dizziness of freedom," experienced with an intensity that is rarely matched in later life. The blank canvas, upon closer inspection, is not just an opportunity; it is a terrifying void. The freedom to be anything quickly collapses into the oppressive and immediate burden of having to be *something*, of having to make a definitive mark. The young person is confronted with the ultimate Sartrean predicament: their existence has preceded their essence, and they are now solely and terrifyingly responsible for creating the person they will be. This task feels particularly cruel because it arrives at the very moment in life when we are least equipped to handle it. We are asked to make the most foundational choices about our identity before we have had the time or the experience to truly know who we are. We are trying to build the ship while already adrift in a stormy sea.

The central source of this terror is the fear of foreclosure, the dread of making an irreversible choice that will close off all other possibilities. For the young person, life has not yet been differentiated into major and minor decisions. Every choice feels monumental, definitive, and potentially catastrophic. The choice of a university major is not just an academic decision; it feels like the choice of an entire life path, the closing of a thousand other professional doors. The choice to enter a serious relationship is not just a romantic commitment; it feels like the final renunciation of all the other people one might have loved. In a world of perceived infinite options, amplified by the endless highlight reel of social media, these early, foundational choices feel impossibly weighty. The fear of making the "wrong" choice, the one that will lead to a life of regret, can be so overwhelming that it leads to a state of profound paralysis.

This is the psychological root of the phenomenon of "analysis paralysis" so common in young adulthood. It is the state of the recent graduate who has a dozen potential career paths and is so overwhelmed by the task of choosing the "perfect" one that they end up choosing none, instead taking a low-stakes job that keeps them in a state of suspended animation. It is the state of the person who drifts from one short-term relationship to another, unable to commit not because they lack love for their partners, but because they are terrified of the finality that a genuine commitment represents. This indecision is not a sign of laziness or a lack of seriousness; it is a deeply meaningful defense mechanism. It is an unconscious attempt to remain in the shimmering, pre-committal world of pure potential for as long as possible. It is a flight from the tragic and necessary reality that to live a single life is to accept the death of a million other possible lives.

This terror is compounded by the lack of a stable, internal compass. The mid-life individual, when faced with a difficult choice, can at least consult a more-or-less stable set of values and a lifetime of experience. The young person has not yet had time to forge this internal compass. They are, in a very real sense, trying to discover their values and make life-defining choices at the same time. This often leads to an excessive reliance on external sources of validation and direction. The young person looks to their parents, their peers, their cultural heroes, or the metrics of social media to tell them what a "good" life looks like. This is a form of automaton conformity born of desperation. The young person conforms not out of a lack of desire to be authentic, but because the burden of creating an authentic identity from scratch, without a guide, feels too heavy to bear. They adopt a pre-packaged identity—the aspiring artist, the tech entrepreneur, the social justice activist—as a kind of provisional self, a way to structure their choices and to feel a sense of direction in the overwhelming openness of their freedom.

The terror and exhilaration of youth, then, are two sides of the same existential coin. It is the life stage where our freedom is at its most absolute and our capacity to handle it is at its most fragile. It is a period of intense and necessary exploration, but also one of profound vulnerability to the deepest of our existential anxieties. To navigate this period successfully is not to find all the right answers or to make all the perfect choices. It is to find the courage to make *a* choice, any choice, and to begin the difficult, imperfect, and lifelong work of building a life. It is the willingness to make the first brushstroke on the canvas, to accept its inevitable imperfection, and to take responsibility for the painting that begins to emerge. It is the moment when the abstract concept of freedom becomes the concrete, demanding, and ultimately meaningful reality of a life that is, for better and for worse, finally our own.

The Odyssey Years: Freedom as a State of Perpetual Drafting

Between the structured identity-building of youth and the solemn commitments of midlife, a new and increasingly normative life stage has emerged: the Odyssey Years. This extended decade (roughly from one's early twenties to mid-thirties) is characterized not by a drive toward a single, fixed destination, but by a series of experiments: in careers, in relationships, in cities, and in worldviews. It is a period of profound negative freedom—freedom from the traditional milestones of marriage, mortgage, and lifelong career.

The promise of this stage is the freedom to draft and redraft one's life story. The young adult tries on identities like outfits, working in a tech startup one year, traveling through Southeast Asia the next, then going to graduate school. Relationships are often "situationships" or intentional partnerships that explicitly resist the label of "forever." This can be a period of incredible creativity, self-discovery, and the building of a rich, diverse portfolio of experience.

Yet, this very freedom creates a unique form of existential vertigo. The lack of a fixed trajectory means there is no external validation for having "arrived." The constant drafting can become a form of avoidance, a refusal to move from the open field of possibility to the fenced garden of a committed life. The pervasive anxiety of this stage is not the fear of failure, but the fear of premature closure: the terror of committing to a path that might not be the "perfect" one, thereby ending the odyssey. The shadow of "what if" looms over every potential commitment. The burden here is the weight of an unfinished story, the exhaustion of constant self-creation, and the quiet dread that one might be drafting forever, never publishing the final version of oneself. The challenge of the Odyssey Years is to eventually gather the courage to stop drafting and to begin the real, irreversible work of living a single, chosen life.

The Commitments of Midlife

If the primary existential task of youth is to stand in the terrifying, open field of pure potential and make a choice, the primary task of midlife is to inhabit the world that has been built by those choices. The boundless, abstract, and often dizzying freedom of the young adult gradually gives way to a different kind of freedom, one that is grounded, defined, and constrained by the concrete commitments of a life in progress. The career has been chosen, the partner has been found, the children have been born, the mortgage has been signed. These are the great, load-bearing walls of a midlife existence. They are the Sartrean "facticity" of our own making, the unchangeable reality that has been created out of our own past acts of freedom. This transition from a life of open-ended potential to a life of structured actuality is one of the most significant psychological shifts we ever undertake. It is here, in the heart of our commitments, that freedom must be radically redefined, moving from a dream of infinite breadth to a project of profound and challenging depth.

This is not, as it is often misunderstood, a loss of freedom. It is a transformation of it. The "freedom *from*" the constraints of family and origin that so defines youth is replaced by the far more substantive "freedom *to*" act meaningfully within a set of self-chosen structures. The artist who has spent two decades honing their craft is no longer "free" to become a neurosurgeon, but they have gained the deeper freedom to express themselves with a mastery and nuance that was impossible in their youth. The parent who has committed to raising a family is no longer "free" to live a life of solitary travel, but they have gained the unique and profound freedom to participate in the growth and flourishing of another human being. The freedom of midlife is the freedom of the master craftsman, not the dabbling apprentice. It is a freedom rooted in expertise, in intimacy, in responsibility, and in the deep, accumulated knowledge of a life that has been lived.

Yet, this mature form of freedom comes with its own immense and particular burden. The very structures that provide our lives with meaning, stability, and purpose—our jobs, our marriages, our homes—can, over time, begin to feel less like a sanctuary we have built and more like a cage that is closing in. The choices that were once made with a sense of hope and passion can, through the slow erosion of time and the accumulation of a thousand minor compromises, come to feel like a life sentence. The career that once felt like a calling becomes a monotonous grind. The marriage that was once a source of joyful connection becomes a predictable and often lonely routine. This is the central existential crisis of midlife: the confrontation with the fact that the life we have freely chosen has become the very source of our feeling of being trapped.

This feeling is, in its essence, a sophisticated form of bad faith. It is the unconscious attempt to escape the responsibility of our own past choices by recasting ourselves as the victims of our present circumstances. We forget that we were the architects of this house. We begin to tell ourselves a story in which the job, the spouse, or the obligations of family are external forces that have been imposed upon us, robbing us of our true, authentic selves. We begin to yearn for the seemingly simpler, more open-ended freedom of our youth, a fantasy of escape from the complex and demanding reality we have created. This is the fertile psychological ground from which the classic, and often caricatured, "midlife crisis" springs.

The midlife crisis, stripped of its clichés of sports cars and illicit affairs, is a profound and often necessary existential reckoning. It is the moment when the bill for our unlived lives comes due. It is the painful, volcanic eruption of all the possibilities we have had to sacrifice in order to live the one life we have. The psyche, which has for years been dutifully repressing the ghosts of our other potential selves, can no longer hold them back. We are haunted by the counterfactuals, by the nagging, tormenting question of "what might have been." What if I had taken that other job? What if I had married that other person? What if I had pursued my art instead of this safe career? This is the sting of finitude, the sudden, visceral understanding that time is not an infinite resource, that some doors are now permanently closed, and that the person we are is, in large part, the person we will be.

The response to this crisis can take one of two paths: the path of escape or the path of re-engagement. The path of escape is an inauthentic and often destructive attempt to recapture the boundless, uncommitted freedom of youth. It is the affair that seeks to find in a new person the excitement that has faded from a long-term relationship, a refusal to do the difficult work of cultivating new forms of intimacy within the existing commitment. It is the abrupt decision to quit a stable job and "find one's passion," an act that often mistakes a change in external circumstances for the much more difficult work of changing one's internal relationship to responsibility. These are acts of rebellion not against the specific job or the specific partner, but against the very nature of commitment itself. They are a desperate flight from the reality of a finite, chosen life back into the seductive but ultimately illusory world of pure potential.

The more difficult, and more authentic, path is one of courageous re-engagement. This path begins not with a change in circumstance, but with a radical act of ownership. It is the willingness to stop blaming our commitments for our unhappiness and to take full responsibility for the life we have created, in all its beauty and all its imperfection. It is to look at the structures of our life and to say, "I chose this. And now, I am free to choose how I will inhabit it." This is the moment when freedom is redefined. It ceases to be about the possibility of escape and becomes about the possibility of transformation from within.

This re-engagement requires us to ask a new set of questions. The question is no longer, "Did I make the right choice?" but rather, "How can I make this choice the right one, here and now?" For the person in a long-term marriage, it means asking, "How can we reinvent our intimacy? How can we become new people, together?" It is the choice to see one's partner not as a known and finished quantity, but as a still-unfolding mystery to be rediscovered. For the person in a stagnant career, it means asking, "How can I find a new sense of purpose within this role? Can I mentor a younger colleague? Can I initiate a new project? Can I change my attitude from one of resentful obligation to one of professional craftsmanship?" It is the search for a new layer of meaning within a familiar structure.

This is the mature freedom of midlife. It is less spectacular than the explosive freedom of youth, but it is far more profound. It is the freedom that is found not in the absence of limits, but in the conscious and wholehearted embrace of them. It is the understanding that a deep and meaningful life is not built by constantly seeking a better set of circumstances, but by bringing a better, more responsible, and more courageous self to the circumstances we have already chosen. It is the difficult, beautiful, and ultimately liberating work of learning to be free not just in the choosing of our life, but in the living of it.

The Freedoms and Constraints of Later Life

The journey through the dense, demanding, and commitment-laden terrain of midlife eventually opens out into a new and unfamiliar landscape: that of our later years. This is a stage of life that our youth-obsessed culture often misunderstands, caricaturing it either as a placid, golden twilight of leisure or as a grim, precipitous decline into infirmity. The reality, from an existential perspective, is far more complex, more poignant, and more psychologically rich than either of these simplistic portraits. Later life is not an epilogue to the story of our freedom; it is a final, challenging, and profoundly meaningful chapter, defined by a dramatic and paradoxical reconfiguration of freedom itself. It is a period characterized by a great and often welcome liberation from the external demands of the world, a freedom that arrives at the very same moment we are forced into our most direct and intimate confrontation with the ultimate, internal constraint: the finitude of our own time.

The first and most palpable experience of this new stage is often one of spaciousness. For decades, the rhythm of our lives was dictated by a demanding set of external obligations. The alarm clock, the work deadline, the parent-teacher conference, the mortgage payment—these were the non-negotiable beats of the midlife drum. The freedom of this era was a freedom found *within* these structures. But in later life, for many, the drumbeat fades. Retirement marks the end of the formal career project. The children, now grown, have their own lives and their own responsibilities. The great, identity-defining, and time-consuming projects of building a career and raising a family are, for the most part, complete. This ushers in a new and radical form of liberty: the "freedom *from.*" It is the freedom from the tyranny of the schedule, from the pressures of professional ambition, from the daily, grinding responsibility for the well-being of others.

This newfound freedom can be profoundly liberating. It is a return, in some ways, to the open-ended possibility of youth, but without the attendant terror of identity formation. It is the freedom to finally read the stack of books that has been gathering dust for thirty years, to take up painting, to learn a new language, to travel not for work but for wonder. It is the freedom to invest one's time and energy based not on external demand, but on internal curiosity and authentic interest. The responsibility is no longer to be a productive employee or an attentive parent, but simply to be a more fully realized human being. For the person who is able to embrace it, this can be a period of immense creativity, personal growth, and quiet joy. It is the earned freedom of a life that has already been built, a chance to finally, and without apology, inhabit the house of the self.

Yet, this expansive new freedom does not exist in a vacuum. It is cast in the long, and ever-lengthening, shadow of our own mortality. The fundamental constraint of later life is the visceral, undeniable, and ever-present awareness of the finitude of time. In our youth and midlife, death is an abstract concept, a distant and theoretical endpoint. In our later years, it becomes a concrete and intimate reality. It is present in the mirror, in the obituaries of our friends and peers, in the subtle (or not-so-subtle) decline of our own physical capacities. The horizon of our future, once seemingly infinite, has now drawn close. The open field of possibility is now a clearly demarcated and finite landscape. This is the ultimate Sartrean facticity, the final, unchosen, and inescapable limit against which all our freedom must now be exercised.

This creates the central, poignant paradox of later life: we are granted the maximum freedom from social and professional obligation at the very moment our biological and temporal freedom is at its most constricted. This paradox fundamentally reorients the nature of choice. The choices of later life are no longer primarily about building a future; they are about inhabiting a present. The calculus shifts from accumulation to appreciation, from investment to expenditure. The question is no longer, "What should I do to get ahead?" but, "Given that my time is precious and limited, how do I wish to spend it?" Each choice—how to spend a day, which relationships to nurture, which commitments to maintain—is imbued with a new and powerful sense of weight and significance. There is a dawning recognition that every moment spent on a meaningless or inauthentic activity is a squandered and irretrievable portion of a dwindling inheritance.

The primary existential task of this stage, then, is one of integration and meaning-making. If the task of youth is to write the story and the task of midlife is to live it, the task of later life is to read it, to understand it, and to make peace with it. This is the psychological process known as the "life review." It is an often unconscious, but profoundly necessary, sifting through of the past, a search for the themes, the patterns, and the ultimate meaning of the life that has been lived. It is here that we must confront our unlived lives, not with the panicked regret of the midlife crisis, but with a more mature and compassionate sense of acceptance. It is the work of owning the totality of our story—the triumphs and the failures, the joys and the sorrows, the choices made and the paths forgone—and finding in that singular, imperfect narrative a sense of coherence and integrity.

The flight from freedom in later life often manifests as a refusal to engage in this difficult work. One common escape is a descent into a bitter and resentful nostalgia, a life lived entirely in the past, endlessly relitigating old grievances and mourning lost opportunities. This is a refusal to accept the reality of the present and to take responsibility for finding meaning in it. Another escape is the frantic, youthful pursuit, a denial of the aging process itself, a desperate attempt to cling to the activities, the appearance, and the values of a life stage that has already passed. This is a flight from the specific and meaningful tasks of old age into a hollow and inauthentic performance of a younger self. And perhaps the most tragic escape is the surrender to despair, the conclusion that it is "too late," that the story is over, and that all that remains is a meaningless waiting for the end.

The authentic and courageous path in later life is to hold both sides of the paradox at once: to savor the new freedoms with gratitude while squarely facing the reality of the final limit. It is the freedom that is found in a conscious and deliberate letting go—the letting go of old ambitions, of past resentments, of the need to be anything other than what one is. The great psychoanalyst Erik Erikson identified the central virtue of this life stage as "wisdom," which he defined as a kind of "detached concern with life itself in the face of death itself." It is a state of being in which we are finally free from the anxious striving of the ego and are able to experience the world with a sense of quiet wonder and deep appreciation. It is the ultimate and most profound form of freedom: the freedom from the fear of our own finitude, and the ability to live the final chapter of our lives with a sense of peace, integrity, and a quiet, dignified courage.

Intergenerational Responsibility

Our journey through the human lifespan, from the explosive potential of youth to the reflective wisdom of later life, can foster a kind of narrative myopia. We are the undisputed protagonists of our own story, and it is natural to view our choices, our struggles, and our search for meaning as a self-contained drama, one that begins with our birth and ends with our death. But this perspective, as compelling as it is, is built upon a profound illusion: the illusion of the isolated self. The life of any single individual is not a solitary monologue. It is a single line of dialogue in a vast and ancient conversation, a conversation that stretches back into the mists of the past and forward into the unseeable horizons of the future. The freedom we exercise in our own lifetime is not a possession we have created for ourselves; it is a temporary stewardship, a precious and fragile inheritance that we have received from those who came before us, and a legacy that we are, whether we choose to acknowledge it or not, actively shaping for those who will come after.

This is the concept of intergenerational responsibility, and it is perhaps the most demanding, most profound, and most existentially significant dimension of our freedom. It is the recognition that our individual lives are not our own private affair. We are born into a world that has been profoundly shaped by the choices, the sacrifices, the triumphs, and the failures of countless preceding generations. The very conditions of our freedom—the political liberties we take for granted, the scientific knowledge we rely upon, the cultural traditions that enrich us, the technological infrastructure that enables us—are not natural features of the world. They are the accumulated capital of human history, a vast and complex inheritance built by the responsible actions of our ancestors. To be born in a society with a functioning democracy, with access to clean water, with a body of medical knowledge that can cure diseases that once decimated populations, is to be the beneficiary of a trust fund we did not earn. Our facticity is not a generic state of being; it is a specific and privileged inheritance.

To awaken to this reality is to feel a profound sense of gratitude, but it is also to be confronted with an immense and sobering weight. If our present freedom is the product of past choices, then it follows with inescapable logic that our present choices are actively creating the conditions of freedom—or unfreedom—for the generations that will follow. We are not just living our own lives; we are, with every collective decision we make, acting as the architects of the future. We are building the house, designing the social and ecological landscape, that our own children and grandchildren and their grandchildren will be forced to inhabit. The freedom they will have, the choices that will be available to them, the very quality of their existence is being determined, in large part, by us, here and now.

Nowhere is this awesome responsibility more starkly and undeniably clear than in our relationship with the natural world. The escalating crisis of climate change is the ultimate and most unforgiving lesson in intergenerational responsibility. Our collective choices in this single lifetime—our patterns of consumption, our reliance on fossil fuels, our failure to act with sufficient urgency—are not just shaping our own present; they are permanently altering the fundamental biophysical operating system of the entire planet. We are, through our actions and our inactions, quite literally determining the habitability of the earth for all human beings who will ever live. The freedoms that future generations will enjoy—the freedom to live without the constant threat of catastrophic weather, the freedom from mass displacement and resource wars, the freedom to experience the beauty and biodiversity of a healthy planet—are being constrained, and in some cases extinguished, by us. This is a burden of authorship on a scale that is almost impossible to comprehend. It is a choice whose full consequences we will never see, but for which we are absolutely and unequivocally responsible.

This dynamic extends to every other domain of our collective life. The economic policies we pursue, the level of national debt we accrue, the investments we make or fail to make in education and infrastructure—these are not just abstract political debates. They are the choices that will determine whether our children inherit a world of opportunity or a world of diminished possibilities and crushing obligations. The political norms we are willing to tolerate, our commitment to the rule of law, to reasoned debate, and to the peaceful transfer of power, determine whether we pass on a resilient and functioning democracy or a fragile and decaying one. We are either the diligent stewards of our inherited political freedom, or we are the reckless tenants who allow a beautiful and ancient house to fall into ruin.

The responsibility is also deeply personal and cultural. It is present in the stories we tell our children, in the values we embody, in the prejudices we challenge or perpetuate. To raise a child to be compassionate, curious, and tolerant is to make a small but real investment in the possibility of a more peaceful future. To pass on our unresolved hatreds and fears is to plant a seed of future conflict. Each individual life, in this sense, becomes a small but crucial battleground in the long, unfolding struggle for a more humane world.

To embrace this intergenerational responsibility is to find the ultimate antidote to the problem of meaninglessness. In a universe without inherent purpose, and in the face of our own certain death, the search for a lasting significance can feel like a futile project. Our individual lives, no matter how accomplished, are fleeting. Our names will be forgotten, our achievements will fade. But the chain of life is long. To see ourselves as a vital link in that chain is to discover a form of transcendence that is both profound and concrete. The meaning of our lives is found not just in our own self-actualization, but in the contribution we make to the lives of those we will never meet. It is to find our purpose not in what we can get from the world, but in what we can give to it.

This is the ultimate maturation of freedom. It is the movement from the youthful, self-centered question, "What will I do with my freedom?" to the more mature, and more profoundly human question, "For what, and for whom, will my freedom be used?" It reframes the entire arc of our lives. The task of youth is not just to build a self, but to challenge the inherited world and to fight for a better future. The task of midlife is not just to maintain our own commitments, but to build durable institutions and communities that will serve the common good. And the ultimate wisdom of later life is to become a conscious and deliberate elder, a guardian of the past and a steward of the future, whose final and most important project is to leave the world a little better, a little freer, and a little more hopeful than they found it. To live with this awareness is to bear the heaviest and most magnificent burden of all: the responsibility not just for our own one and only life, but for our small but sacred part in the great, unfinished story of humanity.

* * *

10

The Body as Both Cage and Key

Our entire exploration to this point has been, in many ways, a conversation about a ghost. We have spoken of freedom, choice, consciousness, and will as if these were the properties of a disembodied mind, a pure, abstract self that floats somewhere behind our eyes, making decisions and authoring a life. We have analyzed the architecture of our thoughts, the patterns of our anxieties, and the structure of our beliefs. But we have largely neglected the house in which this ghost resides. We have failed to grapple with the profound and often uncomfortable truth that every single act of freedom, every choice, every feeling, and every thought is an event that happens in, through, and because of the flesh. We do not simply *have* a body in the way we have a car or a possession; we *are* a body. And this single, undeniable fact is the source of both our greatest limitations and our only possible means of liberation.

This chapter is a journey into that fundamental paradox. It is an attempt to ground our entire discussion of freedom in the most concrete reality of all: the living, breathing, aching, aging, and ultimately finite human body. The body is the ultimate and most intimate site of the existential drama. It is both our cage and our key. It is the cage because it represents the absolute and unchosen limit of our existence, the brute facts of our Sartrean "facticity" made manifest. We did not choose the genes that dictate our height, our health predispositions, or the basic temperament with which we are born. We do not choose to age. We do not choose our ultimate vulnerability to pain, to illness, and to death. The body is the relentless and humbling reminder that we are not gods, that our freedom is not absolute, but is always and forever constrained by the stubborn, unyielding laws of biology. It is the cage of our givenness, the wall against which the fantasy of our infinite potential must eventually crash.

Yet, this very same body is also our only key. It is the sole instrument through which we can experience the world and enact our freedom within it. It is our only point of contact with reality. The entire world of our experience—the beauty of a sunset, the warmth of a loved one's touch, the joy of movement, the taste of food—is a symphony of sensation that is played upon the instrument of our nervous system. Our emotions are not abstract ideas; they are visceral, embodied events, a racing heart, a tightness in the chest, a warmth spreading through the belly. Our capacity to act, to build, to create, to love—all of these are dependent on the simple, miraculous fact of our physical being. Without the body, our freedom would be a silent, powerless, and utterly meaningless concept, a ghost trapped in an eternal, featureless void. To be free is to be embodied. There is no other kind of freedom available to us.

The great flight from freedom, then, often begins with a subtle and pervasive flight from our own embodiment. The deeply ingrained mind-body dualism of Western thought is not just a philosophical error; it is a sophisticated and powerful existential defense mechanism. It allows us to live with the comforting illusion that our "true" self—our consciousness, our ego—is separate from, and superior to, the messy, vulnerable, and mortal animal that is our body. We treat the body as an object to be managed, a machine to be optimized, or an enemy to be conquered. We try to escape its limits through intellectual abstraction or spiritual bypass. But this is a profound act of bad faith. It is a refusal to own the totality of our existence. To be an authentic, responsible human being requires us to abandon this illusion and to accept the difficult and beautiful task of living as an integrated whole, a creature of both mud and spirit, of both absolute constraint and magnificent, if limited, freedom.

This chapter will explore this lifelong negotiation between our transcendent aspirations and our biological realities. We will begin by confronting the ultimate unchosen starting point: the genetic lottery. We will wrestle with the profound tension between the existentialist's insistence on radical freedom and the undeniable fact of our biological inheritance, exploring how we can take responsibility for a self whose foundational materials we did not choose.

From there, we will examine how this dynamic plays out over the course of a lifetime through the universal experiences of health and illness. Expanding on our earlier discussion, we will delve deeper into the subjective, embodied experience of being a physical self in the world, exploring how health provides the silent, taken-for-granted stage for our freedom, and how illness forces a direct and often brutal confrontation with our body's limits, simultaneously constricting our agency and demanding a new and more conscious form of it.

Next, we will turn our attention to our own active attempts to shape and master our physical selves through the practice of discipline. We will analyze how routines like diet and exercise can be powerful tools for creating a kind of "freedom from" the tyranny of our own impulses. But we will also explore the dark side of this project, the point at which the disciplined body becomes a tyrannical obsession, another form of escape from the messy, imperfect reality of our authentic, embodied being.

Finally, we will arrive at the ultimate and most profound embodiment of our finitude: our own mortality. We will argue that the conscious and courageous acceptance of our body's inevitable decay and death is not a morbid resignation, but the final and most crucial key to a fully-lived life. It is the understanding that the very finitude of our physical existence is what gives our choices their urgency, their poignancy, and their meaning. To embrace our mortality is to be liberated from the fantasy of a limitless future and to be returned, with profound force, to the precious and irreplaceable gift of the present moment. This chapter, then, is a call to come home to ourselves, to the simple, profound, and inescapable reality of our own flesh, and to discover that the cage of our finitude and the key to our freedom are, and have always been, one and the same.

The Genetic Lottery vs. Radical Freedom

At the very foundation of the existentialist project lies a bold and defiant declaration of human sovereignty. It is the Sartrean assertion that we are radically free, that our existence precedes our essence, and that we are nothing more and nothing less than the sum of our choices. This is a philosophy of the blank slate, a vision of the human being as a pure, self-creating consciousness, thrown into the world without a pre-written nature, and burdened with the magnificent and terrifying task of inventing a self from scratch. It is a powerful, and in many ways, a deeply empowering vision. Yet, it crashes headfirst into a simple, stubborn, and scientifically undeniable fact: we are not born as blank slates. We are born into a body, and that body arrives with a dense, complex, and entirely pre-written text, a biological script we did not choose and cannot erase: our genetic code.

This is the great, unchosen starting point of every human life, the ultimate and most profound form of our facticity. Before we make a single choice, before we have a single conscious thought, a lottery has already been drawn, and its results will shape the entire course of our existence.

This is the genetic lottery. It is a game of chance in which the stakes are everything: the color of our eyes, the potential height of our bodies, the speed of our metabolism, the innate wiring of our nervous system. But it goes deeper than these surface-level traits. This lottery distributes the raw materials of our very being. It bestows upon one person a predisposition to robust physical health and upon another a vulnerability to chronic illness. It grants one a temperament that is naturally calm and resilient, and another a nervous system that is exquisitely sensitive to stress and prone to anxiety. It deals one a hand rich with innate intellectual or artistic talents, and another a hand that will require immense and patient labor to achieve even a modest level of competence.

This is the cage. It is the most primal and inescapable constraint on our freedom. The reality of our genetic inheritance is a direct and profound challenge to the ideal of a purely self-created life. How can we be held responsible for a character whose foundational traits—our baseline levels of optimism, our introversion or extroversion, our very capacity for focus and discipline—were assigned to us before we ever made a single choice? How can we speak of radical freedom when the very instrument through which we experience and act upon the world is a product of a random biological shuffle? This is not just a philosophical puzzle; it is a deep, lived, and often painful reality. It is the reality of the person who fights a lifelong battle with depression that is rooted in their family history. It is the reality of the individual who struggles with a learning disability, forever feeling that they are running a race with weights on their ankles. It is the reality of anyone who has looked in the mirror and felt a sense of profound alienation from the unchosen face staring back at them.

This tension is not merely a philosophical debate; it is the central drama being played out in the laboratories of modern science. The arguments from fields like neuroscience and behavioral genetics represent the ultimate scientific expression of the body as our cage. Neuroscientific studies, for instance, have famously suggested that the brain initiates action milliseconds *before* we become consciously aware of our intention to act, leading some to conclude that our felt sense of free will is a post-hoc illusion—a story our conscious mind tells itself to make sense of a process that was already determined by our neural machinery. Similarly, behavioral genetics reveals the profound extent to which our personality traits, our vulnerabilities to mental illness, and even our political leanings can be statistically predicted from our DNA. These findings present a formidable challenge: if our choices are simply the predetermined outputs of a biological computer, what becomes of responsibility?

The existential response to this potent critique is not to deny the science, but to reframe the entire question. The existential project is not concerned with proving the existence of a metaphysical "free will" that operates outside the laws of causality. It is concerned with the undeniable *subjective reality* of being a chooser. This is the unshakable truth of the key. Regardless of what a brain scan might reveal about the firing of our neurons, we *experience* ourselves as beings who deliberate, who weigh options, and who must bear the consequences of the paths we take. This lived reality is the ground of our entire moral and psychological world. The existential task is not to solve the riddle of determinism, but to take radical responsibility for our *relationship* to our own determined impulses and predispositions. Our genetics and brain wiring may be the code, but our consciousness is the user, and it is the user who must decide what to do with the program they are running. The flight from freedom, then, is not just a denial of our liberty, but a profound misuse of the scientific story, twisting it into a convenient alibi.

The flight from freedom, in this context, often takes the form of a kind of biological determinism. This is a modern, scientifically-packaged version of bad faith. It is the narrative that says, "I am my genes." It is the attempt to abdicate responsibility for our lives by defining ourselves as the finished and unchangeable product of our biological inheritance. The person who says, "I can't help my bad temper; it's in my DNA," or, "I'm just not a motivated person; my brain isn't wired for success," is using their facticity not as an explanation, but as an alibi. They are treating their genetic predispositions as a life sentence rather than as a starting point. This is a profoundly comforting, if ultimately disempowering, strategy. It transforms the difficult and demanding project of a life into a simple, predictable unfolding of a pre-written script. If our fate is written in our cells, then we are relieved of the terrifying burden of having to write it for ourselves.

The existentialist response to this is not to deny the powerful reality of our biology, which would be a form of delusion. The response is to insist that our facticity, no matter how powerful, is only half of the equation. The other half is our transcendence—our uniquely human capacity to be in a conscious relationship with our own givenness, to interpret it, to struggle against it, to give it meaning, and to choose our attitude toward it. Our genes may provide the raw clay of our existence, but we are the sculptors who must choose what to make of it. The clay may be difficult, filled with impurities and resistant to our touch, but the responsibility for the act of sculpting remains entirely our own. This is the key.

Consider two individuals who have, through the genetic lottery, been given a strong predisposition to anxiety. The first individual succumbs to the narrative of biological determinism. They identify completely with their anxiety, declaring, "I am an anxious person." This is their essence. Their life becomes organized around this perceived identity. They avoid social situations, turn down professional opportunities, and live in a state of chronic, fearful constriction. Their genetic predisposition has been allowed to become their destiny. The second individual, however, takes a different path. They acknowledge the reality of their situation, saying, "I have a biological tendency to experience anxiety." This is a subtle but crucial reframing. The anxiety is not *who they are*; it is a condition they *have*, a challenge they must face. This acknowledgment is the first step in taking responsibility. They are now free to choose their response. They can learn meditation techniques, engage in therapy, practice courage by facing their fears, and build a life of meaning and connection *in spite of* their anxious temperament.

This second path is the essence of an authentic, embodied freedom. It is a freedom that is not found in the denial of our limits, but in our courageous and creative engagement with them. It is the understanding that our responsibility is not for the hand we were dealt, but for the skill, the courage, and the integrity with which we choose to play that hand. The person born with a challenging health condition is not responsible for their illness, but they are responsible for the choice between a life of bitter resentment and a life of grace and resilience. The person born with a difficult temperament is not responsible for their innate wiring, but they are responsible for the lifelong work of cultivating a character that is defined by more than just their primal impulses.

This is the ultimate wrestling match that lies at the heart of our embodied existence. It is a constant, lifelong negotiation between the cage of our unchosen biology and the key of our transcendent freedom. To live an authentic life is to refuse the easy escape of determinism and to take up the difficult, and at times heroic, project of becoming the author of a life, using the very materials we were given but did not ask for. It is to own our existence in its totality, to accept the strange and paradoxical truth that we are, at the same time, a product of a random lottery and the sole, responsible creator of the person we will be.

Health, Illness, and Embodied Agency

For most of us, for most of our lives, the body is a silent partner. It is the quiet, taken-for-granted stage upon which the drama of our conscious life unfolds. We live in a state of what the philosopher Gabriel Marcel called "unproblematic inherence," a seamless, unthinking unity with our own flesh. We do not feel our liver functioning or our neurons firing; we simply *are*. This state of health is the invisible foundation of nearly all our freedoms. The freedom to walk across a room, to climb a mountain, to hold a loved one, to engage in a demanding intellectual task—all of these are predicated on the silent, cooperative functioning of a trillion cells. We treat this profound gift not as a state of being, but as a given, a neutral backdrop. This is a form of existential privilege, the privilege of being able to forget, for a time, that we are fundamentally biological creatures, vulnerable and finite.

The onset of a significant illness or a chronic condition is the violent and unceremonious end of this privilege. It is a summons from the body, a loud, insistent, and often painful demand to be acknowledged. The silent partner becomes a tyrannical protagonist, and the unproblematic inherence is shattered, replaced by a state of intense and often alienated self-awareness. The body is no longer a transparent medium for our will, but an opaque and often hostile object that we must now confront, manage, and negotiate with. This is a direct and brutal confrontation with the "cage" of our existence. The illness becomes the ultimate expression of our facticity, a stark and undeniable limit imposed upon our freedom by the random, indifferent lottery of biology. The boundless horizon of the future, which we once took for granted, suddenly contracts. The world shrinks to the size of a hospital room, a medication schedule, a list of physical limitations.

This experience of constriction, of having our possibilities foreclosed by the brute reality of a malfunctioning body, is a profound form of powerlessness. It is a direct assault on our sense of agency and our belief in a just and orderly world. The initial response is often a state of existential shock, a feeling of profound alienation from the very flesh we inhabit. The body comes to feel like a traitor, a broken machine, a prison in which the "real" self is trapped. This is the source of the immense psychological suffering that accompanies physical illness, a suffering that is often distinct from and deeper than the physical pain itself. It is the anguish of a free consciousness that finds itself tethered to a failing and unpredictable animal.

Yet, it is precisely within this state of profound powerlessness that a new, strange, and demanding form of freedom is born. The illness that robs us of our physical autonomy simultaneously thrusts upon us the full, unmitigated burden of our existential agency. We are suddenly and irrevocably placed in the role of the "chooser," forced to make a series of high-stakes decisions in a landscape of profound uncertainty. The passive, unthinking state of being healthy is replaced by the active, demanding, and often terrifying work of being a patient. While we are not responsible for the fact of our illness, we are, as we have seen, absolutely responsible for our response to it.

The most immediate and obvious form of this new responsibility is the burden of medical choice. The patient is no longer a passive supplicant before the altar of medical authority; they are expected to be an active, informed, and participating agent in their own care. This requires a courageous engagement with the terrifying realities of prognosis and probability. The choices are rarely clean or simple. They are almost always a matter of navigating trade-offs between potential benefits and certain harms. The cancer patient must weigh the possibility of a longer life against the certainty of a debilitating chemotherapy. The person with chronic pain must choose between the risk of addiction to powerful opioids and the certainty of a life lived in constant agony. The individual with a heart condition must decide whether to undergo a risky surgery or to manage their condition through a radical and difficult change in lifestyle.

These are not just technical decisions; they are profoundly existential ones. They are choices that force us to clarify our deepest values. What do I value more: the quantity of my life or its quality? How much suffering am I willing to endure in the hope of a better future? What risks am I willing to take? There are no right answers. There are no guarantees. There is only the lonely, terrifying, and inalienable responsibility of the choice itself. To make these choices is to be engaged in the ultimate act of self-authorship, to be writing the final and most consequential chapters of one's own story in the full and agonizing knowledge of the stakes.

Beyond these medical decisions lies the even more profound responsibility of meaning-making. The illness is a brute fact, a biological event. But the meaning of that event is not given. It must be created. One individual may experience a chronic illness as a divine punishment, a sign of some personal failing. Another may see it as a random, meaningless tragedy, a cruel cosmic joke. A third may, over time, come to experience it as a kind of harsh but transformative teacher, a catalyst for a deeper appreciation of life, a reordering of priorities, and a more profound sense of compassion for the suffering of others. The illness is the same; the meaning is a choice. This is the ultimate freedom that remains even in the face of the most profound physical constraints: the freedom, as Viktor Frankl so powerfully taught, to choose one's attitude in any given set of circumstances.

The flight from this embodied agency can take many forms. It can manifest as the complete and passive surrender to the medical establishment, a form of authoritarian escape where the patient abdicates all responsibility for their own choices. It can take the form of denial or magical thinking, a refusal to accept the reality of the body's limits and a desperate search for a miracle cure that will restore the fantasy of a life without constraints. Or it can manifest as a total identification with the disease, where the rich and complex identity of a person is allowed to collapse into the single, flattened identity of "the patient." This, too, is a flight from freedom, an abdication of the responsibility to live the parts of life that are still available, to nurture the relationships that still matter, and to cultivate the parts of the self that are not sick.

The authentic and courageous path is to embrace the paradox of the body as both cage and key. It is to accept the cage of our physical limitations without being defined by it. It is to take up the key of our own agency and to use it to unlock the possibilities for a meaningful life that still exist, even within those new and often harsh constraints. This is the essence of embodied freedom. It is not the fantasy of a limitless mind, but the difficult, beautiful, and grounded reality of a conscious being learning to live with dignity, courage, and purpose within the fragile, imperfect, and ultimately sacred vessel of a human body.

The Shattered Vessel: When the Body Forces a New Freedom

The theoretical dialogue between the body as cage and key becomes terrifyingly concrete in the event of a sudden disability or the onset of a chronic, debilitating illness. In a moment, the "key" of the body—its capacity to execute the will—seems to break. The future, once a landscape of open possibility, slams shut. The projects, identities, and freedoms that were taken for granted are suddenly revoked. The body is no longer a silent partner in one's freedom; it becomes a loud, demanding, and limiting cage.

This crisis is a brutal, accelerated course in existential facticity. The unchosen reality of one's physical condition becomes the overwhelming fact of existence. The initial response is often one of profound despair and a sense of unfreedom—the very annihilation of one's former life. Yet, it is in this confrontation with the absolute limits of the cage that a new, more profound key can be found. The freedom that remains is the one Viktor Frankl identified in the concentration camp: the attitude one takes toward unavoidable suffering. The project of life is no longer about achieving what one *wants*, but about finding meaning and dignity in what *is*. It is the freedom to choose patience over self-pity, to find a new scale for joy, to redefine what "a good day" means, and to discover a self that is not dependent on physical prowess or health. The body as cage forces a distillation of the spirit. The freedom that emerges is not the freedom of boundless action, but the freedom of unassailable being—the hard-won realization that the essence of who we are is not housed in our temporary, fragile vessel, but in our enduring capacity to choose our response to it.

The Disciplined Body

The body we inherit is a wild and unruly thing. It is a creature of pure appetite, a symphony of primal impulses that know nothing of our long-term plans, our abstract values, or our existential aspirations. It is the seat of our hunger, our fatigue, our lust, our cravings, and our deep, instinctual pull toward the path of least resistance: the comfort of the couch, the immediate pleasure of the sugary food, the seductive embrace of one more hour of sleep. To be purely and simply a body, in this sense, is to be in a state of a certain kind of unfreedom, a slave to the ceaseless and often contradictory demands of our own biology. It is to be an instrument played upon by the random music of our hormones, our blood sugar, and our neurotransmitters.

The project of discipline, then—the conscious and deliberate regulation of our diet, our exercise, our sleep, and our daily routines—can be understood as a profound and quintessentially human act of rebellion. It is a declaration of independence from the tyranny of our own primal impulses. It is the assertion of the transcendent self, the choosing, value-creating consciousness, over the given facts of our biological machinery. The disciplined body is not a denial of our physical nature, but a conscious attempt to enter into a new kind of relationship with it: a relationship not of slavery, but of stewardship. This is the creation of a "freedom from"—a freedom from the chaos of our own cravings, from the prison of our lethargy, from the predictable decay of a neglected physical form.

Consider the simple, daily act of choosing what to eat. In a world of engineered, hyper-palatable processed foods, the path of least resistance is to simply follow the siren song of our cravings for salt, sugar, and fat. To choose, instead, to eat a diet of whole, nutritious foods is a small but powerful act of existential authorship. It is a choice to privilege the well-being of our future self over the immediate gratification of our present self. It is an act of saying, "I am more than my immediate desires. I am a being who is responsible for the long-term flourishing of this body, and I will act in accordance with that responsibility." This choice creates a cascade of freedoms. It frees us from the energy crashes, the mood swings, and the mental fog that so often accompany a poor diet. It frees us, in the long term, from the profound constraints on our agency that are imposed by chronic, lifestyle-related diseases. The discipline of the diet is not a restriction of freedom, but an investment in it.

The same is true of the discipline of exercise. The body's natural inclination, in a world where physical survival no longer requires constant exertion, is toward entropy, toward the conservation of energy. To choose to move, to run, to lift weights, to stretch—this is an act of rebellion against our own inertia. It is a conscious choice to create energy, resilience, and capability where there would otherwise be atrophy. The person who commits to a regular practice of physical exertion is not just building muscle; they are building a more robust and capable platform from which to exercise all their other freedoms. They are creating a body that can say "yes" to more of life: yes to the long hike, yes to the game with their children, yes to the demanding project that requires sustained energy and focus. The discipline of movement is the key that unlocks the door to a wider and more vibrant world of embodied experience.

This freedom created by discipline extends to the rhythm of our lives. To cultivate a routine of consistent sleep, of waking at a regular hour, of creating a structure for our days, is to provide a kind of firm and stable ground for the self to stand on. It is a way of managing the chaotic flux of our own internal states and creating a baseline of stability from which we can act with intention rather than simply reacting to the random weather patterns of our moods. These routines are not a cage; they are the trellis that allows the vine of our life to grow in a strong and focused direction, rather than sprawling aimlessly on the ground.

Yet, this noble project of self-mastery contains within it a dark and dangerous potential. There is a fine and often imperceptible line between a discipline that serves the cause of freedom and a discipline that becomes a new and more insidious form of tyranny. The danger arises when the *means* of discipline ceases to be a tool for a richer life and becomes the *end* in itself. This is the point at which the healthy stewardship of the body collapses into an obsessive and fearful war against it. The disciplined self becomes a rigid, unyielding dictator, and the body becomes its oppressed and subjugated subject.

We see this tragic inversion in the world of diet and exercise when a healthy concern for nutrition metastasizes into an eating disorder, or a commitment to fitness curdles into a compulsive and punishing exercise addiction. The logic of "more is better" takes over. The focus shifts from the goal of well-being to the goal of perfect, and ever more stringent, adherence to the rules. The diet is no longer about nourishing the body; it is about achieving a specific number on a scale, a number that is always just out of reach. The exercise is no longer about cultivating strength and vitality; it is about burning a precise number of calories or meeting a relentless training schedule, even in the face of injury or exhaustion.

In this state, the individual has entered into a profound flight from their own embodied reality. The discipline becomes a powerful tool of alienation, a way of severing the connection between the mind and the body's own innate wisdom. The body's signals of hunger are no longer seen as a call for nourishment, but as a sign of weakness to be suppressed. Its signals of pain are no longer a call for rest, but an obstacle to be pushed through. The body is no longer a wise and trusted partner in the project of life; it has become an unruly and untrustworthy animal to be broken, tamed, and forced into submission. This is a profound and violent form of mind-body dualism, an attempt by the ego to achieve a fantasy of pure, disembodied control.

This self-tyranny is almost always a form of existential avoidance, a displacement of a deeper and more terrifying anxiety. The person who becomes obsessed with achieving a "perfect" body is often fleeing from a profound feeling of internal imperfection or a lack of control in other, more meaningful areas of their life. The world is a messy, unpredictable, and ambiguous place. Our relationships are complex, our careers are uncertain, and our search for meaning is fraught with doubt. The project of perfecting the body, by contrast, seems to offer a world of beautiful, simple certainty. It is a world that can be reduced to quantifiable metrics: calories, pounds, miles, percentages. It is a project that seems to offer a direct and linear relationship between effort and result. In this black-and-white world of physical control, the individual finds a powerful refuge from the messy, grey-scale reality of a human life. The obsession with the body is a way of avoiding the much more difficult and demanding responsibility of cultivating a worthy and meaningful self.

The authentic and mature relationship with the disciplined body, then, is a delicate and lifelong balancing act. It is the path of the wise steward, not the tyrant. It is a discipline that is firm but flexible, one that is in a constant, compassionate dialogue with the body's own needs and limits. It is the understanding that routines are meant to be scaffolds for a life, not the life itself. This is the freedom that is found not in the conquest of the body, but in a respectful and harmonious partnership with it. It is the recognition that the ultimate goal of discipline is not to create a perfect and invulnerable body, but to cultivate a physical self that is a capable, resilient, and willing partner in the difficult, beautiful, and profoundly embodied project of living a full and meaningful human life.

Mortality and Embodied Freedom

Our entire life is a complex, often unconscious, and deeply elaborate negotiation with a single, unalterable fact: our body, the very vessel of our existence, is a temporary arrangement. It is a fragile biological machine that is, from the moment of its creation, in a slow, irreversible process of decay. This is the truth of our mortality, the ultimate and most profound expression of the body as our cage. It is the final, non-negotiable limit against which all our aspirations for permanence, all our fantasies of control, and all our projects of self-creation must eventually break. The awareness of our own inevitable death is the shadow that haunts our every moment, the silent, unspoken knowledge that underpins all our other anxieties. And for this very reason, the denial of death is the most fundamental and pervasive of all our existential evasions.

The flight from our own finitude is the master project of the human ego. It is the invisible engine that drives so much of our culture, our ambitions, and our individual psychological defenses. We see it in the grand monuments we build, the empires we forge, and the fortunes we amass—all attempts to create a legacy that will outlive our fragile flesh, a form of symbolic immortality that whispers to us that some part of us will endure. We see it in our desperate clinging to youth, our medical wars against the natural process of aging, our cultural obsession with extending the lifespan at all costs. On a deeper, more personal level, we engage in this denial every day. We live as if we have an infinite amount of time, perpetually deferring our most important choices, our most authentic desires, and our most crucial conversations to an imaginary future "someday" that we treat as a guaranteed inheritance. We repress the knowledge of our own ending because to truly face it feels like a kind of death in itself, a surrender to a terrifying and overwhelming powerlessness.

This flight, as comforting as it may be, is the ultimate act of bad faith. It is a refusal to live in the world as it actually is. And the profound and tragic irony is that in our desperate attempt to escape the reality of death, we end up escaping the reality of our own lives. By refusing to confront our ultimate limit, we are unable to live with a true sense of depth, urgency, and meaning. It is here that we find the most challenging and liberating paradox in the entire existential tradition, a truth articulated by thinkers from Heidegger to Yalom: an authentic and fully lived life is possible only through a direct, courageous, and ongoing confrontation with the reality of our own death. The acceptance of the ultimate cage is the final and most powerful key to our freedom.

To live with a conscious awareness of our own finitude—what Heidegger termed a "being-towards-death"—is not a morbid or nihilistic resignation. It is not about dwelling on the grim details of our biological end. It is, rather, a profound shift in perspective. It is the act of looking at our life through the lens of its ending, and in doing so, learning to see it with a radical and electrifying clarity. This awareness functions as the ultimate existential filter. When we hold our choices, our commitments, and our daily activities up to the light of our own mortality, the inessential and the trivial are burned away. The things that truly matter—love, connection, meaning, contribution—are thrown into sharp, brilliant relief.

The fear of what other people think, the pursuit of status for its own sake, the accumulation of possessions beyond our needs, the bitter nursing of old grievances—all of the psychic clutter that consumes so much of our time and energy is revealed for the profound waste that it is. The awareness of death is a powerful and clarifying force that calls us to a life of authenticity. It poses the ultimate and most important question: "Given that my time is finite and precious, is this truly how I wish to spend it? Is this the person I truly wish to be?" To live with this question is to be compelled, moment by moment, to make choices that are in alignment with our deepest and most authentic values.

Furthermore, the acceptance of our mortality is the only true antidote to the paralysis of procrastination and the torment of regret. The fantasy of a limitless future is what allows us to endlessly defer our lives. We tell ourselves that we will write the novel, take the trip, heal the relationship, or start the business "someday." The conscious awareness that "someday" is not guaranteed, that our allotment of days is unknown and dwindling, transforms the future from an abstract concept into a finite and precious resource. It returns us, with profound force, to the only time we ever truly have: the present moment. To know that we are dying is to be liberated, finally, to begin to truly live. It infuses our present experience with a poignancy and a richness that is unavailable to those who live in the illusion of a boundless future. The simple act of watching a sunset, of sharing a meal with a loved one, of engaging in a meaningful piece of work, is no longer a mundane event, but a unique, unrepeatable, and sacred moment in a finite and precious life.

This awareness also cultivates a profound and unexpected form of courage. The fear of death is the primal fear, the great, overarching anxiety from which most of our smaller, everyday fears derive their power. Our fear of failure, our fear of rejection, our fear of public speaking, our fear of being seen as foolish—all of these are, in a sense, small rehearsals for the ultimate fear of annihilation. To turn and face the great fear directly, to accept the reality of our own finitude, is to re-contextualize all of these smaller fears. They do not disappear, but they lose their tyrannical hold over us. In the face of our own certain death, the risk of a professional failure or a social embarrassment is revealed for the relatively small thing that it is. The acceptance of the ultimate loss can, paradoxically, make us braver and more willing to take the necessary risks of a fully engaged and meaningful life.

This, then, is the final and most profound meaning of embodied freedom. It is not the freedom of a disembodied spirit, dreaming of an eternal and unconstrained existence. It is the freedom of a mortal creature who has chosen to say a full and courageous "yes" to the totality of its condition. It is the freedom that is found in the loving and responsible stewardship of a body that we know to be both a miracle and a temporary vessel. It is the understanding that the cage of our biological reality—our unchosen genes, our vulnerability to illness, and our inevitable mortality—is not the enemy of our freedom, but the very thing that gives it its structure, its urgency, and its precious, heartbreaking beauty. To be truly free is to accept that we are dust, and then to choose, in the brief and glorious interval between our first breath and our last, to live a life that shines.

* * *

11

The Collective Dimension of Freedom

Our journey to this point has been an intensely personal one, a deep dive into the interior landscape of the individual consciousness. We have mapped the private anxieties of the chooser, the lonely burden of the author, and the silent, internal negotiations of a self at war with its own freedom. The protagonist of our story has been the solitary "I," a heroic, if often tragic, figure wrestling with the fundamental conditions of its own existence on a seemingly empty stage. This introspective focus is essential, for it is only within our own consciousness that the weight of freedom is first felt and its meaning first questioned. Yet, this intense focus on the inner life, if left unexamined, risks perpetuating a profound and distinctly modern illusion: the illusion of the isolated self.

The truth is that no human being is a blank slate dropped into a neutral void. We are not solitary monads, creating ourselves from scratch in a world of our own making. We are, from the moment of our birth, thrown into a world that is already dense with meaning, a world that is crisscrossed with the powerful, invisible currents of history, culture, language, and power. We are born into a pre-existing story, and our freedom is not the freedom of an author before a blank page, but the more complex and constrained freedom of an actor who has been handed a script and thrust onto a stage in the middle of a play that has been running for millennia. Our freedom is not absolute; it is situated. It is a freedom that is both enabled and profoundly limited by the collective context in which it is exercised.

This chapter is a necessary corrective to a purely individualistic existentialism. It is an attempt to zoom out from the microcosm of the single psyche to the macrocosm of the social and political world. It is an exploration of the ways in which our individual burden of freedom is shaped, defined, and often determined by the collective forces that surround us. To be a truly responsible and authentic individual requires us to understand that our private drama is inextricably linked to the public one. Our personal choices are never just personal; they are always, in some way, a response to, a rebellion against, or a reinforcement of the larger social and historical world we inhabit.

Our inquiry will begin by examining the invisible but powerful "social scripts" that are handed to us at birth. We will explore how our gender, our race, our class, and our culture provide us with a set of pre-written roles and expectations, a set of default assumptions about who we are and what we are responsible for. These scripts are not merely suggestions; they are powerful normative forces that shape our desires, limit our possibilities, and define the very meaning of a "successful" or "responsible" life for a person like us. To be free, in this context, is not just an internal struggle, but a social and political one, a fight to write our own lines against the powerful undertow of the pre-written play.

From these pervasive but often subtle scripts, we will turn to the most extreme and brutal of contexts: the reality of systemic oppression. What does freedom mean for a person living under a totalitarian regime, in a society structured by racial injustice, or in the dehumanizing conditions of a concentration camp? Here, the abstract, philosophical nature of freedom is burned away, leaving only its most essential and defiant core. We will turn to the profound wisdom of the psychiatrist and Holocaust survivor Viktor Frankl, whose work stands as the ultimate testament to the "last of the human freedoms"—the freedom to choose one's attitude in any given set of circumstances. We will explore how, even in the face of total external unfreedom, a space for agency and meaning-making can, and must, be found.

Next, from the individual in the cage, we will broaden our perspective to the individual in the global village. The unprecedented interconnectedness of our modern world has created a new and historically novel set of collective responsibilities. The consequences of our choices are no longer confined to our immediate communities; they ripple across the planet. We will examine how massive, complex, and existential challenges like climate change and global economic inequality challenge our very notion of individual choice. In a world where our smallest consumer decisions are implicated in vast and often destructive global systems, the concept of a purely personal responsibility becomes increasingly untenable. We are forced to confront the limits of our individual agency and the profound ethical weight of our collective existence.

Finally, we will bring our inquiry home, to the political structure that is meant to be the ultimate guarantor of our liberty: the modern democratic state. We will explore the idea of civic freedom, the understanding that a democratic society is not a machine that automatically produces liberty, but a fragile and ongoing collaborative project. It is a project that depends entirely on the active, conscious, and responsible choices of its citizens. Democracy does not just grant us the "freedom from" interference; it demands from us the "freedom to" participate, to engage in reasoned debate, to tolerate dissent, and to place the long-term health of the whole above the short-term interests of the part. This is the ultimate collective dimension of our burden, the recognition that the political freedom we cherish is not a permanent inheritance, but a daily, shared, and often difficult responsibility.

This chapter, then, is a journey outward. It is a movement from a psychology of the self to a sociology of freedom. It is an argument that a mature and authentic life requires us to hold two seemingly contradictory truths at once: that we are, as the existentialists insist, radically free and solely responsible for our own lives, and that our freedom is, at the same time, profoundly and inextricably interwoven with the lives and the choices of every other human being, past, present, and future.

The Architecture of Choice: Systemic Constraints on Freedom

Our exploration of freedom has thus far focused on the psychological weight experienced by the individual standing before their possibilities. But to fully understand the burden, we must first examine the room itself—its architecture, its size, and who holds the keys. Our freedom is never exercised in a vacuum; it is always contextual, shaped and constrained by powerful, often invisible, systemic forces. These are the social, economic, and political structures that pre-sort our options long before we become consciously aware of them.

Consider two individuals contemplating their career possibilities. One is born into a family with generational wealth, elite social networks, and a safety net that makes failure a learning experience rather than a catastrophe. The other is born into poverty, facing food insecurity, under-resourced schools, and the constant, grinding stress of economic precarity. Both possess the same existential freedom to choose their attitude and actions. But the concrete, tangible field of choices available to them is radically different. The first faces a room with a thousand doors, each leading to a well-lit corridor. The second stands in a room with a handful of doors, many of them locked, some leading to perilous paths with no safety nets.

This is the difference between existential freedom and practical agency. Systems of class, race, and gender operate as a form of existential facticity on a societal scale. They are the unchosen "givens" that heavily influence the scripts available to us. The burden of freedom for the privileged is often the "dizziness" of too many options. The burden for the marginalized is the "anguish" of having to create a meaningful life within brutally narrow constraints, often while being told by the culture that their limitations are a result of their own poor choices.

To ignore this architectural dimension is to risk promoting a philosophy of freedom that is, in effect, a luxury of the privileged. A mature understanding of the burden of freedom requires this dual vision: the unwavering focus on our inescapable responsibility for the choices we *do* have, coupled with a clear-eyed acknowledgment of the systemic injustices that distribute those choices so unevenly. Our personal responsibility includes the responsibility to see these structures clearly, and where possible, to work to dismantle them—to become architects of larger, fairer rooms for everyone.

Social Scripts of Responsibility

The existentialist vision of freedom, in its purest form, imagines a confrontation between a solitary, sovereign consciousness and a silent, unstructured universe. It is the drama of a single author before a blank page, burdened and blessed with the total responsibility of creating a story from scratch. But this powerful and necessary image is, in the end, a myth. No human being is ever a pure, abstract consciousness. We are not born into a vacuum. We are born into a world that is already thick with stories, a world that is pre-structured by a vast, intricate, and deeply ingrained network of expectations, roles, and narratives. Before we are ever aware of our own freedom, we are handed a script. This script, written by the silent, collective hand of our culture, our class, and our gender, is a detailed and powerful guide to the part we are expected to play. It dictates not only how we should act, but who we should be, and, most critically, for what and for whom we are to be responsible.

These "social scripts" are the default settings of a human life. They are the background assumptions, the taken-for-granted truths that operate so deep within our consciousness that we often mistake them for the natural and unchangeable order of the world. They function as a kind of social gravity, a powerful and invisible force that pulls our lives into a predictable orbit. To follow the script is to move along a path of least resistance, a path that is rewarded with social approval, a sense of belonging, and, most importantly, a profound relief from the dizzying anxiety of having to invent a life from scratch. To deviate from the script, on the other hand, is to push back against this gravity, an act that requires immense self-awareness, courage, and a willingness to bear the social and psychological costs of nonconformity. An authentic life is not lived in a world without scripts;

it is lived in a state of constant, conscious, and often difficult negotiation with them.

Perhaps the most powerful and pervasive of these scripts are those written for gender. From the moment of our birth, and often before, the simple declaration of "it's a boy" or "it's a girl" sets in motion a massive and complex process of social conditioning. The traditional script for masculinity, for example, is a detailed and demanding one. It casts the man in the role of the provider, the protector, and the stoic. His primary responsibility is to be strong, to be competitive, to achieve, and to suppress the so-called "softer" emotions of fear, sadness, and vulnerability. This script provides a clear, if often crushing, path to a socially recognized identity. The man who successfully follows it is rewarded with respect and status. His burden of freedom is channeled into the singular, focused project of material and professional success. But the freedom to deviate from this script is profoundly limited. The man who chooses to be a stay-at-home father, who prioritizes emotional expression over stoicism, or who is not driven by competitive ambition, often finds himself pushing against a powerful and unforgiving social current. He is, in a very real sense, less free to be a full and complex human being, his choices constrained by the fear of being seen as a failure in the fundamental role he was assigned.

The traditional script for femininity is equally powerful and equally constraining. It is a script that is overwhelmingly defined by a responsibility *for others*. The woman is cast as the nurturer, the caregiver, the emotional center of the family, the keeper of social harmony. Her primary project is relational. Her value is often measured by her ability to be desirable to a man, a good mother to her children, and a supportive nexus for her community. This script can be a source of profound relational meaning and deep connection. But it also represents a profound limitation on her freedom. The responsibility for the emotional and domestic well-being of others often comes at the direct expense of her own individual ambitions and her own project of self-actualization. The woman who chooses not to have children, who prioritizes her career over her family, or who is assertive and competitive rather than accommodating, is often judged not just as someone making an unconventional choice, but as someone who is failing at the very essence of what it means to be a woman. The script dictates that her primary responsibility is to others, and the freedom to claim a primary responsibility for herself is a recent, hard-won, and still-contested rebellion.

Beyond gender, our lives are profoundly shaped by the scripts of social and economic class. The very concept of freedom has a different texture and a different weight depending on the material circumstances into which we are born. For the person born into poverty, the script of responsibility is immediate, tangible, and relentless. It is the responsibility to survive. The choices are few, and they are almost all high-stakes. The freedom to choose a career based on passion or self-fulfillment is a distant and unimaginable luxury. The primary choice is to take whatever work is available to keep a roof overhead and food on the table. This is not a failure of imagination; it is a rational response to a world of harsh and unforgiving constraints. The burden of freedom, in this context, is not the dizziness of infinite possibility, but the crushing weight of having to make impossible choices with no margin for error.

For the person born into significant wealth, the script is different, but it is no less powerful. The burden is not the struggle for survival, but the often-unspoken responsibility of stewardship: the responsibility to maintain or grow the family fortune, to uphold a certain social status, to engage in the expected forms of philanthropy. The freedom to walk away from this inherited world, to choose a simple, anonymous life, is often just as socially and psychologically difficult as the freedom of the poor person to enter it. The script provides a ready-made identity and a clear sense of purpose, and to reject it is often to face a profound crisis of identity and a deep sense of guilt and alienation from one's own family and community. In both cases, the accident of our birth has provided us with a role, a set of expectations, and a definition of responsibility that powerfully shapes the landscape of our choices.

Finally, these scripts are embedded in the even larger context of our culture. The fundamental assumptions of Western, individualistic cultures, which have so deeply informed the existentialist tradition itself, are not universal truths. The script of the "self-made man," the heroic individual who forges their own destiny, is a uniquely Western narrative. In many collectivist cultures in Asia, Africa, and Latin America, the primary unit of identity is not the individual, but the group—the family, the community, the nation. The script of responsibility in these contexts is fundamentally different. The primary duty is not to the self, but to the whole. A major life choice, such as a career or a marriage, is not seen as a purely personal decision, but as a collective one, to be made in consultation with, and with consideration for, the well-being of the family. The Western ideal of "following your own path" can, in this context, be seen not as an act of authentic freedom, but as a profound and shameful act of selfishness.

To be an authentic human being, then, is not to somehow magically escape these powerful and pervasive scripts. That is an impossible fantasy. To be authentic is to become aware of the script we have been handed. It is to engage in the difficult and lifelong work of reading it critically, of understanding its origins and its consequences, of discerning which lines still ring true and which have become a hollow and constricting performance. It is the courageous act of taking up the pen and beginning the process of editing, of crossing out the lines that betray our deepest values and writing new ones that reflect the person we are freely and responsibly choosing to become. The ultimate collective dimension of our freedom lies in this shared struggle: the struggle to move from being unconscious actors in a play we did not write, to becoming the conscious and creative interpreters of the roles we have been given.

The Court of Public Opinion: Freedom Under the Watchful Crowd

Beyond the scripts provided by tradition, we now navigate a new and relentless social arena: the digital court of public opinion. This is not the overt oppression of a totalitarian state, but a diffuse, crowd-sourced enforcement of moral and ideological purity. The burden of freedom here is the pressure to constantly self-censor, to perform one's identity in alignment with the ever-shifting consensus of one's chosen tribe, and to live in fear of committing an unforgivable sin of speech or thought.

This environment creates a potent form of existential anxiety. Freedom of expression becomes fraught with peril, not from the state, but from the threat of social and professional annihilation. The responsibility for one's words is no longer just a personal, ethical matter; it is a public performance subject to the swift and often unappealable judgment of the crowd. This forces individuals into a state of hyper-vigilance, parsing every thought before it is uttered for potential missteps. It is a flight from the freedom to be wrong, to be clumsy, to be a work-in-progress. The collective, in its quest for a perfectly just and safe environment, can inadvertently create a culture of bad faith, where individuals disown their complex, contradictory, and evolving thoughts in favor of a safe, pre-approved persona. The burden is the immense cognitive and emotional labor of constantly managing one's public brand, and the deep loneliness of feeling that one's authentic, unpolished self is too dangerous to be seen.

Freedom in Oppressive Contexts

Our entire discussion of freedom has, until this point, operated within the relatively comfortable confines of a liberal, democratic society. The burdens we have examined—the anxiety of choice, the weight of responsibility, the pressures of conformity—are the complex and often painful problems of a people who are, by any historical or global standard, extraordinarily free. They are the discontents of the liberated. But what becomes of freedom when the very architecture of society is designed not to support it, but to systematically crush it? What is the nature of choice for an individual living under the boot of a totalitarian regime, within a system of brutal racial oppression, or in the dehumanizing conditions of a concentration camp? It is here, in these crucibles of extremity, that the philosophical concept of freedom is burned down to its absolute and irreducible essence.

Systemic oppression is more than just the imposition of external constraints. Its ultimate goal is not merely to control the body, but to annihilate the soul. It is a project of dehumanization, a relentless and methodical effort to strip individuals of the very qualities that constitute a human self. The first step is the erasure of identity. The name is replaced with a number. Personal possessions are confiscated. The head is shaved. The unique, individual story of a life is deliberately blotted out and replaced with the uniform, faceless identity of the oppressed group: the prisoner, the slave, the enemy of the state. This is a direct assault on the Sartrean premise that we create our own essence. The oppressive system seeks to impose a new, degraded essence from the outside, to transform the free, choosing, and transcendent "for-itself" into a predictable, manageable, and ultimately disposable "in-itself."

The second step in this process is the annihilation of agency. The freedom to make even the most basic life choices is systematically removed. Where to live, what to eat, when to sleep, what work to do—all are dictated by the absolute and arbitrary power of the oppressor. The connection between action and outcome is deliberately severed. Hard work is not rewarded. Compliance does not guarantee safety. The world is transformed into a chaotic and unpredictable space where the individual's choices seem to have no effect on their fate. This is a strategy designed to induce a state of profound psychological helplessness, to convince the oppressed that they are nothing more than powerless objects, leaves in a storm over which they have no control. The goal is to extinguish the very will to choose.

It is in this absolute darkness that we find the most profound and enduring testimony to the nature of human freedom, in the life and work of the Austrian psychiatrist and Holocaust survivor, Viktor Frankl. Frankl's seminal book, *Man's Search for Meaning*, is not just a memoir of his experiences in Auschwitz and other concentration camps; it is a profound work of existential psychology, a clinical report from the very edge of human endurance. Frankl entered the camps as a trained observer of the human psyche, and even in the midst of his own unimaginable suffering, he never ceased to be one. He watched as the brutalizing conditions stripped people of everything they had, and he saw how some descended into a state of animalistic survival, while others, a rare and remarkable few, seemed to find a way to maintain a core of their humanity, a kind of inner spiritual freedom that the system could not touch.

From these terrible observations, Frankl formulated the central thesis of his entire life's work. He realized that the Nazi project of dehumanization, as total and as brutal as it was, had a fundamental limit. There was one thing, and only one thing, that it could not take away from a person. In his own immortal words: "Everything can be taken from a man but one thing: the last of the human freedoms—to choose one's attitude in any given set of circumstances, to choose one's own way." This is the final, inviolable fortress of the self. The oppressors could control every aspect of a prisoner's external environment. They could control his body, his food, his work, his life, and his death. But they could not control his inner response to those conditions. Between the stimulus of the external world and the response of the individual, there is a space. And in that space lies our freedom, our power to choose.

This is not a freedom of action, but a freedom of meaning. Frankl saw that the prisoners who were most likely to survive were not necessarily the most physically robust, but those who were able to find some kind of meaning in their terrible existence, some "why" to live for. This "will to meaning," Frankl argued, is the primary and most fundamental human drive. In the camps, this search for meaning became the ultimate act of resistance against a system designed to render life completely meaningless. The choice was no longer about what to do, but about how to *be*.

Frankl identified several sources of this defiant meaning. For some, it was the meaning found in love. The intense, vivid memory of a loved one, the holding of that person's image in the mind's eye, could become a powerful anchor, a reason to endure for the hope of a future reunion. For others, it was the meaning found in a future project, a task that was waiting for them to complete. For Frankl himself, it was the manuscript for a book he had been writing, a book he was determined to one day reconstruct and publish. This future goal, this unfinished business in the world, gave his present suffering a purpose; it transformed it from a meaningless ordeal into a necessary trial on the path to a meaningful end.

But the most profound and universally available source of meaning, Frankl realized, was in the choice of how one bore one's suffering. The external suffering was a given, an inescapable part of the facticity of the camps. But the inner response was a choice. He witnessed men who, despite their own starvation, would give away their last piece of bread to a fellow prisoner. He saw individuals who offered a kind word or a gesture of comfort in the face of utter brutality. These were not grand, heroic acts of rebellion. They were small, quiet, and almost invisible choices. But in the context of the camps, they were acts of immense and radical freedom. They were the assertion of a human value—compassion, dignity, fellowship—in a world that was designed to extinguish all human values. The individual who chose to act with dignity in the face of degradation was, in that moment, proving that their inner self was still free, that their spirit was still their own. They were choosing not to become the brutalized animal that the system wanted them to be.

This profound insight is not confined to the extremity of the Holocaust. It is a universal principle that applies to all forms of systemic injustice. The enslaved person who secretly learns to read is engaging in an act of radical freedom, claiming a part of their mind that the system seeks to deny. The citizen living under a totalitarian regime who chooses to share a banned piece of literature or to engage in a quiet act of dissent is asserting their inner autonomy. The individual facing relentless systemic racism who chooses to respond not with the hatred that the system tries to instill in them, but with a proud and resilient affirmation of their own culture and humanity, is exercising the last and most powerful of the human freedoms.

In all these cases, freedom is not the absence of constraints, but the act of conscious and responsible choice *within* them. It is the recognition that while external forces may be able to control our circumstances, they can never, without our consent, control our character. This is a terrible and demanding form of freedom. It offers no promise of a happy outcome. It does not guarantee survival or an end to suffering. But it offers something else that is, in a profound sense, even more important: the possibility of a meaningful existence, even in the most meaningless of situations. It is the ultimate and most powerful testament to the fact that the human spirit, at its core, is a creature of choice, and that the ground of our freedom lies not in the world we are given, but in the world we choose, against all odds, to create within ourselves.

Responsibility in a Globalized World

The traditional landscape of human freedom and responsibility was, for most of our history, a local and tangible affair. The consequences of our choices unfolded within a limited and observable sphere: the family, the village, the immediate community. To be a responsible person was to be a good neighbor, to honor one's debts, to care for one's kin, and to act with integrity in face-to-face interactions. The feedback loop was short, direct, and clear. The farmer who neglected his fields saw his family go hungry. The artisan who cheated a customer lost their reputation in the town square. This was a world in which the weight of responsibility, while often heavy, was at least geographically and morally contained. Our individual freedom was exercised within a knowable world, and the burden of our authorship was largely confined to the local story we were writing.

That world is gone. The forces of globalization, driven by technological innovation and the relentless expansion of a globalized capitalist economy, have shattered the walls of our local realities. We now inhabit a single, vast, and intricately interconnected system, a global village where the distance between cause and effect has been stretched to a planetary scale. The simple, everyday choices of an individual living in a developed nation now send invisible, and often powerful, ripples across the entire globe, touching the lives of countless people we will never meet and shaping the future of ecosystems we will never see. This unprecedented interconnectedness has created a new and profoundly challenging form of responsibility, one that is diffuse, abstract, and almost impossible for the individual psyche to fully comprehend. It has revealed the ultimate limit of a purely individualistic conception of freedom and forced us into a difficult and often unwelcome confrontation with the immense weight of our collective existence.

The central challenge of this new reality is the problem of abstraction. Our moral and psychological hardware evolved to respond to immediate, personal, and visceral challenges. We are wired to feel a sense of responsibility for the suffering person in front of us; we are not wired to feel an equal sense of responsibility for the abstract concept of a million suffering people on the other side of the world, especially when our own connection to that suffering is indirect and mediated by a thousand complex steps. This disconnect between our local, embodied experience and our global, systemic impact is the source of a profound and pervasive form of modern bad faith. It is the quiet, often unconscious, decision to not know, to not think about, the vast and disturbing network of consequences that our comfortable lives depend upon.

Nowhere is this dilemma more stark or more existentially demanding than in the face of global climate change. The climate crisis is the ultimate and most unforgiving lesson in collective responsibility. It is a planetary-scale tragedy of the commons, a slow-motion catastrophe that is being caused not by the malevolent actions of a few identifiable villains, but by the accumulated, everyday, and seemingly insignificant choices of billions of individuals. The decision to drive a car instead of taking public transport, the choice of a diet heavy in meat and dairy, the purchase of a cheap, disposable piece of clothing—each of these is a small, almost invisible, act of individual freedom. Yet, when aggregated on a global scale, these billions of mundane choices coalesce into a force that is actively destabilizing the entire biophysical system upon which human civilization depends.

This creates a psychologically paralyzing paradox. The problem is so immense that our individual actions feel both completely responsible and utterly meaningless. On one hand, my personal carbon footprint is an undeniable part of the problem. On the other hand, my individual choice to recycle, to eat less meat, or to buy an electric car feels like throwing a thimble of water on a raging forest fire. The scale of the problem so completely dwarfs the scale of my individual agency that the most common responses are a descent into either apathetic despair or a kind of performative, virtue-signaling consumption that has little real-world impact. We are trapped in a situation where we are all, in some small way, the authors of a global catastrophe, yet none of us, acting alone, has the power to write a different ending.

This reveals the profound limits of a purely individualistic approach to freedom. The problem of climate change cannot be solved by individual consumer choices alone. It is a systemic problem that requires a systemic solution: a coordinated, collective, and political response on a global scale. This forces a radical redefinition of what it means to be a responsible individual. In this new context, our responsibility is not just to manage our own personal behavior; it is to exercise our civic and political freedom to demand and support the large-scale systemic changes that are necessary. Our responsibility is to be not just a conscious consumer, but an engaged citizen. This is a far more demanding and difficult form of freedom. It requires us to move beyond the private sphere of our own lives and to take up the difficult, often frustrating, and ambiguous work of collective action. The flight from this responsibility is the cynical retreat into the belief that "it's all hopeless" or the self-righteous belief that "I am doing my part," both of which are forms of abdication from the larger, more difficult, and more essential collective task.

This same dynamic of diffuse responsibility and hidden consequence is at the heart of global economic inequality. The freedom we enjoy as consumers in the developed world—the freedom to buy an astonishing variety of products at incredibly low prices—is directly and inextricably linked to the unfreedom of millions of laborers in the developing world. The cheap t-shirt, the affordable smartphone, the readily available coffee—

the production of these goods is often dependent on a global supply chain that exploits low-wage workers, tolerates unsafe working conditions, and engages in environmentally destructive practices. Our economic liberty is subsidized by the economic constraints of others.

To become fully conscious of this reality is to live in a state of profound ethical discomfort. It is to recognize our own complicity in a vast, impersonal system of harm. The most common response to this discomfort is denial and avoidance. We simply choose not to think about the invisible hands that stitched our clothes or mined the rare earth minerals in our phones. We compartmentalize our lives, separating our identity as a "good person" who values justice and compassion from our identity as a consumer who values a good bargain. This is a profound act of bad faith, a necessary lie we tell ourselves in order to navigate the moral contradictions of our daily lives.

Here again, the limits of individual choice become painfully clear. While the choice to be a "conscious consumer"—to buy fair-trade products, to boycott unethical companies—is a meaningful and important act, it cannot, on its own, solve the problem. The system of global capitalism is too vast, too powerful, and too complex to be reformed by individual purchasing decisions alone. A truly responsible engagement with this problem requires, once again, a shift from a purely personal to a collective and political framework. It requires us to support policies that enforce international labor standards, to advocate for fair trade laws, and to challenge the logic of a system that prioritizes corporate profit above human dignity and ecological sustainability.

The globalized world has, in a sense, forced a kind of existential maturation upon us. The simple, adolescent fantasy of a purely individualistic freedom—the freedom to do what I want, as long as it doesn't directly and visibly harm another person—has been rendered obsolete by the very structure of our interconnected world. We have been thrust into a new and demanding form of adulthood, one in which we must learn to be responsible for the invisible, the indirect, and the systemic consequences of our actions. This is a heavy, uncomfortable, and deeply anxiety-provoking burden. It requires us to live with the knowledge of our own complicity, to tolerate the frustration of our own limited agency, and yet to still find the courage to act. It is the understanding that to be free in the 21st century is to be responsible not just for the small garden of our own life, but for our small but undeniable part in the shared and fragile fate of the entire world.

Civic Freedom

The modern democratic state is, in theory, the ultimate political achievement of the existential project. It is a system of governance founded on the radical premise of individual sovereignty, on the belief that human beings are not subjects to be ruled, but free and rational agents who are capable of, and have a right to, self-determination. The great documents of democratic freedom—the constitutions, the declarations of rights, the bills of liberty—are, in essence, a social contract designed to protect the individual from the arbitrary power of the state. They guarantee the "freedom *from*": freedom from tyranny, from censorship, from unjust imprisonment, from the imposition of a state-mandated creed. This negative liberty, the creation of a protected sphere of individual autonomy, is a monumental and historically precious achievement. It is the necessary ground upon which an authentic life can be built.

Yet, this is only half of the equation. To view democracy as a machine that automatically produces and dispenses freedom is to fall into a profound and dangerous state of political passivity. A democratic society is not a finished product to be consumed; it is a fragile, demanding, and perpetually unfinished project. The freedoms it guarantees are not self-sustaining. Their survival depends entirely on the active, conscious, and responsible exercise of a second, and far more demanding, kind of liberty: the "freedom *to*." This is civic freedom. It is the freedom to participate, to engage, to take responsibility not just for our own private lives, but for the health and integrity of the collective whole. If the state is responsible for protecting our right to be free, we, the citizens, are responsible for creating a culture in which that freedom can actually flourish. The great and often tragic irony of modern democracy is that we have become so focused on the freedoms we are owed that we have forgotten the responsibilities we must actively embrace.

The flight from this civic responsibility is one of the most pervasive and consequential forms of existential avoidance in our time. The burden of being an engaged citizen in a complex, pluralistic, and often frustrating modern democracy is immense. It requires us to tolerate ambiguity, to engage with viewpoints we find disagreeable, to accept the necessity of slow, incremental compromise, and to live with the constant, low-grade anxiety of knowing that the future of our shared world is uncertain and that our own small contribution feels, at times, hopelessly insignificant. Faced with this demanding reality, the impulse to retreat is powerful. This retreat takes two primary, and seemingly opposite, forms, both of which are a profound flight from the burdens of an authentic civic life.

The first and most common escape is the flight into apathy and cynicism. This is the posture of the individual who stands apart from the political process, viewing it with a kind of weary, ironic detachment. Their narrative is a familiar one: "All politicians are corrupt. The system is rigged. Both sides are the same. My vote doesn't matter." This cynical posture is not, as it often pretends to be, a sign of a sophisticated and superior intellectual understanding. It is a powerful and highly effective psychological defense mechanism. It is an act of bad faith designed to absolve the self of the difficult and often disappointing work of responsible engagement. By declaring the entire project of democracy to be a meaningless sham, the cynic is able to protect themselves from the pain of caring, from the frustration of a political loss, and from the anxiety of having to make a difficult and imperfect choice.

The declaration that "my choice doesn't matter" is a comforting lie that masks a deeper and more terrifying truth: "I am afraid of the responsibility of my choice mattering." To truly engage, to invest one's hopes and efforts in a political cause or a candidate, is to become vulnerable to disappointment. It is to accept our own small but real complicity in the messy, imperfect, and often morally compromised business of governing. Cynicism is a fortress built to protect the self from this vulnerability. The cynic maintains a sense of pristine, detached innocence by refusing to ever get their hands dirty. They are the permanent spectator in the stands, shouting critiques at the players on the field, forever shielded from the risk and the responsibility of making a play themselves. It is a profound abdication of agency, a flight from freedom into the safe but sterile prison of a self that has chosen to matter to no one.

The second, and increasingly prevalent, escape is the flight into the comforting certainty of partisan fundamentalism. If the cynic flees from the burden of engagement by declaring it all meaningless, the partisan fundamentalist flees from the burden of independent thought by surrendering their consciousness to a tribe. This is Fromm's automaton conformity on a massive political scale. The individual ceases to be a sovereign, critical thinker and becomes, instead, an echo chamber for a pre-packaged ideology. The complex, grey-scale reality of the political world is reduced to a simple, black-and-white morality play, a Manichean struggle between the forces of pure good (our side) and the forces of pure evil (the other side).

This provides an immense psychological relief. The anxiety of ambiguity is replaced by the satisfying thrill of righteous certainty. The difficult and lonely work of researching complex issues, of weighing competing values, and of forming one's own nuanced opinions is replaced by the far simpler and more socially rewarding task of adopting the correct talking points of one's chosen group. The political "other" is no longer seen as a fellow citizen with a different but equally sincere vision for the country; they are dehumanized, projected upon, and transformed into a monstrous caricature, an enemy to be defeated rather than a partner to be engaged with. This is the ultimate flight from the responsibilities of a pluralistic society. It is a retreat from the demanding public square of reasoned debate into the warm, comforting, and intellectually deadening echo chamber of the tribe. It is an escape from the freedom of being an individual in exchange for the security of being a soldier.

An authentic civic freedom requires a courageous and sustained resistance to both of these seductive escapes. It is the difficult middle path between the cynicism that cares about nothing and the fundamentalism that is certain of everything. To be a responsible citizen is to embrace the ambiguity, the frustration, and the profound uncertainty of the democratic project. It is the willingness to remain engaged even in the face of disappointment. It is the intellectual and moral courage to question the dogmas of one's own tribe and to listen with a measure of generosity to the perspectives of the other. It is the understanding that compromise is not a sign of moral weakness, but the essential and life-giving lubricant of a functioning pluralistic society.

This is a profoundly demanding form of adult responsibility. It requires us to hold our own convictions with passion, but also with a measure of humility, an awareness that we do not have a monopoly on the truth. It requires us to place the long-term health of the democratic process—our shared commitment to the rule of law, to free and fair elections, to the peaceful transfer of power—above the short-term, adrenaline-fueled victory of our own side. The ultimate test of our commitment to freedom is not how we treat our friends, but how we treat our opponents. Democracy, in the end, is the political manifestation of a society's collective psychological maturity. Its survival depends not on the perfection of its leaders, but on the capacity of its citizens to bear the immense and often uncomfortable burdens of their own freedom.

* * *

12

Cultivating Existential Strength

Throughout this book, we have undertaken a demanding journey. We have stared into the abyss of our own possibility, felt the weight of absolute responsibility, and mapped the sophisticated labyrinths we construct to hide from ourselves. We have seen how modern life amplifies these burdens with endless choice and digital performance. If the diagnosis feels unsparing, it is because the reality of our freedom is unsparing. But a diagnosis, no matter how accurate, is not an endpoint. It is a beginning. The question that now remains is the most important one: Having understood the burden, how do we develop the strength to carry it? How do we move from a life of avoidance to a life of authentic authorship?

This chapter is an answer to that question. It is not a self-help manual promising seven easy steps to a life without anxiety. Such a promise would be a betrayal of everything we have explored. Anxiety is not the enemy to be eliminated; it is the signal of our freedom, the price of our consciousness. The goal, therefore, is not to lighten the load, but to build the psychological and spiritual muscle required to bear it with purpose, clarity, and even a measure of grace. This is the project of cultivating existential strength.

The path forward is not one of finding answers, but of practicing a way of being. It is built on a series of conscious, repeated commitments—a kind of existential fitness regimen for the soul. We will explore the core practices that allow a human being to stand firm in their freedom, to make choices with conviction, and to find a meaning that is not given, but built.

The Practice of Mindful Choice

The grand, life-altering decisions—the career, the partner, the move—can be so paralyzing because they feel like monumental, isolated events. We wait for clarity that never comes, for a guarantee that will never arrive. The art of choosing, however, is not mastered in these rare, high-stakes moments. It is cultivated through a thousand small, conscious acts. Existential strength is built like physical strength: through daily reps.

This begins with the practice of **mindful choice**. It is the simple, radical act of bringing conscious awareness to the micro-choices that constitute our day. What time will I wake up? What will I eat for breakfast? Will I react to that provoking email with defensiveness or with curiosity? In these seemingly insignificant moments, we are not just choosing an action; we are choosing the person we are becoming. Each conscious choice is a repetition that strengthens the neural pathway of agency. It is a vote for the belief that our actions matter.

The person who mindfully chooses to go for a walk instead of scrolling through their phone, or to respond with patience instead of irritation, is not just improving their afternoon. They are performing a tiny act of existential resistance. They are asserting, "In this moment, I am the author of my life." This daily practice builds the "choice muscle," so that when the larger, more daunting decisions arrive, we approach them not with a flabby, atrophied will, but with a strength forged in the fires of ordinary life.

The Discipline of Commitment

If mindful choice is the repetition that builds strength, then commitment is the heavy weight we must eventually learn to lift. We have seen how the fear of closing doors can lead to a life of perpetual hesitation. The antidote is to reframe commitment not as a prison, but as the most profound and creative act of freedom.

Commitment is the decision to pour our finite time and energy into a single, finite path. It is the courageous annihilation of possibility in the service of actuality. To commit to a craft, a relationship, or a cause is to say, "This, out of all the things I could do, is what I will *do*. This person, out of all the people I could love, is who I will *love*." Commitment is what transforms a vague intention into a tangible life. It is the sculptor's chisel that turns the block of marble (our facticity) into a statue (our lived essence).

The discipline of commitment requires embracing the "good enough." It means accepting that no partner is perfect, no career is without its drudgery, and no creative project will ever fully match the vision in our head. The perfectionist, like the procrastinator, is terrified of commitment because it means the death of their ideal. The existentially strong individual understands that a life lived is always more beautiful than a life imagined. They choose a path, and through the very act of walking it, they make it the right path.

The Courage of Imperfection

This leads directly to the next practice: the courage to be imperfect. Our flight from freedom is often a flight from the vulnerability of being seen to fail, to be judged, to be inadequate. To live freely is to accept that we are a work in progress, and always will be.

This courage is rooted in what the psychologist Carl Rogers called "unconditional positive self-regard," and what we might call, in existential terms, **self-grace**. It is the internal stance of accepting ourselves as the flawed, struggling, and magnificent authors of our own lives, without requiring external validation to grant us permission to exist. It is the willingness to make the clumsy brushstroke, to write the bad first draft, to have the difficult conversation and risk saying the wrong thing.

When we release the demand for a flawless performance, we disarm the primary weapon of the inner critic that fuels procrastination and avoidance. We give ourselves permission to be beginners, to learn, and to grow. This courage allows us to stand by our choices, not because they were perfect, but because they were ours, made with the best understanding we had at the time. It is the foundation upon which resilience is built.

Dialogical Relationships: The Mirrors of Freedom

We cannot do this work in a vacuum. Existential strength is not cultivated in solitude but in relationship. However, not all relationships are created equal. We must seek out and nurture what we can call **dialogical relationships**.

A dialogical relationship is one in which two free individuals meet as subjects, not objects. It is a relationship where both parties are committed to seeing and being seen, to challenging and being challenged. These are the people who reflect our own freedom back to us. They do not collude with our stories of victimhood; they gently ask, "And what is your part in this?" They do not offer easy answers; they help us tolerate the difficult questions. They are the living antidote to the isolation that drives us toward the crowd.

In a world of curated identities, a dialogical relationship is a space of radical honesty. It is where we can take off the armor of our personal brand and reveal the confused, anxious, and authentic human being underneath. These relationships are the gymnasiums where we practice owning our responsibility, where our bad faith is lovingly exposed, and where our courage is bolstered by the presence of another who is engaged in the same struggle.

Finding Structures of Support, Not Submission

Finally, we must learn to distinguish between structures that support our freedom and those that demand our submission. The human psyche needs structure; the "dizziness" of pure freedom is unbearable. The key is to choose our structures consciously, rather than having them imposed upon us.

A **structure of support** is a self-chosen framework that channels our freedom in a productive direction. A daily routine, a meditation practice, a professional code of ethics, a commitment to a community—these are structures we erect to give our freedom form and direction. They are like the banks of a river, which do not stop the flow but give it power and purpose. We can evaluate them, question them, and change them as we grow.

A **structure of submission**, in contrast, is a rigid, external system that demands the surrender of our critical judgment. A dogmatic ideology, a cult, an abusive relationship, or even a corporate culture that demands total conformity—these systems offer certainty at the cost of our autonomy. They promise to carry the burden for us, but the price is our very self.

The existentially strong individual consciously builds and inhabits structures of support while vigilantly resisting the seductive call of structures of submission. They understand that the goal is not to live without a map, but to be the cartographer of their own journey.

The Goal: A Life Chosen

The cultivation of existential strength is a lifelong practice. There is no final state of achievement, no point at which the burden of freedom feels light. There are only days when we stand tall beneath the weight, and days when we stumble. The goal is not to become a different kind of being, free from anxiety and doubt. The goal is to become more fully what we already are: conscious, responsible, and free.

It is to move from a life that happens *to* us to a life that is chosen *by* us. It is to look at the canvas of our existence, with all its mistakes and imperfections, and to see it not as a botched job, but as our unique, unrepeatable, and authentic work of art. The burden is heavy, but it is the weight that gives our life its substance, its dignity, and its meaning. This is the courage to choose. This is the strength to be free.

* * *

V

Part Five: The Path Forward

Having explored the weight of freedom, how do we learn to carry it? This final part offers a path forward. We move from analysis to action: confronting the absurd with courage, forging an ethics of responsibility, and integrating these insights into a daily practice of mature, meaningful living.

13

Living with the Absurd

Our journey to this point has been an act of relentless excavation, a digging down through the comfortable topsoil of our everyday assumptions to the hard, unyielding bedrock of our existential condition. We have stripped away the illusion of a pre-written script for our lives, the fantasy of a world that offers guarantees, and the comforting but ultimately self-deceiving narratives we use to flee from our own authorship. Having performed this difficult work, we are left standing in a stark and silent landscape. We have arrived at the final, irreducible truth of our situation: we are conscious, freedom-bearing creatures who are possessed by an unquenchable thirst for meaning, for reason, and for a sense of ultimate purpose, and we have been thrown into a universe that provides none. It is a universe that is magnificent, terrible, beautiful, and chaotic, but on the great questions of our lives, it remains profoundly and stubbornly silent.

This is the ultimate groundlessness. This is the final and most challenging burden of all. And it is in the direct, unblinking confrontation with this reality that we find the true beginning of a mature and authentic human life. To live without the comforting canopy of a divinely ordained purpose or a guaranteed historical destiny is to live in a state that the great 20th-century French-Algerian philosopher and writer Albert Camus defined as the absurd. The absurd, in this specific philosophical sense, is not the world itself, nor is it the human being. It is not a quality of things, but a relationship, or more accurately, a divorce. It is the irreparable and tragic clash between our passionate, human call for meaning and the world's unreasonable, silent refusal to answer. It is the lover calling out to the beloved in the dark and receiving no reply. The absurdity of our condition lies not in the fact that our lives are meaningless, but in the fact that we are creatures who cannot help but seek meaning in a world that offers none.

The confrontation with this truth is the final and most profound crisis of the human spirit. It is the moment when all our defenses have failed, when all our flights from freedom have led us back to this same stark, empty room. And in this room, Camus argues, we are faced with a fundamental choice, the most important philosophical question of all: faced with a meaningless and indifferent universe, should we, or should we not, commit suicide? For Camus, this is not just a question of physical self-destruction. It is a question of our fundamental response to a life without guarantees. He outlines three primary paths that branch out from this critical juncture.

The first is the path of physical suicide. This is the ultimate act of escape, the decision that a life without inherent meaning is a life that is not worth living. It is a way of declaring that if the game is meaningless, then the only rational response is to refuse to play. Camus, a profound lover of the physical, sensuous world, ultimately rejects this path. He sees it as a form of surrender, a failure to fully exhaust the possibilities of the human condition.

The second path, and a far more common one, is what he calls "philosophical suicide." This is the great leap of faith. It is the act of fleeing from the anxiety of the absurd by dogmatically embracing a pre-packaged system of meaning that promises to resolve the contradiction. This can be a traditional religion that posits a divine plan, a totalizing political ideology that promises a future utopia, or any other closed system of thought that offers absolute certainty and a ready-made purpose. For Camus, this is also a form of evasion. It is an act of bad faith, a refusal to live with the difficult truth of our condition. The person who makes this leap has not solved the problem of the absurd; they have simply chosen to stop looking at it. They have traded the difficult freedom of a life of constant questioning for the comforting security of a life of unshakeable answers.

This leaves only the third path, the most difficult, the most courageous, and, for Camus, the only one that is truly worthy of our humanity. It is the path of rebellion, of lucidly and defiantly living *with* the absurd, of keeping the contradiction alive. It is the path of the individual who refuses both the escape of suicide and the illusion of a transcendent meaning. This is the path of the absurd hero. This hero is a person who looks the silent, meaningless universe squarely in the eye, acknowledges its indifference, and yet, out of a sheer, passionate, and rebellious love for their own existence, chooses to live a life of meaning anyway. The absurd, in this view, is not a conclusion to be despaired over, but a starting point to be embraced.

This chapter is an exploration of this third path. It is a manual for living a heroic life in a world that has no inherent interest in heroes. We will begin by delving into Camus's ultimate metaphor for this heroic struggle: the myth of Sisyphus, the tragic figure whom Camus transforms into the ultimate symbol of a meaningful and even happy human perseverance. We will then examine the common psychological responses to the dawning awareness of the absurd, the maladaptive and life-denying paths of nihilism, cynicism, and escapism, which represent a failure to rise to the challenge.

From there, we will turn to the creative and defiant responses that are the hallmarks of the absurd hero. We will explore how creativity, humor, and a spirit of rebellion can be transformed into powerful tools for forging a meaningful life in the very teeth of a meaningless world. Finally, we will see how the acceptance of the absurd, far from being a call to despair, is in fact the ultimate call to responsibility. The understanding that there is no external, pre-ordained meaning to our lives does not absolve us of our burdens; it makes them entirely and magnificently our own. If the universe has no purpose for us, then we are finally and completely free to create our own. This is the final and most challenging stage of our journey: the transition from understanding the burden of our freedom to learning how to transform that very burden into a source of profound, defiant, and deeply human joy.

Camus and the Absurd Hero

To arrive at a clear-eyed and unshakeable awareness of the absurd is to stand on the edge of a great and silent abyss. It is to finally and fully understand that the universe is not a partner in our search for meaning, that it offers no answers, no justifications, and no ultimate purpose for our brief and passionate existence. This realization is the endpoint of a certain kind of innocence, and it presents us with a profound and dangerous temptation: the temptation of despair. If there is no inherent meaning to the struggle of life, if our labors are ultimately destined to be erased by the indifferent passage of time, then why struggle at all? Why not surrender to the void, either through the finality of a physical death or the living death of a cynical and hollowed-out life? It is in his direct, unflinching, and ultimately life-affirming response to this very question that Albert Camus offers us not a solution to the absurd, but a way to live with it, and to do so with a spirit of rebellion, freedom, and even a kind of hard-won joy.

For Camus, the individual who truly awakens to the absurd condition becomes a stranger in their own life. The familiar, automatic routines of the everyday world—the morning commute, the office politics, the small ambitions—are suddenly stripped of their taken-for-granted significance. They are revealed for what they are: a series of gestures in a play without a final act, a set of habits that we perform against a backdrop of ultimate meaninglessness. This feeling of alienation, of being a tourist in one's own existence, is the starting point. The great error, Camus insists, is to seek an escape from this state. The path of integrity is to find a way to live within it, to hold the tension between our passionate demand for meaning and the world's silence without flinching. This is the path of the absurd hero, and its ultimate and most powerful symbol is a figure drawn from the depths of Greek mythology: Sisyphus.

The myth itself is a portrait of ultimate futility. Sisyphus, a clever king who dared to defy the gods and even managed to chain Death for a time, is given the most terrible of punishments for his hubris. He is condemned for all eternity to a meaningless and hopeless labor. His task is to push a great boulder up the side of a mountain. He strains with all his might, his face pressed against the stone, his muscles bunched, his body covered in sweat and dust. With a final, monumental effort, he reaches the summit. But at the very instant he is about to push it over the other side, the rock, by its own weight, thunders back down into the valley. And Sisyphus must watch it go, and then he must turn, and walk back down the empty slope to begin his task anew. There is no hope of success. There is no possibility of an end. There is only the endless, repetitive, and utterly pointless cycle of his labor.

It is difficult to imagine a more perfect metaphor for a meaningless life. Sisyphus is the ultimate symbol of the powerless laborer, his existence reduced to a single, futile task that achieves nothing. In this, he is the tragic hero of a life without purpose. But it is here, in the very heart of this tragedy, that Camus performs a stunning act of philosophical reversal. He asks us to focus our attention not on the moment of straining and pushing, but on the quiet, often overlooked interval that comes after: the moment when Sisyphus, having watched the rock fall, turns and begins his slow descent back down the mountain. It is in this hour, Camus writes, that Sisyphus is truly conscious. He is no longer one with his rock; he is separate from it, looking down upon the futility of his own fate. He is in a state of lucid, unblinking awareness. He knows the full extent of his wretched condition. He has no illusions. He has no hope. And it is precisely this lucidity, this clear-sighted consciousness, that makes him superior to his fate. The rock is a brute, unthinking object. Sisyphus is a man who knows.

In this moment of conscious descent, Sisyphus is faced with the same choice that confronts every one of us who awakens to the absurd. He can descend in sorrow, consumed by despair and the memory of a better life. Or he can descend with a kind of scorn. This scorn, for Camus, is the essence of the absurd rebellion. It is the defiant refusal to be crushed by a fate that one cannot change. Sisyphus cannot stop the rock from rolling down. He cannot escape his punishment. But he can refuse to weep. He can refuse to grant the gods the satisfaction of his despair. This is the nature of his freedom. It is not the freedom to change his circumstances, but the freedom to choose his relationship to those circumstances. By consciously and willingly embracing his fate, he transforms it. The punishment that was imposed upon him by the gods becomes his own chosen life. The rock is no longer just a tool of his torment; it becomes, in Camus's famous phrase, "his thing."

It is from this defiant act of ownership that Camus makes his final, audacious claim: "The struggle itself toward the heights is enough to fill a man's heart. One must imagine Sisyphus happy." This is not the simple, shallow happiness of pleasure or hope. It is a sterner, more profound, and more durable kind of joy. It is the happiness that comes from a full and passionate engagement with the present reality, however difficult it may be. Sisyphus's happiness is found in the straining of his muscles, in the feel of the rock against his cheek, in the view of the valley from the mountaintop. His world is reduced to this single, repetitive task, and he has chosen to fill that task with the full measure of his being. He has been liberated from the two great thieves of present joy: hope for a different future, and regret for a different past. He exists entirely in the concrete reality of his struggle.

We are all Sisyphus. Our own "boulders" may be less dramatic, but they are no less relentless. It is the repetitive work of an unfulfilling job, the daily, often thankless, labor of raising a family, the quiet struggle of maintaining a relationship, the slow, patient work of honing a craft. These are the tasks that fill our days, the boulders we are compelled to push up our own hills. And like Sisyphus, we are often tempted by the thought of their ultimate futility. What is the cosmic significance of this spreadsheet, this load of laundry, this difficult conversation? The universe offers no answer. The absurd hero is the person who, like Sisyphus, finds the courage to create their own. The meaning is not in the spreadsheet; the meaning is in the integrity and the focus with which we complete it. The meaning is not in the guarantee that our children will be happy; it is in the unconditional love with which we raise them. The meaning is not in the promise of a perfect relationship; it is in the courageous, moment-to-moment choice to show up for another imperfect human being.

The ultimate lesson of Sisyphus is that meaning is not a treasure to be discovered, but a creation to be forged. It is forged in the heart of our struggle, in our passionate and defiant rebellion against a silent universe. The absurd hero is the one who understands that there are no ultimate victories and no final answers, and who chooses to love the struggle itself. It is the understanding that to have a life to live, a boulder to push, and the consciousness to know it, is a strange, tragic, and magnificent fate. And that, in the end, is enough.

Psychological Responses to the Absurd

The confrontation with the absurd is a moment of profound existential crisis, a fork in the road of the human spirit. While the path of the absurd hero, as charted by Camus, is a path of courageous and defiant engagement, it is by no means the most common one. The weight of a meaningless universe is immense, and the psychological gravity of our own anxiety pulls us powerfully toward less demanding, less courageous, and ultimately less authentic responses. These are the maladaptive strategies, the failed solutions to the problem of our existence, the ways in which we choose not to rise to the heroic challenge of our own freedom. These are the dead-end roads of nihilism, cynicism, and escapism.

The first and most philosophically potent of these responses is nihilism. The nihilist is the person who looks into the silent, indifferent abyss of the universe, correctly perceives the absence of any inherent, pre-ordained meaning, and draws what seems to be the most logical conclusion: that if there is no ultimate purpose, then nothing matters. All values are baseless, all actions are ultimately equivalent, and all human striving is a ridiculous and pathetic charade. The nihilist is the prodigal son of the Enlightenment, the one who has taken the death of God to its most extreme and desolate conclusion. If there is no ultimate judge, then there is no ultimate law, and everything is, in a profound and terrifying sense, permitted.

While it often presents itself as a sophisticated and intellectually rigorous position, nihilism is, at its core, a profound psychological defense. It is a flight from the unbearable pain of a wounded love. The nihilist is not a person who never cared about meaning; they are a person who cared so much that the discovery of its absence felt like a catastrophic and personal betrayal. Their declaration that "nothing matters" is not a statement of fact, but a cry of pain, the bitter lament of a jilted lover. It is an act of preemptive emotional surrender. To care about something in a meaningless world is to open oneself up to the possibility of profound disappointment, to risk investing one's heart in a project that is doomed to be forgotten. The nihilist refuses this vulnerability. Their global devaluation of all things is a scorched-earth policy for the soul, a way of ensuring that there is nothing left to lose, and therefore, nothing left to be hurt by.

This is a profound abdication of the central responsibility of a free being: the responsibility of creating value. The nihilist sees the blank canvas of existence and, instead of taking up the difficult and terrifying task of painting, simply declares that the very concept of art is a ridiculous fraud and sets the canvas on fire. This act of destruction provides a fleeting and intoxicating sense of power, the same dark thrill that Fromm identified in his mechanism of destructiveness. But it is the power of a black hole, a power that consumes everything, including the self. To live as a nihilist is to inhabit a cold, grey, and ultimately lifeless world of one's own making, a world stripped of all passion, all commitment, and all possibility of joy. It is the ultimate intellectual suicide, a choice to die of thirst while refusing to acknowledge that it is our own job to dig the well.

A more common, and more socially acceptable, variant of this posture is cynicism. The cynic is a nihilist who has chosen irony as their primary weapon. While the true nihilist may be consumed by a kind of tragic despair, the cynic finds a perch of cool, detached superiority. They stand on the sidelines of life, observing the earnest and often clumsy strivings of others with a world-weary and condescending smirk. The politician who speaks of public service, the artist who speaks of beauty, the activist who speaks of justice, the couple who speaks of enduring love—all are, in the eyes of the cynic, either naive fools or manipulative hypocrites. The cynic is the master of deconstruction, an expert at finding the hidden, self-serving motive behind every seemingly noble act.

This posture, like nihilism, is a sophisticated defense mechanism against the risk of commitment and the potential for disappointment. The cynic is a person who is terrified of being a fool. To genuinely invest in a cause, a person, or a set of values is to risk being wrong, to risk being betrayed, to risk appearing naive. The cynic cleverly avoids this risk by pre-emptively declaring the entire game to be rigged. Their cynicism is a fortress of non-engagement, a way to maintain a sense of intellectual and moral superiority without ever having to put their own beliefs on the line. As we have seen, it is the ultimate flight from civic and personal responsibility. It is the act of a permanent spectator who has found a way to feel powerful simply by booing the players on the field.

The psychological payoff of cynicism is the preservation of a fragile and sterile form of innocence. By never truly committing to anything, the cynic can never truly be wrong. By never truly loving anything, they can never truly be heartbroken. But this safety is purchased at the cost of a full and vibrant life. It is a self-imposed exile from the messy, complicated, and often beautiful drama of human engagement. It is the choice to live in the footnotes of a story rather than in the story itself, a life of clever commentary that is ultimately empty of its own content.

The third, and by far the most pervasive, of these maladaptive responses is not a philosophical posture, but a behavioral strategy: escapism. The escapist is the person who does not consciously deny meaning or ironically detach from it, but who simply drowns out the silence of the universe with a constant and unrelenting stream of noise. If the absurd is the confrontation with a world that fails to answer our deepest questions, escapism is the attempt to never ask the questions in the first place. It is a flight from the demanding and often uncomfortable world of our own inner lives into the easy, frictionless, and endlessly distracting world of external stimulation.

In our modern, technologically saturated world, the tools for this escape are more powerful, more accessible, and more addictive than ever before. We have, at our fingertips, a near-infinite supply of existential anesthetic. It is the endless scroll of a social media feed, a carefully engineered stream of novelty and light outrage that keeps our minds perpetually occupied and superficially engaged. It is the binge-watch of a television series, a total immersion in a fictional world that allows us, for hours at a time, to forget the complex and often unresolved narrative of our own. It is the constant busyness of a life filled with endless tasks, trivial errands, and a workaholism that masquerades as ambition. The goal of all these activities is the same: to fill every empty space, to eliminate every moment of quiet contemplation in which the unsettling questions of our existence might have a chance to surface.

This is a life lived in a state of chronic, self-imposed distraction. The escapist is not running toward something; they are running away from the profound discomfort of being alone with their own consciousness. The silence is terrifying because it is in the silence that we are forced to confront our own freedom, our own responsibility, and our own mortality. The constant stream of entertainment, of information, of work, is a shield against this confrontation. It is a way of keeping the mind so thoroughly occupied with the trivial that it never has the chance to grapple with the essential.

These three paths—nihilism, cynicism, and escapism—are the great refusals. They are the ways in which we say "no" to the difficult and heroic challenge posed by the absurd. The nihilist says no by declaring the game meaningless. The cynic says no by refusing to play. The escapist says no by pretending the game does not exist. While they appear different, they are all rooted in the same fundamental failure of courage. They are all a retreat from the demanding but ultimately life-giving tension of a conscious being in an unconscious universe. They are the choice for a kind of living death, a state of being that is safe from the anxieties of a fully engaged life, but is also, by the same token, devoid of its potential for passion, for connection, and for a deep, defiant, and self-created meaning.

Creative and Defiant Responses

To awaken to the absurd is to find oneself in a state of profound existential tension. The maladaptive responses we have just examined—nihilism, cynicism, and escapism—are all, in their own way, attempts to collapse this tension, to resolve the unbearable contradiction between our need for meaning and the universe's silence by declaring the entire project a failure. They are a surrender. But the path of the absurd hero, the path of authentic engagement, requires a different and far more courageous response. It is the choice not to resolve the tension, but to live within it, to make it the very source of one's energy and one's art. This is a path not of surrender, but of rebellion. The absurd hero does not find meaning; they defiantly create it, using the very tools that are unique to a conscious and free existence: their capacity for rebellion, their drive to create, and their ability to laugh in the face of the void.

The foundational posture of the absurd life is one of metaphysical rebellion. This is not a political rebellion against a specific regime, but a deeper, more fundamental rebellion against the human condition itself. It is the sustained and conscious act of saying "no." It is a refusal to accept the verdict of a silent and meaningless universe. It is a refusal of despair. This rebellion is not expressed through angry protest or violent upheaval; it is expressed through the quiet but radical act of living with passion, with intensity, and with a profound sense of commitment in a world that provides no ultimate justification for any of these things. The absurd rebel is the person who chooses to love with their whole heart, knowing that all love ends in loss. They are the person who commits to a cause of justice, knowing that a perfect and just world will never be achieved. They are the person who seeks knowledge, knowing that the ultimate questions will never be answered.

This is the essence of Sisyphus's scorn. His rebellion is not in trying to stop the rock from rolling down the hill, which is an impossibility. His rebellion is in his choice to walk back down the hill with a clear-eyed awareness of his fate and to push the rock again, not out of a deluded hope for a different outcome, but out of a defiant commitment to the struggle itself. To live in a state of rebellion is to find our dignity not in our victories, but in the integrity of our struggle. It is to care, passionately and without reservation, about the projects and the people of this one, finite life, precisely *because* the universe does not. Our passionate engagement becomes a form of protest, a magnificent and deeply human gesture of defiance against the cold, cosmic silence.

This spirit of rebellion finds its most powerful and concrete expression in the act of creativity. If the universe is a chaotic, formless, and meaningless expanse, then the act of creating something—a piece of art, a garden, a business, a family—is the ultimate act of human rebellion. It is the imposition of a human-made, meaningful order onto a small patch of indifferent reality. The artist who takes a blank canvas and creates an image of beauty or terror is not just making a picture; they are performing a metaphysical act. They are taking the raw, unstructured data of their experience and giving it form, coherence, and significance. The act of creation is a defiant declaration that, even in a world without inherent purpose, a human being can and will create a pocket of meaning.

This understanding of creativity must be broadened far beyond the traditional arts. The scientist who dedicates their life to understanding a small corner of the universe, the entrepreneur who builds a company that solves a human problem, the teacher who cultivates a space of curiosity and growth in a classroom, the parents who create a home filled with love and stability—all are engaged in the same fundamental project. They are all absurd creators. They are taking the chaotic, raw material of the world and shaping it into something of human value. They are pushing back against the entropy of the universe with the focused energy of their own intention.

Crucially, the value of this creative act, from an existential perspective, lies not in the permanence of the product, but in the integrity of the process. The absurd creator knows that their creations are, like themselves, ultimately destined for oblivion. The novel will go out of print, the company will eventually fail, the beautiful garden will be reclaimed by weeds. The absurd hero, like Sisyphus, knows that the rock will always roll back down. But this does not invalidate the act of creation. The meaning is found in the act of painting, of building, of teaching, of loving. It is in the full and passionate engagement with the work itself. The creative life is one that finds its purpose not in the fantasy of a final, immortal achievement, but in the daily, courageous, and deeply satisfying work of making something new in a world that does not ask for it. It is a life that is justified not by its outcome, but by its own, self-generated fire.

The third, and perhaps most subtle and sophisticated, tool of the absurd hero is humor. If the absurd is the clash between our grand, serious aspirations and the humble, indifferent reality of the world, then humor is the ultimate expression of our ability to perceive this clash and not be crushed by it. To laugh at our own predicament is to achieve a kind of psychological mastery over it. It is to step back from our own intense, self-important drama and to see it from a cosmic perspective, to recognize its inherent and often ridiculous disproportion. Laughter is the sound of freedom. It is the sign of a consciousness that is not entirely trapped in its own suffering, a self that can look upon its own fate with a measure of lightness and detachment.

This is not the cold, detached, and superior irony of the cynic. The cynic's laughter is a weapon used to devalue the world from a safe distance. The absurd hero's laughter is a warm, engaged, and deeply human response that is directed, first and foremost, at themselves. It is the laughter that recognizes the ridiculousness of our own seriousness, the comedy of our own tragedies. It is the ability to see the profound humor in the image of a small, bipedal ape on a tiny planet, shaking its fist at a silent universe and demanding to know the meaning of it all. This laughter does not erase the pain of our condition, but it makes it bearable. It creates a space of psychic freedom, a moment of release from the crushing weight of our own significance.

Humor, in this sense, is a form of rebellious intelligence. It is a way of acknowledging the cosmic joke and, by laughing along, refusing to be its butt. It is the final and most elegant proof that we understand our situation completely and have chosen not to be defeated by it. It is the ultimate expression of Sisyphus's happiness. One can imagine him, as he walks back down the hill, not just with a scornful defiance, but with a quiet, knowing smile, a private chuckle at the grand, repetitive, and utterly absurd theater of his own existence.

These three responses—rebellion, creativity, and humor—are not separate tactics to be deployed in isolation. They are the interwoven threads of a single, coherent, and deeply courageous posture toward life. The absurd hero is a person who lives in a state of perpetual, passionate rebellion against their own despair. They channel this rebellion into the creative act of forging a life of self-made meaning. And they sustain this difficult and often lonely struggle with the liberating and life-giving power of a humor that allows them to find joy not in a guaranteed future, but in the magnificent, tragic, and deeply funny business of being human. This is the path of making one's life a work of art, a defiant masterpiece painted on the canvas of a meaningless world.

Absurdity as a Call to Responsibility

The journey into the heart of the absurd is a profoundly destabilizing one. To look upon a silent, indifferent universe and to fully accept the absence of any pre-ordained meaning, purpose, or divine plan is to risk falling into the abyss of nihilism or the comfortable paralysis of despair. The initial, and most common, interpretation of this revelation is that if nothing has any ultimate meaning, then nothing ultimately matters. If there is no final judgment, no cosmic scoreboard, then we are absolved of our burdens. The death of God, in this reading, is the death of responsibility. This, however, is the great and tragic misinterpretation of our condition. It is the final and most sophisticated of all our flights from freedom. The truth, as the absurd hero comes to understand it, is the precise and terrifying opposite. The discovery of the absurd is not the end of responsibility; it is its true and absolute beginning.

The absence of a cosmic plan is the ultimate abdication of all alibis. As long as we can believe, even unconsciously, that there is a higher power, a historical destiny, or a natural law that dictates the course of our lives, we always have a place to defer our ultimate responsibility. We can tell ourselves that our suffering is part of God's plan, that our actions are determined by the forces of history, or that our character is simply a product of our nature. But the moment we accept the absurd, the moment we look into the void and see nothing looking back, all of these escape routes are sealed forever. The final transfer of ownership is complete. There is no one else to credit for our triumphs. There is no one else to blame for our failures. The authorship of our lives, in its totality, is placed squarely and irrevocably into our own hands.

This is the great and challenging gift of the absurd. It does not give us a meaning for our lives; it gives us the far more precious and demanding task of creating one. Life ceases to be a mission to be discovered and becomes a project to be built. The metaphor is crucial. We are not explorers searching for a hidden city of gold; we are architects standing on an empty plot of land, handed a set of tools and the raw, unstructured material of our own existence. The responsibility is now ours, and ours alone, to design the structure, to lay the foundation, and to build, brick by brick, a life that has a meaning of our own making.

In an absurd world, where do our values come from? They are not discovered in a sacred text or handed down from a divine authority. They are forged, moment by moment, in the crucible of our own choices. We are the sole source of the values that will govern our lives. When we choose to act with compassion in a situation that tempts us toward cruelty, we are not adhering to an external moral law; we are, in that moment, creating compassion as a real and tangible value in our small corner of the universe. When we choose to pursue a difficult truth in a world that rewards easy lies, we are casting a vote for a world in which truth matters. Our actions are no longer just behaviors; they are legislative acts. Each choice is an affirmation, a declaration of what we have decided is good, and beautiful, and true.

This is a far heavier, and far more magnificent, burden than any traditional concept of responsibility. The responsibility of the religious believer is to follow the rules that have been given to them. The responsibility of the absurd hero is to invent the rules, to live by them, and to be their sole and lonely guarantor, all the while knowing that these rules have no backing or authority beyond their own free and conscious commitment to them. This is the source of the Sartrean anguish, the feeling of being crushed by the weight of a freedom that is total and without excuse. But it is also the source of our ultimate dignity. Our meaning is not borrowed from the heavens; it is earned, through the difficult and courageous labor of a life lived with integrity.

This returns us, one last time, to Sisyphus. His ultimate heroism lies not just in his defiant rebellion, but in his total acceptance of his responsibility. He is responsible for his own consciousness. He is responsible for his own integrity in the face of a meaningless fate. He is responsible for the meaning of his own suffering. The gods have given him his punishment, but he is the one who chooses to transform it into his life's project. His rock is his responsibility. To take it up each morning is not an act of submission, but an act of profound and personal ownership. He has looked upon the full absurdity of his condition and has chosen not to flee, but to engage, to commit, and to create a world of meaning that is contained entirely within the singular, repetitive, and deeply personal act of pushing his stone.

The final verdict of existentialism is therefore not one of despair, but one of a demanding and heroic humanism. The discovery of the absurd is not an excuse to escape from the challenges of life; it is the ultimate and undeniable summons to create a life of our own. It is the final, liberating realization that if our lives are not a gift from the gods, then they are free to become a gift that we give to ourselves, and to each other. It is a call to take up our tools, to accept the weight of our own creative power, and to begin the difficult, beautiful, and sacred work of building a meaningful home in a universe that has left us profoundly, terribly, and magnificently alone.

* * *

14

The Ethics of Freedom

Our journey thus far has been a descent into the solitary crucible of the self. The figure that has emerged from our exploration—the authentic individual, the absurd hero—is a lonely one. It is Sisyphus, alone with his rock. It is the Sartrean author, alone with the blank page of their own existence. The central drama has been an internal one: the struggle of a single, sovereign consciousness to create a meaningful life in the face of its own groundlessness. The responsibility we have focused on has been a responsibility *for the self*, the profound and demanding task of owning our own choices and forging our own essence. This intense, inward focus is the necessary starting point of any existential inquiry. For if we are not first responsible for our own being, how can we be responsible for anything else?

Yet, if our inquiry were to end here, it would be a profound and dangerous failure. A philosophy that culminates in the heroic but isolated self risks collapsing into a kind of solipsistic narcissism. If the ultimate goal is my own authentic self-creation, what is to stop my authentic project from being one of cruelty, of exploitation, of profound indifference to the suffering of others? If there is no God, no universal moral law, and all values are self-created, what prevents my "authentic" choice from being an act of monstrous selfishness? The silent universe that provides no meaning for my life also provides no inherent reason why I should care about yours. This is the dark and often unspoken shadow of a purely individualistic existentialism, the ghost that haunts the lonely hero. To leave this question unanswered is to offer a philosophy that is not just incomplete, but potentially inhuman.

This chapter is the necessary and decisive turn outward. It is the moment we acknowledge that Sisyphus is not, in fact, alone on his mountain. The world is filled with other people, each engaged in their own absurd and heroic struggle, each pushing their own rock. Our freedom does not unfold in a vacuum; it unfolds in a dense and complex web of relationships. Our choices are never just our own; they ripple outward, impacting, enabling, and constraining the freedom of those around us. This is the truth that moves us from a psychology of the self to an ethics of our life *with others*. The ultimate test of our freedom is not found in the solitary act of creating our own meaning, but in the difficult, demanding, and inescapable encounter with another human being. Responsibility is not just a project of self-authorship; it is our fundamental response to our shared humanity.

Our exploration of this ethical dimension will begin with a profound and necessary challenge to the existential framework we have built so far. We will turn to the work of the philosopher Emmanuel Levinas, who offers a radical reorientation of our entire understanding of responsibility. For thinkers like Sartre, freedom is the foundation, and responsibility is its consequence. For Levinas, this is backward. Responsibility is the primary and most fundamental fact of our existence. It does not arise from our freedom; it is a profound and infinite demand that is placed upon us from the outside, in the simple, vulnerable, and undeniable presence of the "face of the Other." We will explore how this powerful ethical claim precedes and even limits our freedom, suggesting that we are not first free and then responsible, but are, in our very essence, responsible beings who must then learn how to be free.

From this high philosophical ground, we will descend into the messy, ambiguous, and often painful reality of everyday moral choice. We will examine the psychology of moral dilemmas, moving beyond abstract thought experiments like the trolley problem to the real-world situations where our values collide and the path forward is unclear. We will look at the psychological forces that shape our choices in moments of profound moral ambiguity, from the immense pressure to conform that can lead good people to participate in evil, to the immense courage it takes to become a whistleblower and speak a difficult truth to power. This is the landscape where an abstract commitment to "doing the right thing" is tested by the concrete realities of risk, fear, and social pressure.

Next, we will broaden our focus to consider the unique and amplified burden of responsibility that comes with positions of power. Freedom and the weight of its consequences are not distributed equally. The choices of a leader—in politics, in business, in a family—have a vastly disproportionate impact on the lives and the freedom of others. We will explore the unique existential burdens of leadership: the loneliness of final authority, the moral compromises that are often necessary for the "greater good," and the profound weight of being responsible not just for one's own life, but for the well-being and the future of an entire community or organization.

Finally, having explored these different dimensions of our shared moral lives, we will attempt to synthesize them into a coherent and workable ethical framework. This chapter will not offer a new set of commandments, for that would be a betrayal of the very spirit of existential freedom. Instead, it will propose a model for an *existential ethics*, a way of navigating our moral lives without the false comfort of absolute certainty. We will argue that such an ethics must be built upon three core pillars: authenticity, our unwavering responsibility to be the true authors of our own moral choices; responsibility, our infinite and unconditional obligation to the well-being of the Other; and relational accountability, the ongoing, difficult, and deeply human work of negotiating our freedom in a world we share. This chapter, then, is the ultimate maturation of our inquiry. It is the journey from the solitary "I" to the connected "we," the final and most important recognition that a life of authentic freedom is, and must always be, a life lived for, with, and in response to, others.

Responsibility Beyond the Self: Levinas and the moral claim of the "Other"

The entire existential edifice we have constructed up to this point rests on a single, powerful, and deeply modern foundation: the primacy of the individual self. From Kierkegaard's solitary knight of faith to Sartre's radically free author and Camus's defiant Sisyphus, the drama has been an internal one. Freedom is the fundamental given, the first principle of our existence. From this primordial freedom, responsibility arises as its necessary but secondary consequence. We are responsible because we are free. Our ethical life, in this framework, is a project that flows outward from the sovereign self. We choose our values, we create our moral law, and we take responsibility for the world we are creating through our choices. The "I" stands at the center of its own moral universe, a lonely legislator burdened with the task of inventing a good life from scratch. But what if this entire picture is backward? What if freedom is not the beginning of our story, but a secondary and even problematic feature of a much deeper, more fundamental reality? What if we are not first free, and only then responsible? What if, in our very essence, we are first and foremost, responsible beings?

This is the profound and revolutionary challenge posed by the 20th-century Lithuanian-French philosopher Emmanuel Levinas. Writing from a tradition of Jewish thought and phenomenology, and profoundly shaped by the trauma of the Holocaust, Levinas looked upon the self-centered freedom of mainstream existentialism and saw in it the potential for a terrible violence. A freedom that begins and ends with the self's own project of authenticity, he feared, has no inherent defense against a monstrous solipsism. It has no compelling answer to the question, "Why should I care about anyone else?" Levinas's entire philosophical project can be understood as an attempt to answer this question, and in doing so, he performs a radical inversion of our entire ethical framework. He argues that the most fundamental fact of human existence is not the solitary self's confrontation with a meaningless universe, but the immediate, concrete, and inescapable ethical encounter with another human being.

For Levinas, the ethical relationship is not something we choose to enter into; it is a reality that is thrust upon us, a reality that precedes our freedom and calls it into question. This encounter is centered on what he famously calls the "face of the Other." The "face," for Levinas, is not the physical collection of features—the eyes, the nose, the mouth—that we can perceive and objectify. It is not something we can ever fully grasp, categorize, or turn into a concept. The face is the simple, undeniable, and overwhelming presence of another person in all their vulnerability, uniqueness, and transcendence. It is the part of them that always escapes our attempts to possess, to control, or to fully understand them. To truly encounter the face of the Other is to encounter a mystery, a trace of an infinity that lies beyond my own finite world.

This encounter is not a neutral, cognitive event; it is an immediate and overwhelming ethical command. The first and most primary expression of the face, Levinas argues, is a silent, implicit commandment: "Thou shalt not kill." This is not merely a prohibition against the physical act of murder. It is a more profound prohibition against the metaphysical violence of reducing the Other to an object for my own use. It is a command against seeing the other person as a mere tool for my projects, an obstacle to my desires, or a simple component in my grand narrative of self-creation. The face, in its very nakedness and vulnerability, commands me to let it be, to recognize its absolute right to exist on its own terms, separate from my own world and my own freedom.

It is in this moment that the entire existential framework is turned on its head. For Sartre, my freedom is primary. The other person enters my world as an object, another being whose freedom is a potential threat or limit to my own. But for Levinas, the claim of the Other is primary. Before I am even aware of my own freedom, before I have even constituted myself as an "I," I am confronted with this ethical demand from the outside. My responsibility is not something I choose to take up; it is a charge that is laid upon me, a summons that I cannot refuse. In Levinas's radical formulation, I am a "hostage" to the Other. I am, in my very essence, responsible for their vulnerability, for their suffering, for their life. This responsibility is the very thing that constitutes me as a unique and irreplaceable self. I am "me" precisely because I am the one who has been called upon to answer for this other person. My identity is not forged in solitary self-creation, but is awakened by the ethical claim of the world.

This responsibility, crucially, is infinite and asymmetrical. It is not a contract based on reciprocity. I am responsible for the Other regardless of whether they are responsible for me. My ethical obligation to them is not conditional on their good behavior, on their deservingness, or on what they can do for me in return. It is an absolute, unconditional, and one-way street. Levinas writes, "I am responsible for the Other without waiting for reciprocity, were I to die for it. Reciprocity is his affair." This is a direct and profound challenge to the entire tradition of Western ethics, which is so often based on a logic of rights, of contracts, and of balanced scales. Levinas is proposing an ethics of pure, uncalculated, and infinite giving, an ethics where my primary role is not to claim my own rights, but to answer for the needs of another.

This radically reorients our understanding of freedom. Freedom is no longer the highest value, the unimpeachable starting point of our existence. It is, instead, something that is secondary to, and must be justified by, our primary ethical responsibility. My freedom is only good and meaningful insofar as it is a freedom that is exercised in the service of the Other. The question is no longer, "What does my authentic self want to do?" but rather, "What does my responsibility to the Other demand of me?" My freedom is called into question, judged, and ultimately given its meaning by this prior and more fundamental ethical obligation. We are not free beings who must learn to be responsible; we are responsible beings who must learn what to do with our freedom.

Levinas's philosophy, born in the ashes of a century that witnessed the catastrophic consequences of an ethics based on the self, the tribe, and the state, is a profound and difficult call to a new kind of humanism. It is a call to find the center of our moral lives not in the lonely, self-creating ego, but in the humble, demanding, and ultimately sacred space between one person and another. It offers a powerful and definitive answer to the problem of existential solipsism. The meaning of my life is not a project I invent in a vacuum; it is a response I give to the world that calls out to me. The ultimate burden of freedom is not the burden of creating a self for myself, but the much heavier, and far more meaningful, burden of being a self for others. It is the recognition that the entire project of my existence finds its ultimate justification not in my own authenticity, but in my simple, compassionate, and responsible answer to the silent, commanding face of another human being.

Moral Choice in Ambiguous Situations

The ethical vision of Emmanuel Levinas is a profound and necessary corrective to a purely self-centered existence. It places an infinite, unconditional, and asymmetrical demand upon us, a responsibility for the Other that is the very foundation of our humanity. It is a North Star for the moral life. Yet, as with any star, its primary function is to orient us, not to provide a detailed map of the complex and often contradictory ground we must actually traverse. The tragic and beautiful difficulty of a human life is that we rarely encounter a single, solitary "Other" in a vacuum. Our lives are a dense network of overlapping and often conflicting responsibilities. We are responsible to our partners, to our children, to our colleagues, to our communities, to our society, and to the abstract ideal of truth itself. And very often, the ethical claim of one of these "Others" is in direct opposition to the claim of another.

This is the reality of moral ambiguity. It is the landscape where our clear, abstract values collide, where the rules of our ethical systems provide no simple answer, and where every potential path forward involves some form of compromise or even transgression. In these situations, we are stripped of the comfort of a clear and righteous path. We are returned to a state of pure, unadulterated, and often agonizing choice. It is here, in the gray, murky fog of the real world, that the psychology of our moral decision-making is revealed, and the true weight of our existential freedom is most acutely felt.

To understand how our minds grapple with these dilemmas, it is useful to begin with the abstract and highly simplified models used by philosophers and psychologists, most famously, the "trolley problem." In its classic formulation, you are standing by a set of train tracks and see a runaway trolley car hurtling toward five people who are tied to the track and unable to move. You are standing next to a lever. If you pull the lever, the trolley will switch to a different track, where, unfortunately, there is one person tied up. You are faced with a choice: do nothing, and the five people will be killed; or pull the lever, and the one person will be killed.

The overwhelming majority of people, when presented with this scenario, conclude that the correct action is to pull the lever. The logic is a straightforward utilitarian calculation: saving five lives at the cost of one is the greater good. This choice, while tragic, feels rational and justifiable. But then, the scenario is altered. Now, there is no lever. You are standing on a footbridge overlooking the track, next to a very large stranger. The only way to stop the trolley from killing the five people is to push this stranger off the bridge and onto the track below. His large body will stop the trolley, but he will certainly be killed. The utilitarian math is identical: one life is sacrificed to save five. Yet, the overwhelming majority of people in this scenario have a powerful, visceral, and immediate intuition that pushing the stranger is a monstrous and morally forbidden act.

What this thought experiment so brilliantly reveals is the deep, and often irrational, conflict in our moral psychology. We have, on one hand, a capacity for cool, detached, utilitarian reasoning (the "lever" mind). But we also have a powerful, intuitive, and deeply embodied set of deontological rules—rules about what is inherently right and wrong, regardless of the consequences (the "footbridge" mind). For most of us, the rule "thou shalt not kill" is far more potent when it involves the direct, physical, and intentional act of pushing someone than when it involves the more abstract and indirect act of pulling a lever. The trolley problem reveals that our moral compass is not a single, consistent device, but a complex and often contradictory set of intuitions, emotions, and rational calculations.

While useful, the great limitation of the trolley problem is its bloodless abstraction. It is a disembodied, context-free puzzle. The "people" are faceless variables, and the "chooser" has no history, no relationships, and no personal stake in the outcome. It is a game of pure logic, and as such, it fails to capture the true, existential weight of a real-world moral choice. The true test of our moral character is not found in these clean, philosophical laboratories, but in the messy, high-stakes, and socially complex situations where our own lives, our loyalties, and our deepest sense of self are on the line.

Consider the far more common and far more existentially demanding dilemma of the whistleblower. An engineer named Susan, working at a large automotive company, discovers a flaw in the design of a new car's braking system. Her simulations suggest that under certain rare but plausible conditions, the brakes could fail, potentially leading to catastrophic accidents. She brings her concerns to her immediate supervisor, who dismisses them, citing the immense costs of a redesign and the pressure to get the new model to market. She is subtly, but clearly, instructed to drop the issue. Susan is now standing in the heart of a profound and deeply ambiguous moral dilemma. This is not a simple math problem; it is a clash of deeply felt and legitimate responsibilities.

On one hand, she has a responsibility to the company that employs her and to the colleagues she works with every day. She has a duty of loyalty. Her actions could damage the company's reputation, cost thousands of people their jobs, and destroy the careers of her superiors. She is part of a team, a community, and the script of that community is one of solidarity and shared purpose. This is the powerful, gravitational pull of conformity, the deep human need to belong and to not betray the trust of one's own tribe.

On the other hand, she has a responsibility to the faceless, anonymous "Other" of the general public, the thousands of future drivers and their families who will be unknowingly placing their lives in the hands of this flawed technology. This is the Levinasian demand in its purest form, a responsibility to a vulnerable and unknown stranger. Her conscience, her professional ethics, and her basic sense of human decency are all calling her to act.

To choose to remain silent is the path of least resistance. It is the path of bad faith, and the mind will offer a thousand sophisticated rationalizations to make it feel acceptable. "It's not my decision to make; I've done my part by reporting it." "The probability of failure is low; I'm probably overreacting." "I'm just one engineer; I can't change the whole system." "I have a family to support; I can't risk my job." These are the comforting narratives of self-absolution, the stories we tell ourselves to avoid the terrifying burden of a courageous choice.

To choose to become a whistleblower, on the other hand, is an act of profound and lonely existential authorship. It is a choice to privilege a universal, abstract ethical principle over a specific, tangible social loyalty. It is a rebellion against the powerful social script of conformity. The whistleblower knows that this choice will likely come at a tremendous personal cost: the loss of their job, the alienation of their colleagues, a protracted legal battle, a permanent stain on their professional reputation. They are choosing to become a pariah, to be cast out from the comfort of the tribe in the name of a truth that the tribe does not want to hear.

This is the ultimate test of an ethics of freedom. There is no external authority to provide the "right" answer. There is no guarantee of a good outcome. In fact, a good outcome for the public may result in a catastrophic outcome for Susan's own life. The choice is hers alone, and in it, she is not just deciding what to do; she is deciding who to be. To remain silent is to define herself as a person for whom safety and loyalty are the highest values. To speak out is to define herself as a person for whom public responsibility and personal integrity are the highest values. The moral choice, in an ambiguous world, is not the application of a pre-existing rule, but the difficult, courageous, and deeply personal act of creating a self. It is the moment when we are forced to stop asking what we are supposed to do, and to start asking what kind of human being we are choosing to become.

The Burdens of Leadership

The existential burden of leadership is crystallized not in the grand speeches or strategic victories, but in the solitary silence that follows a difficult decision. Imagine a hospital administrator during a crisis, whose decision will allocate limited, life-saving resources to one ward over another. There is no rulebook that can absorb the responsibility for that choice. There is no algorithm to blame. The weight of that decision, with its implicit valuation of human life, rests entirely on one person's shoulders. This is the anguish Sartre described, magnified to an almost unbearable degree. The leader in this moment is utterly alone, condemned to their freedom. They cannot hide behind protocol or a committee vote; they are the final author of an action that will create irreparable consequences for other human beings. This is the essence of leadership beyond technique: the courage to make a choice in the face of radical uncertainty and to bear the moral weight of its outcome, forever, without the consolation of certainty.

The architecture of human society is not flat. It is a landscape of hills and valleys, of concentrated power and diffuse dependency. While it is a fundamental existential truth that every individual is the author of their own life, it is an equally fundamental social truth that some individuals, by virtue of their position, are also the co-authors of the lives of many others. This is the essence of leadership. To be a leader—whether in the halls of government, the boardroom of a corporation, the classroom of a school, or the living room of a family—is to occupy a position where one's freedom is magnified and the weight of one's responsibility is amplified exponentially. The burdens we have been exploring are not distributed equally. For the leader, the anxiety of choice, the agony of ambiguity, and the weight of consequence are not just personal, psychological states; they are the core and constant conditions of their professional and moral existence.

The first and most obvious of these burdens is the sheer scale of consequence. For the private individual, a poor choice may lead to personal regret, financial hardship, or a damaged relationship. The blast radius is relatively contained. For the leader, a single decision can create the defining reality, the Sartrean "facticity," for hundreds, thousands, or even millions of people. The CEO who decides to shut down a factory to maximize shareholder value is not just making a financial calculation; they are, in that single act of freedom, authoring a future of unemployment, anxiety, and dislocation for an entire community. The military commander who sends troops into battle is not just executing a strategy; they are choosing to place the finite and irreplaceable lives of other people's children in the path of mortal danger. The parent who chooses to move their family to a new city for a career opportunity is choosing to uproot their child's entire social world.

This is a weight that is almost impossible to fully comprehend. To live with this level of responsibility is to live with the constant, haunting awareness that one's own imperfections, biases, and moments of poor judgment can have catastrophic consequences for people who have placed their trust, either willingly or unwillingly, in your hands. This is why the flight from this responsibility is so common in positions of power. It often takes the form of a retreat into the sterile, dehumanizing language of abstraction. The employees become "headcount," the soldiers become "assets," and the citizens become "demographics." This is a powerful psychological defense, a way of creating a cognitive and emotional distance from the real, human impact of one's choices. It is a form of bad faith that allows the leader to wield immense power without having to feel its immense and terrible human weight.

The second, and perhaps most agonizing, burden of leadership is the constant necessity of the morally ambiguous choice. The leader is the perpetual resident of the "footbridge" scenario in the trolley problem. Their work is rarely a matter of choosing between a clear right and a clear wrong, but of navigating the murky, tragic space where all the available options involve some form of harm. This is the world of the "greater good," a concept that is clean and elegant in a philosophy textbook, but is brutal and often soul-crushing in practice. It is the world of the necessary evil, the calculated sacrifice, the lesser of two tragedies. The leader is the one who must choose which group to save and which to sacrifice, who must decide which budget to cut, which department to downsize, which principle to compromise in the service of a larger strategic goal.

This is a profound source of what is often called "moral injury." Unlike existential guilt, which arises from a failure to live up to one's own potential, moral injury is the wound that comes from having been forced to violate one's own deeply held ethical principles. The political leader who must authorize a drone strike that will kill a known terrorist but may also result in the deaths of innocent civilians, the doctor who must decide which of two equally deserving patients will receive a life-saving organ, the manager who must lay off a loyal and hardworking employee to keep the company afloat—all are forced to participate in a system that makes their hands unclean. They are responsible for choices that, in a just and ideal world, no one should ever have to make. To be a leader is to accept that one's own sense of moral purity is often the first casualty of the job. The flight from this burden is the retreat into a rigid, ideological certainty, the refusal to acknowledge the tragic trade-offs that are inherent in a complex world. The responsible leader, in contrast, is the one who has the courage to bear the weight of these unclean choices, to live with the wound of their own moral compromises, and to not lose their humanity in the process.

Third, the leader must bear the burden of a profound and inescapable existential isolation. While they may be surrounded by advisors, colleagues, and constituents, the final act of authorship for any significant decision rests with them, and them alone. This is the truth behind President Harry Truman's famous desk sign: "The Buck Stops Here." In the final analysis, a leader cannot defer responsibility. They cannot blame their team, they cannot blame the circumstances; the choice, and its consequences, are ultimately theirs. This solitude of command is a unique and often crushing form of loneliness. It is the state of being the single, final consciousness in which all the competing arguments, all the uncertain data, and all the potential consequences must be weighed and synthesized into a single, decisive, and irreversible act.

This isolation is a breeding ground for anxiety and self-doubt. The leader is perpetually haunted by the knowledge that they might be wrong, that their information might be incomplete, that their judgment might be flawed. The desire to escape this lonely burden is immense. It is the temptation to surround oneself with sycophants who offer reassuring praise rather than challenging counsel. It is the temptation to fall into a state of indecisive paralysis, to perpetually gather more information in a futile attempt to find an absolutely certain, risk-free path. The courageous leader is the one who can tolerate this solitude, who can sit with the anxiety of their own potential fallibility, and who can still, in the end, find the strength to make a choice and to take full and public ownership of it, for better or for worse.

Finally, the leader must carry the burden of being a symbol. They are not just a person; they are a role, an embodiment of the hopes, the fears, and the expectations of the group they lead. This requires a constant and exhausting performance. They must project confidence in the face of uncertainty, calm in the midst of chaos, and unwavering resolve in the face of their own private doubts. This creates a profound and often painful split between the public persona and the private self. It is a form of institutionalized bad faith, a necessary inauthenticity that is required to maintain the stability and morale of the group. The leader's own anxieties, their own vulnerabilities, their own humanity must often be suppressed in the service of the symbolic role they are required to play. The weight of this performance, the constant pressure to be more than one is, is one of the most subtle but most corrosive of all the burdens of leadership. It is the sacrifice of one's own authentic self on the altar of a collective need. To be a leader, then, is to willingly take up a weight that is, by any human standard, too heavy to bear. It is to accept the amplified consequences of one's choices, the agony of moral compromise, the solitude of final authority, and the inauthenticity of a symbolic existence. The great leader is not the one who is untroubled by these burdens, but the one who has chosen to carry them with consciousness, with humility, and with a profound and unwavering sense of responsibility for the well-being of those who have been placed in their care.

* * *

15

Integration: Freedom as a Lived Practice

I f you have journeyed with me through the preceding chapters, you may be feeling a certain kind of weight. It is a feeling that is both intellectually clarifying and emotionally heavy. We have, together, undertaken a profound and often unsettling diagnosis. We have looked squarely at the dizzying anxiety that accompanies our freedom, the crushing weight of a total responsibility for our own lives, the frustrating paradoxes of modern choice, and the cold, silent indifference of an absurd universe. We have dissected the sophisticated psychological defenses we use to flee from these truths and have seen how this flight from freedom is the source of so much of our quiet, modern suffering. To arrive at this point is to have been stripped of many of our most comforting illusions. It is to stand, clear-eyed and without easy answers, in the stark and demanding landscape of our own existence.

The natural and most human question that arises from this stark new awareness is a simple and urgent one: Now what? To be given a profound diagnosis without any prospect of a cure can feel like a cruel and pointless exercise. To be told that our condition is one of groundlessness, anxiety, and a freedom that feels more like a burden, is to risk being left in a state of intellectual paralysis or emotional despair. If this is the truth of our predicament, how, then, are we supposed to live? It is to this crucial and deeply practical question that we now, finally, turn. This chapter marks the great pivot of our entire inquiry. We move from the philosophical work of understanding to the deeply personal and practical work of integration. The goal is no longer to simply analyze the burden of freedom, but to begin the lifelong project of learning how to carry it. This is a movement from theory to practice, from diagnosis to a plan for living.

Let us be clear about the nature of this plan. This is not a chapter that will offer a cure. The existential condition is not a disease to be eradicated. The anxiety that accompanies our freedom is not a pathology to be medicated away; it is a vital sign, a signal that we are alive, conscious, and engaged with the fundamental realities of our own being. The search for a life completely free from anxiety, from doubt, from the pain of difficult choices, is itself a flight from freedom, a desire to return to the unthinking, un-free grace of a life without consciousness. The promise of this chapter is not a life without the burden, but the development of the psychological and spiritual strength to bear that burden with dignity, with courage, and even with a kind of profound joy. It is about transforming the weight from a crushing force that holds us down into a steadying force that grounds us in a life of substance and meaning.

To do this, we must shift our thinking from a language of problems and solutions to a language of practice. A practice is not something we do to achieve a final result and then be done with it. A practice is a conscious, disciplined, and ongoing engagement with a chosen way of being. A musician does not practice the piano to one day solve the problem of music; they practice to be in a deeper and more masterful relationship with music itself. In the same way, we will now explore the elements of an *existential practice*, a set of skills, mindsets, and commitments that allow us to be in a more conscious, courageous, and creative relationship with our own freedom. This is not a program of self-improvement designed to create a perfect, finished product. It is a lifelong discipline of self-authorship designed to support the messy, imperfect, and ongoing process of creating a meaningful human life.

Our exploration of this practice will be structured in four parts. We will begin with the most concrete and accessible level: the development of psychological tools for bearing responsibility. In a world that constantly encourages us to flee from our own authorship through blame, distraction, and denial, we must actively cultivate the mental habits of self-awareness and ownership. We will explore simple but powerful practices like journaling, structured reflection, and values-clarification exercises, not as self-help gimmicks, but as essential psychological technologies for building the "muscle" of responsibility. These are the practical, daily exercises that allow us to move from being the passive victim of our circumstances to the active agent of our own lives.

From these internal tools, we will broaden our focus to the great existential project of meaning-making in an uncertain world. Having accepted the absurd truth that the universe offers no pre-ordained purpose, the responsibility to create meaning falls entirely to us. Drawing on the profound, life-tested wisdom of Viktor Frankl's logotherapy and the empirical insights of modern positive psychology, we will explore the concrete ways in which meaning can be forged. We will see that meaning is not a mysterious substance to be found, but is the practical, observable result of a life dedicated to creative work, to unconditional love, and to a courageous and dignified bearing of our inevitable suffering.

Next, we will address the crucial social and relational dimension of this practice by exploring the nature of a mature freedom. So much of our suffering comes from a clinging to an adolescent, individualistic fantasy of freedom as a state of pure, unconstrained autonomy. A mature life requires us to move beyond this simplistic model and to embrace the profound and challenging truth that a meaningful human existence is almost always found in the delicate and lifelong balance between our need for personal agency and our equally powerful need for relational connection. We will explore how true freedom is not the absence of commitment, but the conscious and wholehearted embrace of it.

Finally, we will synthesize these various threads into a coherent vision of what we might call existential maturity. This is the ultimate goal of our practice. Existential maturity is not a final destination, but a way of being. It is the cultivated ability to live with open eyes in a world of ambiguity, to embrace our freedom without being paralyzed by it, to act with unwavering responsibility for our choices, and to accept the profound and often painful limits of our existence without collapsing into despair. It is the capacity to hold the tragic and the beautiful, the finite and the infinite, the absurd and the meaningful, all at once, in a single, open, and courageous heart. This chapter, then, is an invitation. It is an invitation to move beyond the fear of our own freedom and to begin the difficult, beautiful, and deeply practical work of becoming the person we are choosing to be.

Psychological Tools for Bearing Responsibility

To stand in the full, unshielded light of our own freedom is to be confronted with the total and unwavering responsibility for our own lives. This, as we have seen, is the source of our most profound anxiety, and the primary motivation for our myriad flights into denial, blame, and conformity. The modern world is a powerful and relentless engine of irresponsibility. It offers us a near-infinite buffet of distractions to keep us from our own inner lives, a cacophony of external voices to tell us who we should be, and a culture of victimhood that provides a ready-made and socially acceptable alibi for our own failures to choose. In such an environment, responsibility is not our natural state. It is a psychological and spiritual muscle that, without a conscious and sustained practice of exercise, will inevitably atrophy.

To live an authentic life, therefore, requires more than just a philosophical conviction. It requires a practical discipline. We must actively cultivate the mental and emotional habits of self-awareness and ownership. We must create intentional structures in our lives that force us to confront the reality of our own authorship, to see our choices as choices, and to begin the difficult work of aligning our actions with our deepest values. This is not a project of grim self-flagellation, but one of profound self-respect. It is the decision to take our own one and only life seriously enough to become its conscious and deliberate creator. The tools for this practice are not complex or esoteric. They are simple, accessible, and profoundly effective psychological technologies for building the strength to bear the weight of our own being.

The first, and perhaps most powerful, of these tools is the practice of reflective journaling. This is not the diaristic recording of daily events— "Today I went to the store and saw a friend"—but a more structured and intentional act of self-interrogation. The journal, in this context, becomes a private laboratory for the examination of the self, a dedicated space where we can make our unconscious processes conscious. It is the primary tool for moving from the passive, unexamined question, "What happened to me today?" to the active, responsible, and existentially potent question, "What did I choose today?"

To begin this practice is to commit to becoming the primary and most attentive witness to your own life. It can start with a simple, daily or weekly review centered on a few key questions. At the end of the day, one might ask: *Where did I feel most alive and authentic today, and what choices led to that feeling? Where did I feel most inauthentic or alienated, and what choices led to that feeling?* This simple act of correlation begins to build an awareness of the direct link between our choices and our subjective experience. Another powerful practice is to focus on a single, significant decision made during the day, and to deconstruct it in the journal: *What was the choice I made? What were the alternatives I rejected? What fears were present in this decision? What values was I trying to honor?* This forces a direct confrontation with the reality of foreclosure—the unlived lives we sacrifice with every choice—and begins to train the mind to see choice not as a casual act, but as a definitive act of self-creation.

Over time, this practice of journaling becomes a powerful tool for identifying our own unique patterns of existential avoidance. It is in the written record of our own thoughts that our favorite narratives of bad faith are revealed in all their repetitive and self-defeating glory. We begin to see, with undeniable clarity, the patterns of our blame: the way we consistently attribute our professional frustrations to our "incompetent boss" or our relational unhappiness to our "needy partner." By writing these stories down, we create a space of critical distance. We can begin to question them, to ask, "What is my role in this dynamic? What part of myself am I refusing to see by casting this other person as the villain?" The journal becomes the place where we can have the difficult conversations with ourselves that we are too afraid to have in the open. It is where we can confess our fears, admit our complicity, and begin to dismantle the comforting but ultimately imprisoning stories of our own innocence.

The second essential tool in this practice is a more focused exercise: the conscious and deliberate clarification of our core values. So much of our existential guilt and our feeling of inauthenticity comes from a fundamental misalignment. We are living a life that is in conflict with a set of values that we have never taken the time to consciously articulate. We often inherit our values by osmosis from our family, our culture, or our peer group, and we mistake these adopted beliefs for our own authentic commitments. The project of values clarification is the act of sorting, of distinguishing our own chosen values from the "social scripts" we have been handed. It is the essential work of building our own internal compass.

This is not an abstract, philosophical exercise. It is a concrete and often surprising process of self-discovery. A powerful way to begin is through a guided imaginative exercise. Imagine yourself at the end of your life. What are the three to five words you would hope could be used to truthfully describe the person you were and the life you lived? Was it a life of courage, of compassion, of creativity, of security, of adventure, of service? The answers that arise in this contemplative space often cut through the noise of our everyday, socially-conditioned desires and point toward a deeper, more authentic sense of what truly matters to us.

Another, more analytical, approach is to work with a comprehensive list of values—words like honesty, freedom, connection, achievement, stability, growth, etc.—and to engage in a process of forced choice. The task is to narrow the list down to the five that feel most essential, most non-negotiable, to your sense of a life well-lived. The crucial, and most difficult, step is then to rank them in order of importance. This act of ranking is a powerful simulation of real-world moral ambiguity. It forces us to confront the reality that our values will often come into conflict, and that we must be clear about our ultimate priorities. Is security more important to you than adventure? Is compassion more important than achievement? There are no right answers, only your answers. The clarity that emerges from this process is the foundation of an authentic life.

Once these core values have been identified, they cease to be abstract nouns and become a powerful and practical tool for decision-making. They become the metrics for an honest "life audit." We can look at the major domains of our existence and ask, with radical honesty: *How does my current career allow me to express my primary value of creativity? How do my daily habits reflect my stated value of health? How does the way I spend my money align with my commitment to community?* This process will almost always reveal a series of painful and uncomfortable gaps between our professed values and our lived reality. This gap is the precise location of our existential guilt. But it is also the location of our freedom. The awareness of this gap is not a verdict; it is an invitation. It is a clear and unambiguous call to begin the difficult but deeply meaningful work of making new choices, choices that will slowly and deliberately begin to close that gap and bring our lives into a state of greater integrity.

These two tools, reflective journaling and values clarification, are the yin and yang of a responsible life. The journal is the diagnostic tool; it is the practice of seeing *what is*. It reveals our actual behaviors, our patterns of avoidance, and the stories we tell ourselves. The clarified values are the navigational tool; they are the practice of defining *what ought to be*. They provide the compass, the North Star that gives us a direction for our choices. To engage in these practices is to take up the dual roles of the honest scientist and the courageous artist of our own lives. It is to commit to a life of seeing ourselves clearly and, in the light of that seeing, to begin the lifelong, never-finished, and ultimately sacred project of creating a self that is worthy of our own deepest respect.

A third, indispensable tool for this practice comes from a powerful and evidence-based contemporary approach known as Acceptance and Commitment Therapy (ACT). Resonating deeply with the existential and Buddhist themes we have explored, ACT offers a practical and compassionate framework for dealing with the very anxiety that our freedom provokes. It provides a direct answer to the question: How do I move forward when my own mind is screaming at me to retreat into the safety of avoidance? The practice is built on a few core principles.

First is the practice of Acceptance. This is not resignation or a passive surrender to misery. Acceptance, in the ACT sense, is the conscious and courageous choice to make space for our difficult inner experiences. It is the willingness to allow the uncomfortable feelings—the anxiety of choice, the dread of uncertainty, the guilt of past failures—to be present in our bodies without launching a war against them. We spend so much of our psychic energy trying to control, suppress, or eliminate these feelings, a struggle that, like fighting in quicksand, only exhausts us and pulls us deeper into the muck. Acceptance is the radical act of ceasing the struggle. It is the choice to let the waves of anxiety wash over us without being swept away, to acknowledge their presence without obeying their commands. This is the practical antidote to both repression and spiritual bypassing. We are not trying to bury the anxiety or to prematurely transcend it; we are learning to carry it.

Second, and inseparably from acceptance, is the practice of Cognitive Defusion. This is the art of separating ourselves from our own thoughts. Our minds are relentless story-generating machines, constantly producing a stream of judgments, predictions, and self-criticisms ("You're going to fail," "You'll make the wrong choice," "You're not good enough"). We tend to treat these thoughts not as mental events, but as objective reality. Defusion is the process of learning to see our thoughts for what they are: just bits of language, images, and sounds passing through our awareness. Instead of saying, "I'm a failure," we practice saying, "I'm having the thought that I'm a failure." We can visualize our thoughts as leaves floating down a stream or clouds passing in the sky—we can notice them without having to become them. This small shift in perspective is profoundly liberating. It creates a space between our conscious self and the noisy chatter of our inner critic. It allows us to see that our thoughts do not have to dictate our actions.

This leads to the final and most crucial step: Values-Driven Action. Once we have made space for our discomfort through acceptance and unhooked from our paralyzing thoughts through defusion, a critical question emerges: Now what? With this newfound psychic freedom, in which direction do we move? The answer, for ACT, is found in the very values we have just clarified. The purpose of this entire practice is not to feel better, but to live better. It is to take committed action in the service of what matters most to us, even in the presence of anxiety and self-doubt. The goal is to choose to move toward the person we want to be, and to bring our uncomfortable thoughts and feelings along for the ride.

This three-part practice—Accept, Defuse, and Act—is the psychological engine of a mature, existential life. It is the practical, moment-to-moment work of being an absurd hero. It acknowledges the full weight of our condition, the full noise of our anxious minds, and yet still insists on our freedom to choose. It is the discipline of showing up for our own lives, not when we feel ready, not when the anxiety has subsided, but now.

Meaning-Making in Uncertainty

To accept the absurd is to find oneself standing in a profound and intimidating vacuum. The traditional pillars of meaning—divine purpose, historical destiny, natural law—have crumbled, leaving us in a world that is silent, indifferent, and without a pre-written script. This is the ultimate groundlessness, the condition that can so easily lead to the despair of nihilism or the frantic distraction of escapism. The declaration that "life is meaningless" is, however, not the end of the human story, but the true beginning of our most profound responsibility. If the universe does not provide a meaning for our lives, then the task of creating one falls entirely and magnificently to us. Meaning is not a treasure to be found; it is a structure to be built, and the tools we use are the very choices we make in our daily lives.

No one understood this more profoundly or tested this truth in a more terrible crucible than Viktor Frankl. As a psychiatrist imprisoned in the concentration camps of the Holocaust, Frankl had a front-row seat to the complete and systematic stripping away of everything that normally gives a life its meaning: professional identity, family connections, personal possessions, health, and the basic guarantee of a future. In this living laboratory of despair, he observed a stark and life-altering truth: the individuals who had the greatest chance of survival were not necessarily the most physically robust, but those who were able to hold on to some kind of meaning, some reason to endure the otherwise unendurable suffering. From this experience, he developed his powerful and deeply practical therapeutic approach, which he called logotherapy, or "healing through meaning."

Logotherapy is built on a single, foundational premise: the primary motivational force in human beings is a "will to meaning." This stands in direct contrast to other schools of thought, such as the Freudian emphasis on a "will to pleasure" or the Adlerian focus on a "will to power." For Frankl, the deepest human craving is not for happiness or for status, but for a life that makes sense, a life that feels significant and worthwhile. When this will to meaning is frustrated, when we feel that our lives are empty and pointless, we fall into a state he termed the "existential vacuum." This is the psychological breeding ground for a host of modern ailments: depression, apathy, addiction, and aggression. The cure, Frankl argued, is not to seek pleasure or to amass power, but to take up the active, responsible work of discovering the meaning that is potentially present in every moment of our lives.

Crucially, Frankl insisted that meaning is not something we invent out of thin air. It is something we *discover* in the world. It is an objective potential that is waiting to be actualized by our choices. He outlined three primary avenues through which we can discover this meaning. These are not abstract philosophical concepts, but concrete, lived pathways available to every human being, regardless of their circumstances.

First, we find meaning by creating a work or doing a deed. This is the path of giving something to the world. It is the meaning that arises from dedicating ourselves to a task that is larger than our own immediate gratification. This can be the grand, creative act of the artist, the scientist, or the builder. But it is just as readily found in the humble, everyday work of the teacher who cultivates a young mind, the craftsman who takes pride in a well-made object, or the parent who creates a loving and stable home. This is the meaning of Sisyphus, the meaning that is found in the integrity and the commitment of the struggle itself. To engage in a creative work is to take responsibility for a small piece of the world and to make it better, more beautiful, or more functional than it was before. It is an act that transforms our focus from the self-centered question, "What can I get from life?" to the more meaningful question, "What is life asking of me?"

Second, we find meaning by experiencing something or encountering someone. This is the path of receiving something from the world with a spirit of openness and appreciation. It is the meaning that can be found in a moment of profound connection with the beauty of nature, in the transformative power of a great piece of art or music, or, most importantly, in the love of another human being. For Frankl, love is the ultimate and highest way of grasping another person. To love someone is to see them in their absolute uniqueness, to see the potential within them, and to, by our very act of loving, help them to actualize that potential. This is a profound echo of Levinas's ethics. Meaning is found not in the solitary project of the self, but in the self-transcendence that occurs when we truly turn toward the Other. It is the recognition that a life finds its deepest significance in the connections it forges.

Third, and most radically, Frankl argued that we can find meaning in the attitude we take toward unavoidable suffering. This is the final and most powerful of the human freedoms, the one that can never be taken away. When we are faced with a fate that we cannot change—a terminal illness, an irreversible loss, an oppressive situation—we are still, and always, free to choose how we will respond. This is the point at which life ceases to be about doing and becomes purely about being. To face one's suffering with courage, with dignity, and with a concern for others is to find a meaning of the highest order. It is an act that wrests a human victory from a biological or political defeat. The suffering itself is meaningless; the meaning is found in the character we choose to forge in the face of it. This is the ultimate call to responsibility, the understanding that even in our most powerless moments, we are still the authors of our own character.

Frankl's logotherapy, born in the crucible of extremity, finds a remarkable and validating echo in the more recent, data-driven field of positive psychology. Thinkers like Martin Seligman have sought to empirically study the components of a "flourishing" life, and their findings powerfully align with Frankl's insights. Seligman's PERMA model, for example, identifies five key elements of well-being: Positive Emotion, Engagement (the "flow" state of deep absorption in a task), positive Relationships, Meaning (belonging to and serving something that you believe is bigger than the self), and Accomplishment. The pillars of Engagement, Relationships, and Meaning are, in essence, scientific validations of Frankl's three pathways.

This convergence has led to a number of simple, evidence-based practices that can be understood as a kind of modern, secular logotherapy. The practice of gratitude journaling, for instance, is a direct and powerful tool for cultivating the capacity to find meaning in experience. By regularly taking note of the good things in our lives, however small, we train our minds to see the world not as a source of threats and deficiencies, but as a source of gifts to be appreciated. Similarly, the well-documented psychological benefits of altruism and acts of service are a testament to the truth that meaning is a byproduct of self-transcendence. The choice to volunteer our time, to help a neighbor, to contribute to a cause we believe in, is a powerful way of moving from the existential vacuum of the self to the meaningful world of our connection with others.

Finally, the field of narrative psychology offers a powerful tool for finding meaning in our past, particularly in our past sufferings. This is the practice of consciously re-writing the story of our own lives. It is the choice to see our past traumas and failures not as a story of victimhood and damage, but as a "redemptive narrative," a story in which our struggles have been the very source of our strength, our wisdom, and our compassion. This is not an act of self-deception; it is a profound act of meaning-making. It is the responsible and creative work of taking the raw, often painful, data of our past and shaping it into a story that is not just bearable, but empowering. It is the ultimate act of authorship, the declaration that we are not defined by what has happened to us, but by the meaning we choose to create from it.

Ultimately, the practice of meaning-making in a world without guarantees is a practice of attention and intention. It is the intentional choice to turn our attention away from the self-centered anxieties of our own ego and toward the world of potential meaning that surrounds us: the work to be done, the people to be loved, and the attitude to be chosen. It is the understanding that meaning is not a feeling to be pursued, but a consequence to be created. It is the final and most liberating paradox of our existence: a life finds its deepest and most enduring meaning only when it is dedicated to something beyond itself.

The Nature of Mature Freedom

The Western cultural imagination, and indeed much of the existential tradition we have explored, is built upon a heroic and deeply seductive myth: the myth of the sovereign individual. This is the figure of pure, unencumbered autonomy, the lone cowboy on the frontier, the self-made entrepreneur, the solitary artist. It is a vision of freedom as a state of radical independence, a "freedom *from*" all external constraints, obligations, and dependencies. This adolescent fantasy of a life without limits is a powerful and, in some ways, a necessary developmental stage. It is the fuel of our youthful rebellion, the engine of our separation from the unthinking conformity of our childhood, the defiant assertion of our right to be the sole author of our own lives. To claim our autonomy, to declare our independence, is the first and most crucial step on the path to an authentic existence.

But it is only the first step. And to mistake this initial declaration of independence for the final destination of a human life is the source of our most profound relational suffering and our most persistent feelings of loneliness and alienation. A freedom that is defined solely by the absence of constraints is a shallow, brittle, and ultimately empty freedom. It is a freedom of the void. The raw, untamed autonomy of youth, if it does not evolve, curdles into the cynical detachment of the person who trusts no one, the restless dissatisfaction of the person who can never commit, and the profound isolation of a self that has successfully walled itself off from the very connections that make a life meaningful. A life lived in the pursuit of pure, unconstrained personal freedom is a life that will, in the end, find itself profoundly and terribly alone.

The great and difficult task of a mature life is to move beyond this adolescent fantasy and to embrace a more complex, more paradoxical, and far more substantive understanding of what it means to be free. Mature freedom is not a static state of being, but a dynamic, lifelong, and often difficult negotiation. It is a dialectic, a dance between two seemingly contradictory but equally essential human needs: our need for personal autonomy and our need for relational connection. It is the recognition that a truly flourishing human life is not found in the victory of one of these needs over the other, but in the courageous and constant effort to hold them in a creative and life-giving tension.

Autonomy, in this mature sense, is the unwavering commitment to our own existential authorship. It is the responsibility to cultivate our own inner life, to clarify our own values, to think our own thoughts, and to not surrender our consciousness to the crowd, the algorithm, or the expectations of our loved ones. It is the courage to set boundaries, to say "no" when our integrity demands it, and to bear the social discomfort that often accompanies a life of authentic conviction. Without this robust sense of an autonomous self, our relationships become a flight from freedom, a desperate and formless merging with others in an attempt to escape the anxiety of our own aloneness. We become a chameleon, a people-pleaser, a hollow echo of the people we seek to love. A healthy and responsible self is the necessary foundation for any healthy and responsible relationship.

But this autonomy must be held in constant dialogue with its counterpart: relationality. This is the recognition of the fundamental truth of our interconnectedness, the Levinasian insight that we are, from the very beginning, responsible beings, called into our very selfhood by the presence of the Other. Relationality is the willing and conscious choice to have our freedom limited by the needs, the reality, and the well-being of another person. It is the understanding that our own project of self-creation does not unfold in a vacuum, but in a shared world, and that an authentic life must, by necessity, be an ethical life, a life that is accountable to the community in which it is embedded. A freedom that is not tempered by a sense of responsibility to others is not freedom; it is a form of sociopathy.

Mature freedom, then, is the art of balancing these two poles. It is the freedom that is found not in the absence of constraints, but in the conscious and wholehearted choosing of them. Let us consider the domain of love. The immature view of freedom sees a committed relationship as a cage, a loss of autonomy, a final and tragic closing of doors. The mature view understands that the act of commitment is not the end of freedom, but its highest and most meaningful expression. To choose to build a life with another person is a profound act of existential authorship. It is a choice to voluntarily circumscribe the boundless, shallow freedom of infinite options for the deep, demanding freedom of a singular, committed love. This chosen constraint does not destroy freedom; it gives it a place to land, a ground upon which something of substance can be built. A mature partnership is not a fusion of two selves into one, but a dynamic interplay of two sovereign individuals who have freely chosen to align their paths, who support each other's autonomy while simultaneously holding each other accountable to the shared project of their relationship.

We see this same dynamic in parenting. The immature self experiences the birth of a child as a catastrophic loss of personal freedom, a hostile invasion of their autonomous world by a creature of pure, relentless need. The mature self understands that the act of parenting is a freely chosen commitment to place another's needs above one's own. The parent willingly, and even joyfully, accepts the profound constraints on their time, their energy, and their resources, because they have chosen a project that is larger and more meaningful than their own unencumbered liberty. The freedom they find is not the freedom to do whatever they want, but the profound, generative freedom of helping another human being come into their own.

Ultimately, the nature of mature freedom is paradoxical: it is only in the act of binding ourselves that we become truly free. The person who refuses all commitments, who keeps all their options open, who jealously guards their own autonomy against the claims of the world, is not free. They are a prisoner of their own indecision, a slave to the fear of foreclosure, a ghost drifting through a life of shallow encounters and unrealized potential. It is the person who has the courage to choose their constraints—to commit to a partner, to a craft, to a community, to a set of values—who is truly liberated. For in the act of commitment, the frantic, anxious energy of choosing is finally put to rest, and the deeper, more focused, and more powerful energy of living can begin. A mature freedom is the understanding that a finite life can only find its meaning not by trying to be everything, but by choosing, with courage and with love, to be something. It is the discovery that the only walls that truly imprison us are the ones we build to keep the world out, and the only freedom that truly matters is the one we find in the brave and responsible act of letting it in.

Defining Existential Maturity

The long and often difficult journey of this book has not been a quest for happiness, for success, or for a life free from pain. It has been a quest for something far more fundamental, more durable, and ultimately more meaningful: a state of being we can call existential maturity. This is not a final destination to be reached, not a certificate of enlightenment to be earned, but a dynamic, ongoing, and deeply personal practice. It is the art of living a fully human life in a world that is not designed for our comfort, a world that is rife with ambiguity, uncertainty, and the constant, demanding pressure of our own freedom. Existential maturity is the cultivated capacity to stand, without illusion and without despair, in the very heart of our existential condition and to create from it a life of substance, integrity, and self-generated meaning.

This maturity is not a function of chronological age, of worldly success, or of intellectual knowledge. It is a function of courage and consciousness. It is defined not by the absence of anxiety, but by our relationship to it. The existentially immature individual is one who is in a state of perpetual flight, their life organized around the unconscious project of evading the fundamental truths of their existence. Their energy is consumed by the maintenance of their defenses: their blame, their denials, their conformities, their distractions. The existentially mature individual, in contrast, is one who has chosen to turn and face these truths. They have decided that a life of courageous, clear-eyed engagement, however difficult, is preferable to a life of comfortable self-deception. This mature posture toward life is characterized by four core, interwoven capacities.

First, the existentially mature individual embraces their freedom. This is the fundamental turning point. They have moved beyond the youthful paralysis of infinite options and the chronic resistance of procrastination. They have come to understand that the anxiety of choice is not a pathology to be cured, but the necessary and unavoidable friction of a life in motion. They accept their role as the author of their own existence, not with a sense of grim resignation, but with a kind of solemn, creative energy. They understand that every choice is an act of creation, a brushstroke on the canvas of the self, and while this is a heavy responsibility, it is also their greatest and only true power. They are no longer terrified by the blank page; they have come to see it as an invitation. They have learned to make their choices not with the frantic, maximizing search for a guaranteed "perfect" outcome, but with the quieter, more grounded intention of making an authentic one, a choice that is a true and honest expression of their own, self-clarified values.

Second, and inseparably from the first, the mature individual acts with unwavering responsibility. They have consciously and deliberately abandoned the most seductive of all human alibis: the narrative of victimhood. They have taken the difficult but liberating step of ceasing to blame the external world—their parents, their partner, their boss, "the system"—for the state of their own inner life. They have taken full ownership of their choices, their feelings, their actions, and their consequences. This is not a form of self-blame, but a profound act of empowerment. The mature individual understands the crucial distinction between fault and responsibility. They may not be at fault for the painful events of their past or the unjust constraints of their present, but they know that they are, and always will be, 100% responsible for the meaning they create from those events and the choices they make in response to them. This sense of ownership extends beyond the self. It is a responsibility that is relational, a recognition of the infinite ethical claim of the Other. They understand that their freedom is not an isolated possession, but a force that has a real and tangible impact on the world, and they strive to wield that force with compassion, with integrity, and with a deep sense of accountability.

Third, the existentially mature individual accepts their limits without despair. This is the crucial and paradoxical counterpoint to their embrace of freedom. Their life is not a fantasy of limitless potential; it is grounded in a courageous and unsentimental acceptance of the real. They have made peace with their own facticity—the unchosen facts of their biology, their history, and their place in the world. They have stopped fighting a war against their own imperfections and have begun the more difficult and more fruitful work of creating a meaningful life with the materials they have actually been given. Most profoundly, they have learned to live in a conscious and ongoing dialogue with their own mortality. They have turned to face the ultimate and most terrifying limit of all, and in doing so, have been liberated. The awareness of their own finitude is not a source of morbid despair, but a source of urgency, of clarity, and of a deep, poignant appreciation for the precious, unrepeatable gift of the present moment. They have, like Sisyphus, learned to find their joy and their meaning not in a hypothetical, guaranteed future, but in the struggle itself, in the rich, tangible, and deeply embodied reality of a life that is being lived, here and now.

Finally, and as a synthesis of all the above, the existentially mature individual has the capacity to live in a state of creative tension. They have developed the psychological strength to hold the great, opposing truths of the human condition in their mind and heart at the same time, without the need to collapse them into a simple, premature, and false certainty. They can be both autonomous and deeply connected, both a sovereign self and a responsible member of a community. They can act with passion and total commitment while simultaneously knowing that the universe offers no guarantee of success. They can feel the profound sadness and tragedy of the world without surrendering to a cynical despair. They can laugh at the absurdity of their own predicament without devaluing the seriousness of their own struggle. This ability to tolerate ambiguity, to live with paradox, to inhabit the gray areas, is the ultimate hallmark of a wise and resilient mind. It is the inner freedom that allows one to navigate a complex world with a measure of grace, of flexibility, and of profound, unshakable peace.

To cultivate this state of being is the work of a lifetime. It is not a final achievement. Existential maturity is not a permanent plateau of wisdom from which one never stumbles. We will all, until our final day, have moments of bad faith, of cowardice, of blame, of escape. We will all, at times, flee from the weight of our own freedom. Maturity, then, is not the absence of these flights; it is the ever-quickening speed of our return. It is the practice of noticing our own evasions with a gentle and compassionate self-awareness, and of choosing, again and again, to come back to the difficult but life-giving ground of our own responsibility. It is the humble, ongoing, and deeply human work of showing up for our own one and only life, and of choosing, in the face of all that is difficult and uncertain, to make of it something of substance and of worth.

* * *

16

Conclusion

The Courage to Choose

We began this journey together with a simple and unsettling paradox: that the very condition we celebrate as our greatest human endowment, our freedom, so often feels less like a gift and more like an unbearable burden. We have, in the pages of this book, pursued that paradox down into its deepest philosophical roots and traced it back up into the most familiar and mundane corners of our modern lives. We have walked the lonely streets of Kierkegaard's Copenhagen and felt the dizzying anxiety of a life of pure potential. We have sat in the Parisian cafes with Sartre and felt the crushing, absolute weight of being "condemned to be free." We have journeyed with Camus into the heart of the absurd and stood with Sisyphus as he watched his rock thunder back down the mountain. And we have returned from these philosophical depths to the brightly-lit, over-abundant aisles of our own supermarkets, to the glowing, demanding screens of our digital lives, to the quiet, anxious chambers of our own hearts, and we have found this same ancient drama playing out in a thousand new and modern forms.

We have seen that to be a conscious being is to be thrown into a world without a script, a world that offers no ultimate guarantees, no final answers, and no pre-ordained purpose. We have seen that this "groundlessness" is the source of our deepest anxieties. In response to this anxiety, we have charted the myriad and ingenious ways we flee from our own freedom. We have seen our own reflections in the comforting submission to authority, in the quiet camouflage of conformity, in the sterile superiority of cynicism, and in the frantic, hollow busyness of a life of perpetual distraction. We have diagnosed our own universal human tendency to blame the external world for our internal state, to project our own shadows onto others, and to cling to the rigid certainty of a fundamentalist belief system as an anesthetic against the pain of doubt. We have, in short, held a mirror up to our own flight.

To arrive at this point, to see these patterns in the world and, more importantly, in ourselves, is a difficult and often painful awakening. It is an intellectual and emotional stripping away of our most cherished defenses. And it can, in its initial stages, feel like a profound loss. To be stripped of our alibis, to be robbed of our comforting illusions, is to be left standing naked and exposed before the full and demanding truth of our own existence. It is to feel the full weight of our freedom, perhaps for the very first time. And in this moment of stark, unshielded awareness, the temptation of despair is immense. If this is the truth of our condition, if we are truly this alone, this responsible, this untethered in a silent universe, then what hope is there?

It is here, at the very bottom of this abyss, that the entire project of this book pivots from a diagnosis of our burden to a celebration of our capacity. For the truth is that the human spirit, in its deepest and most authentic expression, is not defined by its need for comfort, but by its capacity for courage. The final and most important lesson of the existential tradition is not that we are condemned to a life of anxiety and despair, but that we are blessed with the power to create a life of meaning and dignity *in spite of* these conditions. The absence of a cosmic plan is not a verdict; it is an invitation. It is the ultimate and most radical permission to become the authors of our own lives.

The burden of freedom, when we finally stop running from it and turn to face it, reveals itself to be the most precious and generative gift we have ever been given. It is the raw material of our humanity. The anxiety that we feel is not a symptom of a pathology; it is the energy of life itself, the signal that we are awake, conscious, and engaged with a world of real and consequential choices. The responsibility that weighs upon us is not a punishment; it is the very source of our dignity, the recognition that our choices matter, that what we do with our one and only life has a significance that is entirely of our own making. The uncertainty that haunts our future is not a curse; it is the necessary condition for hope, for creativity, and for the very possibility of a life that is not a foregone conclusion but a genuine and unfolding adventure.

To live in the light of this understanding is to recognize that the central virtue of a human life is not happiness, nor is it success, nor is it purity. The central virtue of an authentic human life is courage. And this is not the grand, theatrical courage of the battlefield or the heroic myth. It is a quieter, more persistent, and far more demanding form of courage. It is the courage to choose.

It is the courage to choose our own values in a world that offers a thousand ready-made identities. It is the courage to ask ourselves, with radical honesty, "What do I truly believe in?" and to begin the difficult, lifelong work of building a life that is in alignment with those beliefs, even when it is inconvenient, unpopular, or frightening to do so.

It is the courage to choose commitment in a culture that celebrates the shallow freedom of infinite options. It is the courage to say "yes" to one person, one path, one community, one project, and in doing so, to say a brave and necessary "no" to all the other lives we might have lived. It is the understanding that a deep life is not built by keeping our options open, but by having the strength to close them.

It is the courage to choose to take responsibility for our own lives in a world that is always offering us a more comforting and convenient alibi. It is the courage to stop blaming our past, our parents, or our circumstances and to ask the terrifying but ultimately liberating question, "What will I do now?" It is the choice to be the protagonist of our own story, rather than the victim.

It is the courage to choose to love another person, not as a solution to our own loneliness, but as a separate and mysterious being, with a freedom and a destiny of their own. It is the courage to make ourselves vulnerable, to risk the profound pain of loss, and to find our meaning not in a fantasy of perfect fusion, but in the difficult, beautiful, and ongoing work of building a shared world.

It is the courage to choose to engage with our world, in all its imperfection and its injustice, rather than retreating into the sterile safety of cynicism or apathy. It is the courage to care about something beyond ourselves, to cast our small and seemingly insignificant vote for a better world, and to find our purpose not in the guarantee of victory, but in the integrity of the struggle.

And finally, and most profoundly, it is the courage to choose to face the final and most absolute of our limits, our own mortality, and to not be broken by it. It is the courage to look upon the finite and precious nature of our own existence and to decide that this fact, far from rendering our lives meaningless, is the very thing that gives them their urgency, their beauty, and their sacred, unrepeatable worth.

This, then, is the ultimate challenge with which this book leaves you. The insights we have explored are not a set of doctrines to be believed, but a set of tools to be used. The work is not to understand the philosophy; the work is to live it. The final and most important choice is now yours. You can choose to set this book aside and return to the comfortable, anesthetic sleep of an unexamined life, the life of quiet conformity, of subtle blame, and of endless distraction. It is a path that offers a measure of peace, a freedom from the heavy burden of your own freedom.

Or you can choose the more difficult path. You can choose to begin the practice of a more courageous and more conscious existence. You can choose to take up the tools of self-reflection, to clarify the values that lie dormant in your own heart, and to begin the slow, imperfect, and magnificent work of bringing your life into alignment with them. You can choose to embrace your freedom, not as a problem to be solved, but as a project to be lived. You can choose to accept the weight of your own authorship, and to find in that weight not a burden, but the very ground of your own strength. You can choose, in this one and only life you have been given, in this one and only world you will ever know, to live without illusion, to act with responsibility, and to create a meaning that is entirely, magnificently, and defiantly your own. The choice, as always, is yours. Choose well.

* * *

About the Author

RJ Starr is an academic psychologist, professor, and author whose work examines the emotional, cognitive, and existential foundations of human life. His scholarship explores how individuals construct meaning, assume responsibility, and sustain psychological clarity within conditions of uncertainty. Integrating psychological theory with cultural and philosophical analysis, Starr's writing situates questions of identity, emotion, and resilience within the broader challenges of contemporary existence.

In his teaching and public lectures, Starr emphasizes critical inquiry, conceptual precision, and emotional maturity as essential capacities for navigating modern life. His website, https://profrjstarr.com, serves as a repository of his work, including essays, research papers, courses, podcasts, and educational tools. Across these projects, his central aim remains consistent: to advance a psychologically grounded framework for engaging the complexities of the human condition with intellectual rigor and existential depth.

You can connect with me on:

🌐 https://profrjstarr.com